Emotional Clearing

A Groundbreaking

East/West Guide to

Releasing Negative Feelings

and Awakening

Unconditional Happiness

Emotional
Clearing

John Ruskan

BROADWAY BOOKS   NEW YORK

EMOTIONAL CLEARING. Copyright © 2000 by John
Ruskan. All rights reserved. Printed in the United States
of America. No part of this book may be reproduced or
transmitted in any form or by any means, electronic or
mechanical, including photocopying, recording, or by any
information storage and retrieval system, without written permission from the publisher. For information, address Broadway Books, a division of Random House, Inc.,
1540 Broadway, New York, NY 10036.

Broadway Books titles may be purchased for business or
promotional use or for special sales. For information, please
write to: Special Markets Department, Random House,
Inc., 1540 Broadway, New York, NY 10036.

BROADWAY BOOKS and its logo, a letter B bisected on the
diagonal, are trademarks of Broadway Books, a division of
Random House, Inc.

Originally published by R. Wyler & Co.

Visit our website at www.broadwaybooks.com

Library of Congress Cataloging-in-Publication Data applied for.

First Broadway Books edition published 2000.

Designed by Lee Fukui

ISBN 0-7679-0406-0

00 01 02 03 04 10 9 8 7 6 5 4 3 2 1

*dedicated to
spiritual seekers
everywhere*

Contents

Part 4: Working on Yourself

Acknowledgments

I would like to extend my most heartfelt appreciation to the people who have helped me in the crystallizing of this book . . .

The Kriya Yoga tradition and the spiritual master Babaji, for my first guidance on the path.

Gurudev Amrit Desai and his ashram family of 1987–88, for showing me how to love myself.

Therapists who have provided invaluable support for the book: Martha Crampton, Robert Hall, Richard Moss, Sharry Rose, Hazel Stanley.

Liam Watt, who has been endlessly supportive and was the first certified Integrative Processing therapist.

Editors Peter Gault and Tony Hoffman, for helping make the manuscript into a book.

Agent Diana Finch, for her patient guidance.

Tracy Behar and everyone at Broadway Books, for their wonderful enthusiasm and for being the key to bringing the book to the large audience for whom it was destined.

Disclaimer

The author of this book does not presume to offer psychological therapy or advocate the use of any technique for the treatment of any specific or traumatic psychological condition without the approval and guidance of a qualified psychologist. The intent of the author is only to relate his personal experience in the hope that it may help you in your quest for emotional and spiritual health. If you use any of the information as a form of self-therapy, the author and publisher assume no responsibility for your actions.

Preface

Throughout my years of involvement in the spiritual and healing communities, I have noticed something that has prompted the writing of this book: Many people who are earnest seekers after spiritual growth tend to be unfamiliar with the methods or the importance of working with the emotional component of the psyche. They – as well as myself for a long while in the past – approach inner growth by concentrating only on the "higher" idealistic aspects that they hope to develop, such as love, and ignore the more unpleasant emotional aspects of the self. Often there is a tremendous gap in awareness about the emotional self and even the assumption that the emotions are not really important. At the same time, those involved in psychological therapy, where emotional healing is the main concern, often cannot see how to combine spiritual arts with inner work.

The premise of this book is that no real growth into higher consciousness can occur unless working with the emotions becomes a central part of inner work. Moreover, I hope to show that working with emotion as well as feeling in general can become a most vital and even primary path to self-realization, enabling us to release the inner forces that keep us blocked and from our full potential.

This book is the product of the merging of two cultural, intellectual, and spiritual traditions. As I have worked, I have felt these two lines of tradition meeting in my thoughts and then converging into the writing, like a prism in reverse. Like female and male, mother and father, yin and yang, each element has been necessary to fully actualize the other. In the broadest terms, the East has represented the mother – the mystical, nurturing connection to the inner source of spiritual replenishment, healing, and growth. The West has represented the father – the rational intellect, the organizing, pragmatic principle that gives form and structure to the healing force.

What has resulted is not a comparison or analysis of these two ways but a synthesis. It has been my intention to show how both paths may be unified into a single approach that will provide a system of self-work that can be followed intellectually and will lead to an opening of the Heart. I feel that this approach can be vital for us of the West in our quest for spiritual wholeness and resolution of the ever-present pain of existence.

Emotional Clearing first appeared in consciousness bookstores in 1993 as a self-published book. It was one of the first books of the decade to identify the vital importance of releasing negative feelings as a key part of spiritual growth. I am pleased that the audience it has found has been steadily growing. In this latest edition I have extended the sections on meditation, practice, depression, the correlation between chakras and feelings, and have updated and clarified the writing wherever I felt it was needed.

If this book, my gift to you, can be of any value to you, you have in turn helped me as well as all of us, because the pain you feel is not only your pain but the pain of the world. Separateness is an illusion. When you heal yourself, you heal the world.

I wish you continual fulfillment in every aspect of your life. I wish you the wisdom to make the most of the limitless possibilities that life offers. Most important, I wish you the power to activate the love and healing that lie so close within.

John Ruskan

I understand that my love for myself is the greatest possession I will ever have. Love for myself comes into being only when I accept and experience my feelings as they are, at this very moment, both pleasant and unpleasant. As I welcome my painful self, it heals. Loving myself provides the power for transformation.

INTRODUCTION

The Art of Loving Yourself

People sometimes envy the artist's life. They feel the artist's life is an exciting one, expressing the instinct to break free. The artist is seen as struggling with the essential problems of human existence, facing those issues within, and bringing them into concrete expression. The courage to engage in the inner confrontation is admired. I know I felt like this before deciding to devote much of my time to the understanding and practice of art. It is one reason I became an artist.

The real artist – one who is truly exploring issues of the self and not just exploiting a technique – is operating on a high level of consciousness. Artistic expression comes from the Creative center of consciousness, which, in Eastern psychology, is even higher than the Heart, accounting for the unusually intense experience of the artist.

Artists can run into problems with their work, however. Often problems begin when the artist tries to establish a sense of social identity and acceptance through the art. The motivation shifts from pure self-expression to concern with whatever is being gained from the work. The shift of motivation can be subtle but still can result in hampered creativity and eventual self-defeat.

Even though I was strongly drawn to art and the quest for inner growth at about the same time in my life, the spiritual principles that I was learning did not prevent me from falling into the destructive cycle I am about to describe. I had been taught that happiness did not come from the results of one's work, or from the approval of others, but from the joy of the doing. I agreed, and in my own work as an artist, I felt that I was coming from the heart, not looking for approval. Art for me meant going inside and bringing forth. Creative expression was exhilarating and ecstatic. I felt I was developing the capacity to mobilize the incredible energies I perceived.

Because for me, the essence of the creative act was *perception.* I could find ecstasy in just looking at painting, dance, architecture, or listening to music. I later realized that the power is in the perceiver. The work of art is simply the framework onto which we project our artistic experience, much like life in general.

From the act of perception it was natural for me to go to actual creation. Yet it wasn't really me who created. I just watched while some other creative power came forth. My role as the artist was to perceive, to be moved by what manifested. My skill as the artist was in getting my conscious mind out of the way so the process could occur. If something happened in this process that moved me, then I had produced a piece of "art," something interesting enough to share with others. And sharing was something I wanted to do.

For while I was aware of the pitfalls of using art as a means of bringing attention to myself, it seemed natural to want to share what I had created with others. I allowed that I was not perfect and that there was bound to be a certain amount of ego attachment to my work. If I needed to have a minimum of recognition, I felt I should accept the need, along with whatever limitations it might bring.

The incident that helped me become aware of the destructive cycle in which I was enmeshed occurred during a weeklong workshop on Body Wisdom I was attending. By the third day, there had not yet been much catharsis in the group. Our leader guided us into an extended holding of a yoga posture, the Mountain. Holding this posture puts a great strain on the body, and many people started trembling and shaking. Energy was starting to move in our bodies. We finally released the pose and were instructed to move around the room in any manner we chose.

As I moved, I suddenly began to sense the energy in my body. The energy was taking the form of classical ballet positions I could not name. Although I have not had any ballet training, and I am not at all what might be called a "ballet" type of person, I have always had a natural aptitude for dancing, and many of my friends have been dancers. I always had assumed that somewhere in the past, if there really were past lives, I had been a dancer. Still, I had never gone beyond the intellectual assumption.

This experience was not intellectual. The energy in my body was assuming perfect classical positions, drawing my imperfect physical pose into as close a correspondence as possible. The inner seeing and feeling of the energy taking the archetypal ballet positions, the realization that the positions were indeed archetypal, and the ecstasy from the inner perception were all overwhelming. I was taken through a beautiful and moving artistic experience.

Nevertheless, linked with the beauty that I was witnessing inside myself was the sense of pain – the pain of isolation. I realized that I was reliving my pain from the past life as a dancer. I went into a major catharsis of emotion. I knew that whenever catharsis is linked to what might be past life recall, there is a good possibility that the recall is real and not imagined. I knew I was tying into my suppressed pain from the previous life and that it was being released.

I saw that a large part of my present life had been the same as the previous life, except now I was involved mostly with music. I was again consumed with the ecstasy of creation and the pain of isolation, without understanding that the two – at least for me – are inseparable, that they are dualistic complements. The suppressed pain from the previous life was the source of the present pattern.

The incredible experience of creation on which artists are focused does not come without its complement. The act of creation brings with it the sense of isolation and inner emptiness from having exhausted energies. The ecstasy is balanced by the pain.

After understanding the dualistic nature of my creative experience, my life came into focus. I had spent much of my life taking in the ecstasy and then not understanding what the pain was all about. The pain of isolation, from both the present and the previous life, was the motive behind sharing my work and the strong, partly unconscious motivation for establishing a social identity as an artist. I felt if I could reach out with my work, the terrible pain of isolation would be relieved. That it never was relieved added to my confusion because even when my work received acceptance – when I got recognition – the pain was still there. I became confused and hurt. Recognition became pointless. I questioned the value of what I was doing and became self-destructive, probably in more ways than I realize even now.

The problem came into being when I allowed myself to be motivated by the pain of isolation; when I tried to seek its relief through recognition – what I thought was my desire to share. In similar ways, we all try to avoid our pain, without understanding that when we are motivated by the desire to avoid negativity, there is no escape from it.

I had spent much of my life unconsciously locked into a cycle of addiction to creative work. From the ecstasy of the creation, I would fall into its complement, the isolation of the creator. Seeking to avoid the negative aspect, either I would turn to sharing my work as the antidote for the isolation or, not finding relief there, I would again go back to the creative experience to escape the pain. I became compulsive about creating as a means to escape the isolation that came with creating. Not being released, the isolation was only suppressed. It built to the point where I became compulsive in other areas of my life as well, such as relationships. Eventually, the suppressed pain became so great that I had to stop work, reaching the point of burnout. The catharsis I had in the workshop helped me understand that it was the buildup of suppressed pain, from both the present and previous life, that had contributed to blocking me and holding me back.

How do we get rid of the isolation that may come with the act of creating as well as other emotional problems we may have? That is what this book is about. The first step is to *integrate,* to reclaim and accept, the feelings we are concerned with. When something has been integrated, it has not gone away but is no longer perceived as disturbing. Most of the pain is there because the feelings are unintegrated. Integration starts the process of healing and clearing. All aspects of life, not just the creative, have both positive and negative complements. We must learn how to integrate, not avoid, the negative. In so doing, something may be learned from the artist.

Artists are concerned with the unwholesome side of life as well as the beautiful. Often artists portray ugliness, disharmony, strife; indeed, many artists today live in the ghettos of our cities. They appear to have some connection to the sordid side of life that goes beyond the low rent. This is because the artist accepts, celebrates, and expresses the negative aspect of existence, both in the outer world and the inner feelings. The artist does this primarily to achieve his or her integration of it but also to show us that we cannot escape the responsibility of integrating our own personal experience. When we try to escape, we only suppress, and whatever we try to escape from or fight keeps building.

The inclination to escape is a problem inherent to the New Age. When first attracted to New Age activity, we may approach it with the intent of enjoying peace and harmony. This may be an important first step, especially if we are stressed out, but we miss the point if we continually try to avoid the negative in favor of the positive. We must learn how to integrate what we seek to avoid, with the courage of the artist.

We can all become artists, for art does not depend on technique but on the sensitivity of the perceiver. You can change your mode of perceiving so that life is not seen as something outside yourself that you must battle and control. Life becomes a reflection of yourself, which you may either accept or reject, in turn accepting or rejecting yourself.

When you perceive with acceptance, you allow the creative process to begin. Just as when an artist produces a painting by stepping aside and letting another power come through in the creation, you can use the same approach in ordinary life. You become the artist, with life as your canvas. You become the witness to creative transformation. You experience the exhilaration of the creative act and find beauty in the most miserable parts of existence.

When you perceive with acceptance, something else is accomplished. You learn that acceptance is love and that, in accepting yourself and your feelings as they are, you build the experience of love for yourself in a way that could never be done through any other means. Loving yourself becomes the healing power that transforms your inner world. Loving yourself is the highest art.

part

Emotional Clearing

1

When I accept myself and my feelings as they are, I become whole. I am no longer split – fighting or condemning part of myself. The power of self-acceptance and self-love builds within me. I acquire the ability to heal myself and the conditions of my life. I awaken the power for transformation.

1

The Acceptance of Feeling

We all want to be whole. We would like to have an approach that can help us in the quest to wholeness. We are all too familiar with the sensation of being split, of working against ourselves in spite of our best intentions. A path to inner growth that invites us to accept all aspects of ourselves as a means to becoming whole would appear to be reasonable. Yet when we learn exactly what is to be accepted, confusion and doubt may arise.

The acceptance of joy seems natural, but it may not be clear why we should accept heartbreak or fear. Negative feelings like these are exactly what we want to avoid. Normally we think of negative feelings as preventing or interfering with happiness. We all have some concept of ourselves as we would like to be – without certain faults, limitations, or emotional "problems." We fight these conditions, expecting to be happier if only we could get rid of the negative aspects of ourselves, if we could only improve ourselves. We fight unhappiness itself.

Nevertheless, contemporary psychology teaches that there is a place for acceptance of negative feelings and conditions. In fact, by not accepting, we perpetuate negativity instead of releasing it. Acceptance is a difficult concept to grasp, because we have been trained to resist and fight what we don't like. Indeed, the understanding of acceptance is subtle, and the basic questions remain: How? How do I accept my anger? What does it mean to accept my helplessness? How can I resolve my problem if I am to accept it?

Feelings are painful and become problems only because they are not accepted, or *integrated*. We create pain through resistance and nonacceptance. To go beyond pain and to enjoy wholeness, we must learn to integrate those parts of life we find painful and would like to avoid. Once integrated, they are no longer painful. Instead, they add new dimensions to our existence. These new dimensions cannot be foreseen. Life becomes richer, resulting in real, not pseudo, spiritual and material prosperity consciousness. The creative is allowed to manifest. Happiness becomes unconditional. We become artists of life and realize that what we were resisting was really inside ourselves, not in the outside world.

Integrative Processing is a method of inner work that will enable you to transform your emotions and your life simply and effectively. You will learn exactly *why* acceptance is important and *how* to accept in a way that does not mean you must try to like something you don't. The essence of processing is to accept your feelings, whatever they are, even your feelings of dislike. The problem is that you usually resist and reject the feelings, thus creating the pain.

We will explore concepts that may be new and challenging but are of immense value. You will learn a definite and clear method of resolving any psychological or material problem. Moreover, you will learn a highly practical approach to life that enables you to use all your experiences, both negative and positive, in the most productive way possible. You will awaken your latent potential for love and creativity, and initiate personal growth.

THE THERAPEUTIC ENCOUNTER

For the past fifty years or so, psychological therapy has been the most common means for people in the West to receive help in dealing with stressful emotional conditions or simply to become more sensitive to themselves. Before therapy became available, such help was provided by the church. Today the psychological has largely become separated from the spiritual. Spirituality is often overlooked, or not desired, by persons who turn to psychology for assistance.

The therapeutic effort is devoted, first, to uncovering or making conscious the feelings and patterns that are unconsciously influencing the client in undesirable ways. Second, therapy is directed toward releasing stored negativity through various approaches, depending on the school.

The therapist accepts the client

Regardless of the approach, therapists who are effective share a common quality: They accept the client without conditions. Unconditional acceptance can be startling and transformative, because the problem is not what the client usually thinks it is. The real problem is that the client is not self-accepting, often not even having any concept of self-acceptance. Through the therapist, the client learns how to accept him- or herself, outgrowing negative patterns.

During therapy, blocks are uncovered and loosened up, and the client becomes aware of self-limiting tendencies. This happens primarily because of the therapist's attitude of acceptance, not because of incredible insights or wonderfully effective techniques. The therapeutic use of acceptance can be understood and applied only by one who has mastered self-acceptance on a deep level; it is fallacious to assume that one who is not whole within could ever provide this kind of healing for another. A successful outcome to therapy is achieved when the client no longer needs the supportive energy of the therapist but can provide support through self-acceptance. The client has not become a perfect human being but is now self-sustaining, able to provide nurturing and healing from within.

The role of therapist in the West closely corresponds to the traditional role of guru in the East. The guru provides the same kind of nurturing relationship that the therapist does, for the same reasons. The guru accepts the disciple unconditionally, knowing that acceptance from another is what the disciple needs to learn self-acceptance and to grow as a human being. In the East, however, the role of guru is more comprehensive, including not only psychology but philosophy, religion, and physical culture, all addressing the question of spiritual growth.

This broadness of perspective does not in the least render the psychological aspect shallow or unstudied. The Eastern understanding of the mind has a history and tradition thousands of years old. The ancients of the East were, indeed, master psychologists. Western psychological thought is, for the most part, a few hundred years old and is still being formulated; Eastern thought has been formulated and offers much to be learned.

Psychology's connection
to spirituality is critical

Psychology in the East has a built-in connection to spirituality. In contrast, Western psychology is limited exactly because it usually has no such link. Many psychologists are now coming to this realization and are trying to establish a spiritual connection. For some, this may mean turning to organized Western religion, which to me is like going one step forward and two steps back. Certain religious institutions of the East also may be considered dogmatic and outdated but, when we come to yoga or Buddhism, we find a flexible and intelligent approach to both psychology and spirituality.

We are not going to discuss spirituality directly in this book. The principles of psychology that we will discuss, however, are related to developing the capacity for spiritual experience. The overwhelming contribution of Eastern thought is that as we go within, we discover the Infinite. Nothing more needs to be said about spirituality. Some Western thinkers have come to a similar conclusion, notably Jung, but he was deeply influenced by Eastern thought. Please note, then, that when I refer to "spirituality," I am referring to the inner meeting with the self, not to the trappings of any organized religion, East or West.

We have touched on the function of the therapist or guru in awakening the power of self-acceptance in the client or disciple. It is noteworthy that in the East, this guidance traditionally is considered to be a normal requirement of education; in the West, it usually is reserved for those in a stressful or unstable condition. Lest we romanticize the East, it should be recognized that in modern times only a small percentage of people there are exposed to traditional teachings, just as in the West, only a small percentage are exposed to psychotherapy. Still, we should reconsider the conservative view that therapy is primarily for the mentally ill. Therapy of some sort is the choice of the sensitive and intelligent individual concerned with personal growth.

The student of the East learns, in this basic training for life, a vast and refined system of knowledge, including disciplines for strengthening and purifying mind and body. "Purifying" has exactly the same purpose as in Western psychology, that of bringing to the surface suppressed material and dissolving unconscious blocks that interfere with the productive enjoyment of life. Nevertheless, in the East it is understood that techniques for personal growth are most effective when the disciple has direct contact with a guru. This is not because only the guru can give correct instructions in technique but because the disciple learns self-acceptance through personal interaction. The concept of acceptance is at the core of both Eastern and Western psychology.

ACCEPTANCE

Why is acceptance so powerful and transformative? We will explore this question at length throughout the book. No short explanation can hope to convey a real understanding. Still, I will say a few things here to introduce you to the topic.

Acceptance means
opening to your feelings

Acceptance does *not* mean automatic approval of any event, whether an inner feeling or the interaction with another person or happening in the outside world. Acceptance means rather that we are open to the experience of the event. We may retain our intellectual discrimination, preferring that something be different from the way it is manifesting; however, we do not allow our preference to interfere with the experience. This is possible because experience takes place on a *feeling* level, not an intellectual level. As we open ourselves fully to experience on the feeling level, we accept it.

The capacity for feeling is of utmost importance. Feelings are our connection to life; without them we are stale, hollow, and cut off from true fulfillment. Self-blocking occurs on the feeling level, not the mental or intellectual level. The feeling level is where we are most unconscious. People who have achieved self-acceptance have developed the capacity for feeling deeply, without resistance, whatever is happening in their inner life. Most of us do not do this but block feelings from entering consciousness, resulting in emotional imbalance and confusion.

Unconditional love is
unconditional acceptance

When we interact with a person who is self-accepting, we sense that this relationship differs from most. A self-accepting person has the ability to accept others, to be open to others, and to receive their energy without resistance. A person who is not self-accepting cannot accept or be open to others. Because we seldom encounter self-accepting people, we have no real sense of what a relationship based on acceptance is like. When we meet a self-accepting person who accepts us, who does not unconsciously resist us, we experience a revelation. We can *feel* that we are being accepted on a deep energy level. We are disarmed. There is no reason to resist back. We sense love. Unconditional love is nothing more than unconditional acceptance, whether of yourself or another person.

When unconditional acceptance is part of the therapeutic

encounter, it supplies the power for transformation. Healing occurs because of the power of love. Psychological blocks dissolve; there is no need to fight them. The relationship with the therapist intensifies, and the potential problem of dependency arises.

Awakening Self-Acceptance

The real purpose of the therapeutic relationship is the ultimate awakening of self-acceptance in the client. This happens magically in the interaction, through a kind of resonance. The result is what has been called self-actualization in the West and self-realization in the East. In either case, what has been awakened is the ability to love oneself. One gains the ability to evoke healing power from within, through self-love.

There is no longer any craving or searching for love outside oneself; one is complete as one is, feeling love from within. Relationships are approached as a vehicle through which the love within is expressed rather than as a context in which one seeks to be loved. Life has become essentially, miraculously changed.

Must you find a therapist or guru before you can learn to love yourself effectively? This is a controversial question; authorities advocate both sides. There is no doubt that the kind of relationship I have described can be instrumental in awakening self-love. Yet finding such a relationship can be difficult and is customarily thought of as "happening" rather than being found through active search.

I have seen through my own experience and that of others that it is possible to make substantial, if not completely adequate, progress on our own. For that reason, I have formalized the system of Integrative Processing, a self-therapy devoted to awakening the power of self-acceptance and self-love as well as the higher centers of consciousness and realization. You will learn how to activate yourself through the intellectual approach rather than through the personal influence of a teacher.

If you have a personal healer, therapist, or guru with whom you are working, however, feel free to stay with them if you so desire. Processing is nondogmatic and compatible with any humanistic psychology with which you may be involved. As you learn processing, you will gain a technical knowledge, both theoretical and practical, of powerful psychological principles. If you have no personal teacher, assume that you don't need one at this point. You will surely draw someone into your life at the right time, if you need such a relationship.

WORKING ON YOURSELF

Many people have never been exposed to either a therapist or a guru. Yet virtually all of us need to learn how to awaken the qualities of self-acceptance and self-love. I feel this is the tremendous spiritual challenge of our time.

Life is evolutionary, and we are all "works in progress." The purpose of life is to awaken and expand our dormant capacities for love, creativity, and intelligence, but a program is needed to support us in the awakening. When you get in sync with this natural evolutionary urge, you will immediately feel more at peace with yourself – you are no longer purposeless. The joy that comes from growth itself is enough to keep you interested in life.

To seek personal evolution means you must work on yourself. Most people understand that effort is required and apply themselves with enthusiasm. No one, not even your therapist, can do the work for you. You must be at the point where you understand that working on yourself is a priority – that you are tired of functioning (or not functioning) as you are. Even so, many people tend to make a significant mistake when beginning to work on themselves. It is normal to question one's life and perhaps decide that changes are required, but questioning can carry over into a nonproductive habit – the habit of excessive thinking.

*Working on yourself is not
constantly thinking about yourself*

The issue of excessive thinking is crucial. Working on yourself is not primarily analyzing yourself and your motives, or being thoughtfully introspective, or trying to control yourself and do better, or trying to be something you are not. Using the mind in this manner is self-defeating. You must learn to substitute feeling for thinking. *You must learn to sense what is through the feeling center rather than evaluate experience through the thinking center.*

Many people who think they are working on themselves are deceiving themselves, because they do not have an accurate understanding of how to proceed. They spend their time in constant self-evaluation, which merely makes them absorbed in themselves. After you have read this book, you will have a definite understanding of how to work on yourself.

INTEGRATIVE PROCESSING

To integrate means to form into a whole; to reclaim, accept, and include what was previously apart from. "Processing" is a psychological term that refers to the concept of accepting and staying with experience as it manifests, allowing it to unfold by itself in the here and now. Integrative Processing is the name I have given to the system of self-therapy that has evolved from my own work on myself. It is derived from the traditional wisdom of the East as well as the contemporary psychological knowledge of the West. I have tried to combine the strongest and most compatible elements from each tradition.

Integration means accepting yourself and your feelings as you are

Integration is the condition of accepting and including, of not resisting, parts of yourself or your experience. When something is not integrated, it forms the basis of conflict. We resist something – a feeling, for example – because we believe the feeling is bad for us. It makes us uncomfortable. In fighting the feeling, we further the split between ourselves and the feeling, and thus we increase the sense of conflict.

Resistance creates pain

The conflict that is created through resistance causes pain. This is a key concept. What causes most of our pain is our resistance to a feeling, not the actual feeling itself, even a "negative" feeling. A certain amount of pain may be inherent in negative feelings, but we amplify, exaggerate, and prolong that pain through resistance. Learning how to accept experience is the means to minimizing pain.

Experiencing takes place in the moment

After we have learned to accept, however, experience is not yet completely integrated. It must be digested in a certain way, called *direct experience,* in which it is absorbed or dissolved completely. The ability for direct experience is gained through the cultivation of "being in the moment." Being in the moment is a mystical perspective. *Witness consciousness* is activated, and we function on a new and higher plane that results in a sense of well-being and euphoria as well as calling into play transpersonal powers that have been blocked by the personal ego. These powers operate on a very practical level, effecting *transformation* in situations that we previously resisted. By accepting, we go beyond. We reach the spiritual through the mundane. We discover the spiritual *in* the mundane.

It is essential to learn how to open up on the feeling level. You may think you are feeling your pain right now. The problem, however, is that you continue to resist the pain with unconscious self-rejection, which prevents the pain from being resolved and intensifies it. Developing the capacity to accept leads to unobstructed feeling, catharsis, and the release of pain.

Processing consists of four steps, each step corresponding to a level of our individuality. The steps are taken to achieve integration of any event. The event can be an inner feeling or emotion or a happening in the external world. We can use processing especially in stressful circumstances but also as an approach to all life's happenings, "positive" as well as "negative." Once integrated, we no longer fail to experience the event completely. The energy of the event is dissolved, having run its natural course, instead of being trapped and continuing to affect us. We become "clear." In Part 2, we will go through these steps in detail.

THE STEPS OF INTEGRATIVE PROCESSING

Step	Plane	Function
1. AWARENESS	Intellectual	Knowing
2. ACCEPTANCE	Mental	Thinking
3. DIRECT EXPERIENCE	Body	Feeling
4. TRANSFORMATION	Spiritual	Transcending

1. AWARENESS. Intellectual plane: Basic awareness of the event, whether a feeling or an external happening. Awareness includes "owning" of the event; the recognition that the event corresponds to a projection of suppressed energy held in the subconscious. Awareness also includes understanding the basic principles of how to work on yourself and consciously deciding to apply them.

2. ACCEPTANCE. Mental plane: Ceasing resistance to the event. Normally, experience is blocked unconsciously through various self-rejecting maneuvers of the mind. In accepting ourselves, these mechanisms become conscious and are dropped. In so doing, self-love is awakened, and the gate to direct experience of feeling is opened.

3. DIRECT EXPERIENCE. Body plane: Being in the feeling center, or "in the moment" with the event. Feelings are entered completely, without resistance, analysis, or blame. The event is experienced on a body level until the energy is dissolved.

4. TRANSFORMATION. Spiritual plane: Witness consciousness is activated, and the higher transpersonal intelligence guides the energies, leading to internal catharsis and unexpected creative external change. The flow of life is not obstructed. Adjustment occurs spontaneously and without conscious control.

Thus, we sequence through the various levels of experience in logical order, culminating in the spiritual. What may be surprising to many is that the spiritual is reached through the body, or the feeling center, not through the mind or intellect. Of course, I am not referring to the sensual nature of the body but to the higher centers of consciousness that are approached only through feeling.

Our common misconception is that fulfillment, peace, and happiness can be reached through knowing, accomplishment, or possession. As we survey the twentieth century, the fallacy of this position should be most evident. True happiness is unconditional; it is achieved when we use the intellect to understand that knowledge is important but ultimately not fulfilling; when we go beyond the self-orientation and possessiveness of the mind; when we enter the direct experience of ourselves and the universe; when we have the perception that we *are* the universe.

I understand that when I don't accept myself or my feelings, I create a debt to myself. The feelings don't go away, but become hidden in my subconscious, only to come out later. When I accept my feelings as they are, I no longer create a debt. I experience life fully and allow growth to occur.

2

Creating the Subconscious

RESISTING OUR EXPERIENCE

It is human nature to strive for a sense of well-being. We have basic, legitimate needs for sustenance, shelter, companionship, love, self-expression. We work to satisfy these needs. In acting with goals in mind, we become concerned about how we expend our energy and about the results of our work. We find it natural to accept certain circumstances and to resist others.

Our selective orientation toward experience becomes associated with pleasure or pain. We develop a natural predisposition to choose conditions that are either pleasurable in themselves or lead to pleasurable outcomes and to resist conditions that are painful or lead to painful outcomes. What could be wrong with this? It seems to be a basic description of what life is all about.

Philosophers through the centuries, however, have addressed the implications of a life based on seeking pleasure and avoiding pain, because experience has demonstrated that such a life does not lead to happiness. These philosophers then conceived of other systems of values that might be more helpful in fostering the sense of fulfillment we seek. Of course, our level of maturity has much to do with what we consider to be worth pursuing. As we grow, we outgrow certain needs and adopt – it is hoped – broader, less self-centered ones. Still, the basic needs of security, power, sensation, and relationship are what most of us revolve around.

Many of our "needs" are the result of social conditioning. They are artificial – programmed into us by society. We assign the same urgency and feel the same anxiety about the attainment of artificial needs as we do with more genuine needs. This mistake is the result of our level of consciousness, our lack of vision, our susceptibility to be programmed. However, there is no point in my trying to describe what I think these false needs might be. My opinions would not do the slightest to change anyone else's perception of their needs, nor should they. We are all at our own individual and proper level of growth.

BELIEFS

Needs result from beliefs. Beliefs are the filters through which we perceive reality. Along with instinctual beliefs, such as the belief in basic survival, and beliefs that society has conditioned into us, we hold beliefs that have developed from personal experience in meeting life. Many beliefs are irrational, limiting, and destructive. Once we become aware of them and their counterproductive nature, we may want to change them – but deliberate change is difficult.

Beliefs are maintained by
suppressed energy

Beliefs are conditioned states of mind, occurring mostly on the unconscious level. What may be a limiting belief is difficult to reprogram directly, even with the use of techniques such as affirmations, because it is held in place by suppressed energy formations; the suppressed energy supports and maintains the belief. In our work, we do not attempt directly to uncover or change unconscious beliefs. I consider such action to be invasive and disvalidating. Instead, in accepting ourselves, we accept our beliefs as they are. Processing of feelings will release the energy that is behind the belief and maintains it. The limiting or destructive belief is outgrown naturally, instead of in a forced manner.

Much of what we consider important is important only because we consider it so. Our outlook will change as time goes by and as growth occurs, but for now we accept that we assign an emotional value to the attainment of circumstances that our beliefs call for and to the avoidance of whatever threatens the circumstances. Thus, the teenager buying his first car agonizes over what model to get; the scientist agonizes over the results of his work. They are at different levels of growth concerning their goals. Still, both may undergo unnecessary anxiety because of a misplaced, compulsive attachment to the outcome of their respective endeavors, unconsciously believing that their self-worth depends on the approval of their peers. In this respect, they are at psychologically similar levels of growth.

It may be assumed, therefore, that the individual has an extensive, intensive, self-projected belief system which is considered primary in attaining happiness. The belief system creates needs. Through subjective pain when these needs are not realized, the individual learns to strive for conditions to satisfy the needs. The habitual orientation of evaluating which elements of experience will be allowed or resisted to satisfy needs carries over into the inner life: feelings, emotions, and attitudes. A strong judgmentalism develops toward inner experience as well as toward outer experience.

We have fallen into a trap. We must resist certain conditions to

23

survive, but unwittingly we extend this logic to areas where resistance is inappropriate, leading to unresolved energies, entanglement, and sickness. Resistance of experience occurs on a subtle yet powerful level and is the beginning of what is called *suppression*.

SUPPRESSION

Suppression is the primary psychological mechanism that leads to emotional and spiritual dysfunction. The central purpose of all psychotherapy is to clear suppressed material that is affecting us adversely. Suppression is something that we all do. Those who reach the point of severe distress have merely gone further in suppressing than the average person; those who are considered well balanced suppress less than normal. The standard of emotional health in our society, therefore, is far below the potential possible for humankind, but this just has to do with our current evolutionary level of growth.

*Suppression begins
with resistance*

It is important to understand how suppression works. When something is resisted, a condition is set up within us that affects us deeply. The electromagnetic field surrounding the individual, known as the aura, actually becomes steeled against letting in any outer experience that is resisted. In effect, resistance builds a shield to the exchange of energy on the psychic level, where experience primarily takes place. This shield is quite tangible on the psychic level, and may be felt and seen by a psychic. A person with ordinary but sensitive perceptions often can sense the shield, or "wall," around people who are particularly suppressed.

With inner feelings, resistance has a similar effect. A kind of energy shield is built around the feeling centers, so feelings will not be allowed into consciousness. As experiences occur and are resisted, the energy of the feeling encounters the shield. The energy is unable to be released because it has been blocked rather than absorbed; it cannot complete its cycle; *it cannot discharge into consciousness.* What we don't realize is that when the energy of a feeling is not released, it does not go away but stays with us, in latent form, as part of the psychic energy body.

The motive behind resistance to an unpleasant experience is that we would rather not feel the pain involved. Avoidance of feelings is not always done out of deliberate choice but often because we lack the knowledge to confront life directly. We don't know why or how to experience fully so that there are no loose ends, no lingering or unresolved energies. Over time, the habit of resistance results in chronic blocking of the centers and accumulation of the suppressed energy. Thus, we do not succeed in avoiding the feeling, as we intend, but merely prevent the energy from entering our field of awareness.

Suppression operates both inwardly and outwardly

Suppression is the act of rejecting experience from the field of awareness. Outwardly, we suppress awareness of aspects of other people, happenings, and conditions that are displeasing. We close ourselves off to vital parts of life, becoming judgmental and self-centered. We call something evil when it merely conflicts with our "need." Inwardly, we suppress awareness of painful feelings, including anything about ourselves that we dislike, such as perceived faults or weaknesses. External suppression can make us limited and bigoted, but the consequences of internal suppression can be more severe.

We think that it is possible simply to close the door on negativity and walk away from it. We forcefully try to exclude pain from our awareness by any number of evasive maneuvers. What we are doing, however, is rejecting ourselves, because the pain *is* part of ourselves. In our rejection, we deepen the inner split; we go in the opposite direction from integration and wholeness; and we ultimately feel the consequences in depression, despair, and hopelessness.

When we suppress an unpleasant feeling, we interrupt the natural flow of energies. We do not allow the feeling to clear itself, to resolve itself, to regain its natural equilibrium. The energy becomes trapped, held in storage in a static condition. Where does the energy get stored? It is held in what has come to be called "the subconscious."

Suppression creates
subconscious Karma

The mechanism of suppression, therefore, creates much if not all of the mysterious subconscious that has been puzzled over and glamorized since Freud. The subconscious is nothing more than a buildup of energies, potential forces that lie dormant because they were never adequately resolved when they originally occurred. In rejecting our experience, we have created the reservoir of the subconscious. In Eastern terms, the buildup of subconscious forces is called *Karma*.

THE SUBCONSCIOUS

The subconscious is simply a part of ourselves from which we have turned away. The capacity of the mind to achieve withdrawal of awareness and subconscious containment of energies is itself remarkable, and although it appears to be mostly unbeneficial, the habit of suppression and the influence it has had on us has been a major factor in shaping our life and history. We have chosen to turn away, but we can easily turn back to the feelings in the subconscious if we so desire. The inner wall that has grown to divide ourselves is not that solid; it is more like a gray area, where tips of the iceberg are always coming into view. We have only hypnotized ourselves not to fully see and feel those hidden things.

The problem with suppression of feelings is that the feelings are not resolved but merely hidden. When something is suppressed, it is made temporarily unconscious, only to accumulate and break forth at some later time. Anger, for example, does not dissolve when suppressed but remains as forceful as when originally felt, except that it is no longer within the field of awareness. When it erupts, it is likely to cause much more damage because of the buildup that has occurred.

Suppressed feelings influence us in even more far-reaching

ways. They leave us much in the position of being ruled by hidden forces – forces that at times can seem uncontrollable, like a separate entity with an independent intelligence and will. We become guided by neurotic, unconscious urges that lead to irrational, self-destructive behavior. We are attracted to the wrong people, reject the right people, and become compulsive, addictive, and unreliable, all in spite of our best intentions. Our urges are strong and difficult to oppose. Indeed, opposition is impossible because the suppressed energy eventually has to come out. Holding it back will only bring a more destructive release later. We go through life leaving more or less a shambles behind us, accumulating more unresolved energies and adding to our Karma.

Energy is what
becomes suppressed

Unpleasant feelings as well as unresolved situations are the kinds of things that are suppressed, but when we suppress, it is *energy* that is being put into storage. Emotions can run high, and emotions are nothing but energy moving through the centers of consciousness. When people interact, there is an energy exchange between them. Energy is what enables us to have experiences. Experiences are kinds of energy that we assimilate. Of course, I am referring to psychic energy, which is not yet generally recognized by science. Nevertheless, subconscious energy can build to a considerable strength. It becomes part of our personality, affecting us as well as others.

Since we suppress in consistent yet individual ways, we build a reservoir of negative energy of a specific type. Some people suppress mainly anxiety; some, the sense of worthlessness or sexual frustration, for example. The suppressed energy then creates patterns: unconscious, individualistic ways in which we meet life. Patterns would not be a problem, except that they are often negative, keeping us from full realization of our creative power. Because patterns are usually unconscious, we don't know that it is we who are limiting ourselves.

Suppression leads
to addiction

To suppress requires psychic energy. It takes energy to suppress energy; it takes energy to block. The demand for energy becomes a drain on our resources, creating conditions that encourage the addictive cycle. Because addiction provides energy, taken either from outside sources or inner reserves, it facilitates suppression. When this additional energy is not available, it is not as easy to suppress, and we come face to face with our pain. Thus, when we suppress, energy is diverted from its positive and constructive expression; we become split, working against ourselves, unaware of our self-undoing.

Repression

When the suppression syndrome becomes unconscious, it is called *repression*. Repression is the same as suppression, except that there is no awareness of feelings or the avoidance of them. For example, if you are sad but do not consciously recognize your sadness, it becomes repressed. Proper release is not possible, and the sadness is stored subconsciously. Repression, unfortunately, is common in the modern world. Freud, in *Civilization and Its Discontents,* said that he thought it was unavoidable. His statement is even more appropriate today. Repression comes about because of all the desensitizing that we undergo. Life is so busy, so anxiety ridden, with our attention constantly enticed outward, that we do not realize what our real feelings are. We have lost touch with ourselves.

Continual repression results in neurosis and extensive blocking of the human organism. The result on the emotional level is addiction, depression, and unconscious destructive patterns; and on the physical level, disease. Blocked energy easily can reach the level where it affects the physical, and what is disease but blockage? Looking at prevalent twentieth-century ailments such as heart disease and cancer, I can't help but feel that a main cause is the buildup of subconscious negative forces that the modern way of life encourages. However, it should not be forgotten that humans have been creating their subconscious all throughout history, so modern life should not be condemned outright. The average person, now and in previous times, has always had personal blocking and Karma to contend with.

We are all so similar when looked at from a distance. We all have unconscious yet individualistic tendencies that keep us from reaching our maximum potential. Rarely do we fully realize the higher side of our nature, the love and creative centers. Rarely do we relate to others or ourselves directly, without distorting grossly through our own particular filters of suppressed energy. We must recognize the truth without becoming pessimistic. We are as we are because life and consciousness is evolutionary. We are growing, and in progress. Our capacities only reflect our current levels of growth.

Let's look specifically at what kinds of feelings are commonly suppressed or repressed, becoming buried in the subconscious. Our feelings usually relate to the following areas:

SURVIVAL: Fear, anxiety, insecurity about health, money, possessions, death

POWER: Anger, hostility, aggressiveness, helplessness

SENSATION: Sexual and sensual feelings

NURTURING: Cravings for food, alcohol, smoking, drugs, general emotional neediness

SIGNIFICANCE: Worthlessness, lack of self-esteem and meaningful social identity

HEART: Loneliness, jealousy, hate, sadness, grief

Different feelings may be linked, forming complex systems of suppression and blocking. Thus, sexual issues may be associated disharmoniously in one person with security issues and in another with power issues. The accumulation of these negative energies results in stress. If we knew how to dissolve and avoid the buildup of negative energies, we could avoid stress.

The buildup of suppressed energy can vary over short or long intervals. Short-term emotional suppression can happen with fears, sexual impulses, or any feeling that cannot be dissolved immediately. For example, a person may experience frustration in the workplace and not know how to release it, and then go home and take it out on the family. The attempt to release the energy by venting on a neutral party is known as *displacement.* Displacement is common, resulting in hurt feelings, miscommunication, and damaged relationships.

Long-term avoidance of feelings builds a structure of a quite different and unsuspected magnitude. It can build to the extent that a person's whole life is shaped by internal forces of which there is no conscious knowledge. Conditions that were unresolved in the past have a way of recurring with new faces or circumstances, and we have the choice of taking responsibility and experiencing, or avoiding and suppressing once again.

The subconscious is carried
over from previous existences

It may seem remarkable that such complex systems of avoidance, suppression, and blocking could be formed in one short lifetime. My feeling is that they aren't, but that they have formed over extensive periods in prior existences. Whether you choose to believe in reincarnation is a personal decision. For me, it seems obvious that there is some sort of preexistence to physical birth. Just looking at how quickly and definitely children form their individualities is enough to convince me of a previous life.

I believe that Karma, the subconscious, is carried over from previous existences. Life's events are then formed by subconscious forces, to be played out. It is not necessary to agree with the doctrine of reincarnation to have success with processing, but the notion of a previous existence may help clarify a few things for you. For one, you will find it easier to take responsibility for yourself and where you are at, rather than blaming your childhood and your parents. You will realize that early incidents with family, no matter how painful, were merely catalysts to make you conscious of what was already latent within you. In fact, you chose those very circumstances for just that opportunity.

*Focus on present
feelings, not causes*

Because there is usually no conscious memory of previous existences, and because the causes of most emotional suppression are
in those existences, it is difficult to pinpoint the source of any current condition. However, understanding the cause is not required
to release feelings. In our work, we focus on present feelings, not
causes.

Accepting the possibility of a previous existence also implies
the continuity of life after "death." This idea greatly helps me –
intellectually at least – in working with the fear of death, which is
really the primal fear. Psychics have brought back much documen-
tation of life on the "other side." I personally find their reports,
taken as a whole, to be adequate evidence of something beyond
the earthly shell.

PROJECTION

Projection results from the accumulation of energy generated by
suppression. It is an automatic, unconscious mechanism, which
assigns subjective value and identity to persons or events in the
"outside" world. Feelings that are suppressed are experienced
indirectly through the other persons or events – it appears as if the
feelings are caused by or coming from others. In addition, suppressed qualities are attributed to others. Others are usually then
criticized for the feelings or qualities that we have projected onto
them. In advanced cases of projection, we actually attract people
and circumstances to us that correspond to the feelings we are
holding within.

*In projection, we try to avoid
responsibility for certain feelings*

When we project, we unconsciously assign responsibility for
our feelings to other persons or situations, and we think that they
"caused" our feelings. We generally choose persons or situations
skillfully, to appear justified to others and to ourselves. We fail to

see that the other is only "bringing up" suppressed material from inside ourselves. They are not the cause of our feelings, although they may be considered to be the stimulus. If that feeling or reaction was not already latent within, we would not have responded in that particular way. Think of how differently various people · react to the same situation. In projecting, we see through the distorting filters of our own suppressed energies. We do not see reality as it is, and we react inappropriately.

For example, if you have suppressed your anger, you will see others as responsible for "making" you angry because of what they do. You will blame them. You also will perceive others as being angry and directing their anger toward you when you are not angry. You will be likely to condemn them for their anger. If you have suppressed your sexual feelings, you will perceive others as making uncalled-for sexual approaches toward you, and you will judge them harshly as well as condemn other forms of sexual expression not directly concerned with you. If you have suppressed your feelings of rejection toward others, you will think others are rejecting you, and you will blame them.

Similarly, after you have blocked your power through suppression of your energies, you will assign that role to outside agencies, thinking they are responsible for blocking you. You will appear to be entirely justified in your blame. Even an impartial observer might agree that you are contending with an outside force.

The truth is that there is no outside force. Miraculously, we project our subconscious energies onto what appears to be the outside world, creating our entire experience. We are literally responsible for our perceptions as well as whatever happens to us. Accidents that happen "to us" are, unfortunately, only extreme cases of the negative forces that are hidden and stored within building to the point where they can affect us physically. Remember, *energy* is what gets stored in the subconscious, and energy can build to powerful levels if not released.

We never see *what is*. We see only what we have projected. Because of the hidden magnitude of the built-up subconscious, the extent and significance of the suppression-projection mechanism cannot be clearly perceived. To succeed in processing, you must accept intellectually the condition of suppression-projection as a working axiom, even if you have to do so on faith. As you begin to integrate material that was previously suppressed, the truth gradually will become evident, and you will be astounded as well as fascinated.

Up to now, we have examined the suppression of negative feelings and interactions. However, positive events also are suppressed and then projected onto the "outside" world. The shield that was created to avoid negative feelings also blocks positive feelings, and projection becomes the sole means to connect to the feelings. Your most cherished times, someone you thought really loved you, was just the love already within you. Someone who helped you was you helping yourself.

To succeed at self-transformation, you must make the leap from perceiving the universe as a collection of separate individuals and objects acting on you, to perceiving it as a field for your energies, which you project and then take back as if there were an objective outside world. Incredibly, other individuals also have the exact same capability of creating their own universes, simultaneously with you. Try this right now to develop your feeling capability.

EXERCISE

Feel your energies as they go out into the world. Assume that you assign the value and identity to everything you perceive. Your impression of the external world comes to you through your filters of suppressed energy, and your suppressed energy draws corresponding events to you. Assume that when something happens, it has not happened by itself but you unconsciously created it through projection or attracted it to you. If a person seems to behave in a certain way, it is your perception. Focus your awareness on your energy field, and feel the connection you have with your perceptions and reactions. I am not referring to intellectual understanding but to feeling. Simply feel your connection to what you perceive as the qualities of the other.

While you should cultivate a sense of responsibility for your feelings and experiences, based on an understanding of suppression-projection, *by no means should you assume guilt or be self-condemning*. Remember that others are also ultimately responsible

33

for what happens to them, although this does not excuse us from hurting them.

We have taken the concept of suppression-projection further than psychology usually goes with it. We have entered the mystical realm where reasoning and thinking do not apply. This is necessary to reach our goal of inner integration. Fulfillment can never be found through the analytic faculties of the mind; fulfillment comes through the feeling center.

When we project, the world becomes a mirror, reflecting our own qualities back to us. Of course, a great deal of independent activity does go on outside of ourselves, and other people do have a basis of independent character. When we project, we carefully select the appropriate "screen" – a person or situation with some element of what we are projecting – and we load our perception of them with our own energy.

If we try to analyze how much of our perception is projected, and how much is "real," we become distracted from our work on ourselves. No objective evaluation is possible anyway, because we are not clear within ourselves. Therefore, we assume that we are projecting the entire contents of our perception when we use processing techniques. It is very likely that after the issue has been integrated, we will spontaneously see exactly what the other is bringing and what we are bringing to the situation.

The client projects onto the therapist

In light of our discussion of projection, we may more completely understand the value of the relationship with the enlightened therapist. In contrast to an interaction with an average person, where both people normally project onto each other, the therapist ideally does not project subconscious energies onto the client, or at least remains aware of and nonreactive to these projections. This includes having no demands or expectations. In addition, the therapist does not react to or reject but maintains awareness and acceptance of the projections of the client onto the therapist. This is the essence of therapy and the catalyst for the healing transformation. The client is able to become aware of projections more clearly than in relationship with other people, because the mirror is now exceptionally clear. Nonetheless, you should not become discouraged from processing interactions with people in general.

Whenever you react strongly to the stimulus that another person provides, it is safe to assume that suppressed energies within you are surfacing. If you were clear within yourself, you would not be so affected by the negativity of others. Your reactions would not be as pronounced or as judgmental. You might then experience a "normal" amount of negative emotion in response to certain circumstances, but processing techniques are still an excellent approach for clearing these feelings.

CLEARING

On the psychic level, the purpose of projection is clearing. The psychic body, which stores the suppressed emotional energy, naturally wants to clear, or cleanse, itself of this negativity. Projection automatically occurs to bring the energy to a conscious level. However, projection by itself does not result in clearing. If it did, all the world would be liberated. The projected feelings must be handled correctly, or it is all in vain – the projected experiences are resisted and resuppressed, and the amount of negative energy in the subconscious grows. The opportunity to learn through projection is lost.

*Feelings must be experienced
in order to clear*

Clearing of suppressed material takes place only when you finally allow yourself the experience that you have been avoiding. The energy, the feeling, must be allowed into consciousness without resistance in order to be integrated. With painful events, the pain must be accepted and experienced, but you will learn how to minimize and neutralize pain by observing it from the Witness vantage point. The Witness capacity brings about a *nonidentification* with painful feelings, making them more easily integrated and released.

Suppressed energy is released through conscious experience of it. As you allow yourself to have the feeling, the feeling will change. Pain will dissolve, becoming neutralized. Facing feelings is all that is necessary to clear suppressed negativity, and once something is faced, it can be cleared in a surprisingly short interval. The problem is that our unconscious self-rejection prevents us from really facing our feelings, even when we want to – we have lost the capacity for feeling. Exploring and regaining that capacity is what we are learning here.

Life becomes your therapist

As you go through life, you will have various encounters that bring up your subconscious energies into conscious awareness. These energies surface when conditions are appropriate for them to be released. If you can learn to integrate these energies as they come up, you will be meeting life most creatively. You will be *using* your circumstances instead of being abused by them. It is for this opportunity that we incarnate on the Earth plane.

Amazingly, each individual's life is designed to provide just the right circumstances for the clearing of hidden negative forces within. By correctly utilizing these circumstances, you can work on yourself very effectively without a therapist. Life becomes the therapist, and indeed, life is the best and ultimately the only therapist. Your circumstances at this very moment are the ones you need. They are bringing up negative energies from your subconscious to be cleared. When you integrate them, that is, when you accept and experience them without resistance, clearing takes place.

Projection may lessen if you practice contacting your feelings directly, as in meditation. However, you should not expect to stop projecting, because projection is a natural way of clearing. You must learn to become aware. Realizing what is happening, you will smile to yourself. You will not "buy into" thinking that the other is responsible for your experience; you will "own" your experience, meaning that you take responsibility for *what is* before you. In so doing, you achieve the control over your life that you seek.

I recognize that the nature of life is balance – that I will always experience the "up" as well as the "down." If I fight and try to avoid the "down," I fight life itself. If I accept both in an understanding way, I will be at harmony with life and with myself.

3

The Play of Opposites

Projection can be taken one step further by relating it to the concept of duality. Duality is a theory; there is no way of conclusively proving it. For me, duality is something to which I refer as I observe and learn from life. It is a concept to use when taking a long look at your ups and downs; it is not a dogma or rule to adopt blindly, to which you try to fit your life. Still, if you feel sympathetic toward the idea, it will give you a new perspective. You will gain a more balanced insight into the nature of existence.

DUALITY

The theory of duality states that the manifest world is composed of opposites. However, these are not really opposite, as they might appear, but are in fact complementary. Each of any pair of complementary qualities depends for its existence on the other; neither could exist by itself. Examples of these pairs are day and night, hot and cold, up and down, solid and soft. If something were to exist without its complement, there would be no way of perceiving it, because the experience of both qualities is needed to know either one separately. It is impossible to imagine day without knowing night. Certain things are not obvious because their complements are hidden. Thus, we are not usually conscious of the atmosphere, but we would be if we were transported into space. We have never been without the atmosphere, so we are hardly aware of it, and it normally has no emotional content.

Duality is understood and agreed with most easily in terms of physical examples. Controversy begins when feelings are considered, because I believe the exact same principles apply to our inner life: the day and night of emotions, the hot and cold of relationships, the up and down of what we usually call "happiness," the ceaseless entanglement of pleasure and pain. We would not recognize pleasure if our experience did not also include pain of equal degree. The hungrier we are, the more we enjoy eating. The lonelier we are, the more meaningful the closeness we find. The obstacle in our path makes possible the joy of overcoming. Our ecstatic highs are balanced by our depressive lows.

The mind creates duality

Why does it have to be this way? Duality is simply the nature of perception and feeling; it is not a form of punishment. The mind perceives by sensing a pair of complements. When anything affects the mind, the mind must also have an experience of similar intensity with its complement – not simultaneously, but near in time – in order even to be aware of it. Moreover, it is *we* who unconsciously assign the positive and negative value to each side of the experience, in an almost arbitrary manner at times. The mind *creates both* the pleasure and the pain. Dualistic experience, therefore, will vary between individuals.

Take any experience, and the mind will divide it into two parts: one part pleasure and one part pain. We are not normally aware of how extensively the mind categorizes our experience. It appears as if the event is genuinely composed of both "positive" and "negative" elements. We don't realize that we make something painful or, rather, we assign pain to some aspect of the event, only to achieve the required balance of experience. Thus, pain has no real existence but, of course, we perceive it as real.

Because of duality, the emotional value of any experience will vary as it is repeated. You may like something, but as you repeat it, trying to recapture the original feeling, it changes. You go through unexpected painful stages, alternating positive and negative, without being aware that you are the one who is making the experience change and assigning the feelings to it.

Duality affects whatever is most important to you

I do not ask you to accept the theory of duality without question. Rather, try to look at your experiences from this viewpoint, and judge for yourself if it has any credibility. You probably will agree that there is at least something to it, especially when you examine the issues that you expect will give your life meaning, such as relationship or career. Important issues are the very ones in which dualistic experience is most strongly evoked.

Romantic relationships are notorious for their love-hate aspects. Relationships start with the best of feelings and intentions, but before long, the negative side becomes apparent. There will always be a negative side, because we can't feel love *on a dependent level* without resentment. Actually, we have projected both our love and our hate, because they are suppressed and inaccessible. We assign both qualities to aspects of the other person that best accept the projections. If there is nothing really objectionable to attach the resentment to, we will exaggerate something out of proportion or invent something.

Success in career or attainment of ego needs in general – security, power, sensation, or recognition – is always experienced dualistically. Perceived success is followed, or even accompanied, by perceived failure. The failure may occur in the same field as the success or in an apparently unrelated area of life. If nothing happens that might be taken as failure, we either project failure or become blatantly self-destructive, causing real loss in order to balance the experience. Either way, the sense of failure balances success.

Do not be motivated by duality to avoid negativity

Please note that I am not describing the mechanism of duality to encourage you to be more careful in avoiding negativity. Negativity cannot be avoided; it can only be suppressed. There is a deep, inextinguishable need in us to live through the negative; we do not rest until this need is filled. We go out of our way to create negative, complementary conditions.

Realizing that any move toward security, pleasure, or success is bound to include its opposite, it is possible to fall back into an overriding pessimism. People become cynical without ever hearing the theory of duality, because they have known success to be accompanied by failure. They decide to avoid failure by avoiding success and end up missing life. This nonconfrontational attitude is fairly common and usually unconscious.

But we should not stop striving after happiness. As human beings, it is our nature to pursue happiness, in whatever form we individually conceive. If you just can accept that your highs always will be balanced by lows – that you would not even recognize the highs without the lows – you will maintain a balanced, positive outlook about life. You will be able to relax when things become uncomfortable, instead of reacting in panic. In accepting unhappiness, you ultimately transcend it. You paradoxically achieve a higher, more *unconditional* form of happiness.

Addiction exaggerates duality

We are subject to the law of duality most strongly when addicted to the satisfaction of any desire. Addicted, we are compulsive; we must have the object in question. Addicted, fulfillment is highly dualistic, alternating between pronounced, neurotic pleasure and pain. Our need and belief systems are artificial, compulsive, and addictive, setting us up for strong dualistic experiences. When not addicted to outcomes, we do not go through the same intensity of dualistic swings, if only because we do not look for intense satisfaction to come from the activity. We are more relaxed and don't need as much to be happy.

Processing brings growth

Growth is gradual; we learn we don't need this and then that. The elimination of compulsive needs, or what we think we just have to have, is an important part of personal liberation. But exactly how is growth achieved? You cannot free yourself from compulsive, addictive needs by an act of will. It is only when you use the intellect to move to a place of *processing* that growth and real change begin. Processing and clearing of the feelings associated with addictive and unsatisfied needs results in a gentle, natural outgrowing of them. Do not force yourself to be something you are not; do not want to be something other than what you are. In accepting yourself as you are, you allow growth to occur.

DUALISTIC PROJECTION

The purpose of the projection mechanism of the mind is to clear the subconscious. But as it projects, the mind must create a balance of positive and negative to be able to perceive at all. The primary "negative pole" of the projection usually brings up the suppressed energy; the compensating "positive pole" is created spontaneously to balance the energy experience and does not represent clearing of the subconscious. The positive pole may be internalized and may become the focus of our compulsiveness. Let's go over a few examples that detail how this works.

Anger/Celebration

A man has a run-in with someone during the day. He projects his anger and perceives someone as being angry with him for no good reason, or becomes angry himself and believes that the other person "caused" it. Then he goes to his favorite bar and carouses with his buddies, telling them of the episode. Feelings of camaraderie ensue, wherein they all denounce the villain, balancing the whole episode. The initial argument was the primary negative pole of the projection, based on the suppressed energy trying to release, and the good time in the bar was the compensating positive pole, constructed to balance. Of course, before he went to the bar, he could have gone home and kicked the dog in an attempt to displace the still-unreleased anger.

Love/Rejection

A woman has repressed her feelings of rejection for other people. Traditional psychologists might say she is inclined to reject others because of the rejection and lack of love she received as a child. However, if we acknowledge the influence of previous-life Karma, we would say she came into the present life with these subconscious tendencies intact and that her childhood only served as the catalyst for her condition. She represses (unconsciously) the feelings of rejection for others because the feelings do not fit in with her self-image. She projects, therefore, and perceives others as being cold and rejecting toward her. This is the primary negative projection, and it is experienced painfully. The compensatory, positive pole of the projection assumes the form of her "love" for one person. She idealizes the image of her lover, searching for the proper person, or screen, on which to project. If she finds the person, her love affair will be ecstatic to the degree that her perceived rejection by others has been painful.

She will not see her lover as a real person or will give only token attention to the real person, because she is in love with her projection. Her "love," being dependent and unreal to begin with, will change as well, according to duality, becoming fear and resentment, affording new opportunities for suppression.

She also could have internalized the secondary projection, seeing herself, for example, as a martyr, someone who loves and sacrifices for humanity but who is misunderstood and rejected. She receives support and pleasure from the internalized self-image to the extent that she feels pain from the primary projection – the coldness she experiences from others.

Hostility toward authority/
Rebellious self-determination

A child grows up in a military family and "reacts" badly. Traditional psychology might say he developed a suppressed hostility toward authority because of the restraint imposed on him in childhood. Our viewpoint would be that he came into the present life with authority issues, choosing an early environment that would serve as a catalyst for them. He grows up becoming a rock singer, intent on demolishing authority with his message. His perception of authority as evil is a projection based on the suppressed hostility. If originally he had been able to release the hostility instead of suppressing it, there would be no latent energy available to form the projection.

The original cause of the suppressed condition is not known, but possibly because of previous-life difficulty in a similar situation, suppression on a large scale occurred. He may have had his personal power severely limited by an authority figure and was unable to release the resulting resentment; but this in itself would have been the result of Karma from yet another previous life. Possibly, there never was any outer restraint, but he limited himself with his own inner blocking, projecting the responsibility onto outside authority. Trying to trace back to the original cause is difficult, if not futile, as well as irrelevant for the purposes of processing.

His primary projection is that he is being controlled, manipulated, and limited by authority, toward which the suppressed irrational hostility is directed. His compensating projection is internalized. He styles his self-image as that of a free agent: unbound, spontaneous, defiant, rebellious – a rock star. His enjoyment of the positive projection is dependent on and balanced by the pain of the negative projection. He suffers real pain in the primary projection, the experience of authority as tyranny. He finds real pleasure in the rebellious self-image, the compensating projection. They are balanced.

His audience consists mostly of people who share a similar authority conflict. They identify with both sides of the projection, seeing themselves as victims of authority and also unconsciously identifying with authority because they assign their self-blocking functions to it. In the performance, they gain a heightened sense of participation through the dramatic presentation of both poles of the energy projection.

In much the same way, we go through life projecting and balancing our experience. This is not something only "neurotics" do, but something we all do, all the time. Some events balance out immediately; some dictate the course of our entire lives. The great novelists concern themselves with circumstances and themes such as these; that is why there is always a mixture of fulfillment and frustration in the lives of their characters. Indeed, the inevitability of duality is a large part of their message.

INTEGRATION OF DUALITIES

The key to resolving the problem of duality is integration of the negative. By trying to avoid the negative, it becomes suppressed and part of our subconscious Karma; we become addicted to the positive. If the theory of duality is at all valid, the futility of continual avoidance of the negative becomes plain. We are trying to avoid the unavoidable and creating a debt that eventually must be paid. By choosing to avoid the negative now, it will affect us even more subversively in the future, keeping us bound to the irrational and destructive urges of the subconscious that suppression creates.

You cannot eliminate the negative
by attaining more of the positive

An important insight for us is how we become trapped in any one particular dualistic projection. In an effort to avoid the negative, we become compulsive about the positive. We do not see that they are related, that one depends on the other for its existence, that they are two sides of the same coin.

We think that we can do away with the negative by attaining more of the positive, but eventually we come to realize that the negative can never be eliminated by more of the positive; in fact, when we attain more of the positive, the negative only increases; they must balance each other. The negative must be faced and released directly. Understanding this is one of the turning points of inner work.

When you realize that you have been pursuing some particular attainment compulsively, whether it takes the form of relationship, money, or recognition in order to eliminate an inner feeling such as loneliness, insecurity, or worthlessness, you begin serious work. You see the futility of what you have been doing; you confront the feeling that has been driving you, often unconsciously. You begin to work with the feeling itself, and your life begins to change.

Integration means accepting
and including the negative

Instead of trying to separate one part of life from another, we acknowledge that the negative is integral to any particular experience; that the experience could not be without it; indeed, that we ourselves have unconsciously assigned the negative value to balance the forces. We accept and surrender to the negative. As we stop running from the negative, there is bound to be suppressed pain in the subconscious. There is no other way to get rid of this pain except to bring it to the surface and experience it. This is what is done in therapy. Facing the negative is a necessary part of the healing process.

Integration brings
freedom from pain

Our goal is not merely to endure pain but to go beyond pain. Integration does not mean endless confrontation with pain. Once suppressed pain is cleared, it is gone forever. Integrated dualities are not painful, because both poles are balanced. When dualism is integrated, life becomes whole, or "holistic." We become free from duality, the trap of pleasure and pain. We transcend, no longer frantically clinging to the positive and fearfully trying to avoid the negative. We find ourselves with a new awareness and freedom; we have grown; happiness is unconditional.

Integration does not mean that the negative side of any dualistic experience is eliminated, but that our perception of the negative changes so it is no longer disturbing. Life is still encountered in terms of dualities, but in a noncompulsive manner – a natural ebb and flow. Just as day and night, hot and cold are not regarded as problems, the poles of feeling are experienced as nonproblematical. We use the "negative" productively. This is the goal of processing and other growth therapies.

A good example of one of the basic dualities that most of us need to work on is relationships: Unintegrated, we experience the poles of isolation/dependency; integrated, we enjoy autonomy/relatedness. Unintegrated, we fear being alone. Lonely and anxious, we seek to escape from the isolation through relationship. We are driven by the fear of being alone and depend on the other to eliminate our loneliness. We become addicted to the other. If the other is lost, we experience and exhibit symptoms that would be present in withdrawal from any addiction. When integrated, we enjoy our aloneness. We become creative when alone, recharging our energies, and even look forward to being alone. We then are able to relate to others nondependently, which makes our company even more pleasant.

Each aspect of life may be broken down and understood in terms of its dualistic complements. The integration of dualistic experience becomes an art in itself.

My body is the most important friend I have. It is always with me, to support and serve me. It is the center of my feelings. If I love my body, I will love myself. If I am aware of and accept my body, I will be aware of and be able to accept my feelings. I will grow and become whole.

4

Feeling Through the Body

Our discussion so far has been concerned with what might be called the workings of the mind. I would now like to direct your attention to another aspect of our individuality, the body. In our culture, the body usually is viewed either as a servant of the mind or as a source of pleasure or vanity, but it is not given the status it deserves. If we are to develop sensitivity to ourselves, we must do so through both approaches, that of the body as well as the mind.

The study of both body and mind leads to the conclusion that they are not unrelated but that there is, after all, a deep connection between them. Each influences the other, each may be observed and understood through the other, and each blends into the other, almost eliminating the distinction between them.

Therefore, learning to approach ourselves through the body is an important aspect of our self-work. If this emphasis were omitted, we would be at a disadvantage in our effort to integrate ourselves. The same serious disadvantage, I feel, is incurred in any therapy or inner growth practice that does not include work with the body. The importance of the body in psychological therapy comes about in the following ways.

STORING NEGATIVITY

We have discussed the fact that suppression stores unreleased negative energy. Storage begins on the psychic level, but as suppressed energy accumulates, it carries over into the physical body. For practical purposes, therefore, the physical body can be seen as an accurate representation of the suppressed psychic energy, and working with the physical body can release energy stored in the physical-psychic continuum. As a result, various types of "body-work" have emerged, each effecting the release of negative psychic energy through work with the physical.

The interfacing of the physical and psychic has become known as the body/mind connection. Even though the concept of body/mind has been a fundamental part of Eastern psychological theory for thousands of years, it is relatively new in the West. Wilhelm Reich is generally credited with being the first to bring this concept into contemporary psychological practice. It is largely through his discoveries that the various schools of psychology have grown which emphasize working with the body to effect psychological change.

Our attitudes toward the body affect us more than we realize. We learn to think of the body as the means to achieve goals. We become "mind-oriented," because goals are of the mind, instead of "feeling-oriented." We don't pay attention to feelings because they don't help us accomplish goals. In turning away from feelings, we turn away from body awareness, because feeling is a body function. We become unconscious in our bodies and tacitly allow the buildup of negative energies.

THINKING AND FEELING

People working in the psychological field usually state that the body reflects the mind, but this is not quite accurate. The body really corresponds to the psychic feeling capacity, which includes the emotions. Emotions are felt in the body. Blocks in the emotions "set up" in the body.

The mind, on the other hand, has somewhat of an antithetical function to feeling. The mind is composed of thoughts. Thoughts have no emotional value in themselves, except as they act on feelings. Thoughts are cold; they are composed of judgments, comparisons, evaluations, reasoning, plans, and so on. The common quality of all thoughts is that they deal in the past, in learned and remembered values. Then, based on the past, thoughts extend into the future, creating goals. The mind acts like a computer, essentially learning to associate pleasure or pain with memory.

The mind, however, does not have the capacity to experience. Experiencing is the function of the feeling center. We run into trouble when we attempt to experience through the mind. Instead of experiencing, we end up comparing *what is* to some remembered event in the past or anticipated event in the future, and we never fully perceive the actual event taking place before us.

The feeling center is the proper function to use in experiencing

In direct experience, there is no thought present, no comparison or evaluation, just awareness of *what is*. This could be an inner event or the interaction with someone or something in the outer world. In either case, the experience is allowed to occur as a feeling, without resistance or blocking. We allow ourselves simply "to be" with the experience.

The feeling centers correspond to the *chakras*. The chakras are psychic centers located in the body. They are centers of energy, consciousness, and feeling. When we block ourselves from experiencing – which happens when we try to experience through the mind – we block ourselves from these centers of consciousness and, therefore, from the body. Feelings of alienation from the body result. This tendency can be reversed, and sensitivity to feelings developed, by getting in rapport with the body.

Thus, if you are too much in the mind and not enough in the body, you will feel alienated or out of touch with yourself. You will have the sense of being an identity with a body instead of the sense that, on a certain level, you *are* the body. Being out of touch with yourself is also why you feel out of touch with others. As you increase your connection to the body, you increase the capacity for feeling, self-acceptance, self-love, and the ability to love others.

The body is always in the moment

While the mind is always in either the past or the future, the body is always in the moment because of its feeling nature – feeling is inherently in the moment. Being in the moment is a condition that you should strive to develop, because life is taking place in the moment. When locked in the mind, in expectations of the future based on the past, you do not confront and experience life.

Not being in the moment contributes to the sensation of being an isolated "I," an ego. If asked to locate the "I" physically, we typically feel that it is somewhere above the neck, out of touch with the body, which is considered to be merely the dumb beast that carries the "I" around. This is characterized by our modern dress code for men of a tight collar and tie around the neck, and also the belt around the waist. It is interesting to note that women's fashion allows freer-flowing, nonconstrictive designs, supporting the observation that women are generally more in touch with their bodies and feelings than men. Men tend to drive their bodies from the mind, while women tend to feel their way through situations.

One who feels a connection to the body will not feel like an isolated "I," a separate ego, but will feel a deep connection within, both to the self and to others. The connection to the body is felt on a profound and fulfilling level; energies are contacted that are unknown to the isolated person.

The sense of isolation, the "I" or the ego, is of central concern in Eastern psychology. One of its goals is to expand the ego to the point where the oneness of creation is perceived. However, we should not attempt to be something we are not but should accept and celebrate ourselves as we are. As we develop our consciousness, which can be effectively thought of as developing contact with the feeling centers of the body, we naturally will increase our sense of perspective.

Western psychology uses the term "ego" differently. The ego is thought of more as the core of the individuality, not as something to be outgrown. Western psychology traditionally is dedicated to strengthening and making the ego function more smoothly. This approach may have to do with the lack of contact with spiritual values that I mentioned earlier but is more likely due to the urgency of the cases with which it must contend as well as a reflection of our culture.

Eastern psychology recognizes that a strong ego is required before higher work can be undertaken, but it is concerned more with developing our evolutionary potential than with just making us functional. The developing of higher qualities necessarily involves the loosening of the ego. However, there is no need to become fixated on ego/nonego disputes or aspirations. We only have to allow ourselves to grow naturally.

RELEASING NEGATIVITY

Negativity stored in the body becomes trapped in the muscles, chakras, and organs. Working with these areas is the primary concern in all types of bodywork. Bodywork usually is done in any of several ways – manipulation, energy work, or stretching.

Manipulation

Manipulation consists of therapeutic massage. The stimulation releases the trapped energy, and emotional releases are common on the massage table. There are many different bodywork techniques and schools, and I feel they all have something to offer. The only drawback is that a practitioner is required, involving a certain inconvenience and expense, but getting bodywork treatments when possible will prove to be beneficial.

Energy work

Nonmanipulative energy techniques involve balancing of the body's functional energy system and can result in significant release of suppressed emotional energy. These techniques usually are applied by a practitioner directing a flow of energy from the hands, either touching the body or not. The intent is to affect primarily the psychic energy body. The practitioner's energy will nurture the recipient where needed, break up congestion in the chakras, and implement release of trapped negativity.

Stretching

Stretching of muscles has been found to be effective in releasing blocked energy. The technique of releasing stored negativity through stretching has been worked out most systematically and beautifully in the age-old system of yoga postures, which is my personal favorite form of bodywork. Yoga has a marked advantage in that it can be practiced alone, making it inexpensive and convenient, as well as effective in achieving its intent. Tension from daily living as well as long-term suppression is held in the muscles, and yoga addresses both.

In addition to stretching muscles, yoga postures work directly on the chakra system, releasing blocks that have built up. The spine is kept flexible. The condition of the spine is important for good health; keeping it flexible maintains the energy flow in the body and between the chakras. The arteries are stimulated, counteracting hardening and congestion. Joints are kept loose. For our purposes, however, the most important aspect of yoga postures is their suppression-releasing capabilities. Normally, it is not emphasized that yoga will release trapped feeling energy, but if you are conscious of using it for this purpose, you will find that it can be an extraordinary tool. When combined with breathwork, the result is a physical approach that is unsurpassed for stimulating the release of suppressed negativity stored in the body. A regular practice of yoga will help keep you relaxed as well as gently uncover layers of the subconscious.

With any body-centered approach, the effectiveness is enhanced when you understand that suppressed energy is being released into consciousness for clearing. However, clearing does not happen automatically. You must process the material as it comes into awareness in order to complete the release; the function of the bodywork is just to make it conscious. If you handle the material incorrectly or are not concerned with the emotional aspect of the work, there will be minimal emotional benefit. The release of suppressed material is sensed as negative feelings coming into consciousness. When the feelings come up, you should not be alarmed but should welcome the opportunity to clear them and process the material with the techniques you are learning.

*Bodywork clears
negativity directly*

The advantage of using any body technique to implement clearing is that imbalances are approached deeply and directly on the energy level. Clearing is stimulated by working with the blocks in the psychic body, through the physical body. The need for clearing through projection onto other people or events is reduced. We become more balanced when interacting with others, because clearing takes place in our private practice. We develop a sense of connectedness with the body and feeling centers.

Even so, bodywork is not all that is needed to facilitate personal growth. As you work on yourself, you must approach from other directions as well. Other approaches include processing, psychotherapy, meditation, spirituality, group work, or any growth technique that develops sensitivity to feelings, bringing suppressed material into awareness. Remember, these techniques should not be primarily of an analytical, thinking nature. The feeling side must be developed. Use your intellectual and thinking functions to understand the principles involved, and then leave thinking behind as you train yourself to feel.

It should be noted that exercise in general, while important, does not have the same effect as bodywork. Exercise can keep you in shape and perhaps help blow off some nervous energy, but muscle-held tensions will not be released. Actually, exercise such as weight lifting and bodybuilding do exactly the opposite, tightening the muscles and driving muscle-held suppressed negativity deeper, increasing insensitivity to the feeling nature of the body. If you are involved in weight training, it is doubly important for you to include stretching in your routine. A good rule of thumb is equal time for both, stretching after weights.

Bodywork involves getting the energy "unstuck" in the body. You must cultivate the ability to allow the loosened energy to flow as it would prefer, not as your conscious mind would dictate. You must surrender to the innate intelligence of the body, the "wisdom of the body."

THE WISDOM OF THE BODY

Choiceless awareness is the capacity for feeling directly *what is* – inner and outer – with no thought of wanting anything to be different. We accept, we don't block, experience. We become the Witness, refraining from choosing or controlling.

Choiceless awareness is essential
for higher consciousness

As choiceless awareness is maintained during bodywork, we begin to get more in touch with the body and the feeling nature. Going further, we sense the presence of an intelligence previously unrecognized. This intelligence is nonverbal, nonmental, and non-dualistic; it may be compared to instinct but is higher on the scale of evolution than conscious intelligence, while instinct is lower. This intelligence, which is activated through feeling, not thinking, is referred to as the wisdom of the body.

We become aware of the working of the wisdom of the body through sensation. Sensations are feelings; they may not always be pleasant, but their occurrence indicates that the body is balancing itself. When sensations reach a particular level of intensity, we call them "symptoms." If you do not understand that unpleasant symptoms are beneficial, you may become alarmed and attempt to suppress them in an effort to feel better. However, if you know that symptoms are signs that the body is healing and purifying itself, you will be able to relax, letting the body's process occur as it will. If you accept the feelings with love, you allow self-healing. If you fight the feelings, you fight your own healing energies.

Allow the body
to purify itself

A most basic example of the body's self-healing capacity is the common cold. A cold is the body's attempt to clear itself of mucus (largely caused by dairy products) and other contaminants. If you allow the cold to go through its complete cycle, a thorough cleansing occurs. If you fight the cold with excess antihistamines, you block the cleansing, and the body will need to have another cold soon.

The same logic can be applied to any "disease," although the connection between symptoms and cleansing may not be as apparent. The disease represents a psychic cleansing in progress. Allowing the cleansing to occur and the wisdom of the body to work as it will is basic to *homeopathic* healing on the physical level and also to healing on the psychological level.

Strong feelings are the psychic body's attempts to purge suppressed negativity. If you accept and process both physical and emotional feelings, you begin psychic healing. You allow the wisdom of the body to heal you when you accept and experience your feelings as they are, with no thought of changing them. The wisdom of the body is identical to the power that is invoked in the last step of processing, when the Higher Self guides transformation.

LOVING YOUR BODY

In contemporary society, there exists an enormous focus on body culturing. We normally approach body culturing with an idea of how we think the body should be – or, more accurately, should appear – since most of our concern about the body is from a cosmetic viewpoint. We think our bodies are too fat, too thin, need to be in better shape, need more muscle. Esthetic considerations do have a legitimate place in the concern for health, but generally we are much too superficial in our goals.

Behind the concern with the appearance of the body is a sense of dislike, which can grow to the point of hatred. Hatred of the body is common. It is what motivates us to work so strenuously to change the body. Plan after plan – exercise, dieting, etc. – is entered upon to force the body into becoming the ideal that we hold in our mind. This forcing becomes a kind of violence that we do to ourselves.

When we try to force the body to change, we are coming from the mind center, not the feeling center. We are in the mind because we have a goal, an ideal, a picture of what we want to be, what we think will bring us happiness. We relate to the body as an object that should be a certain way to please us. We therefore experience the body from a dualistic standpoint, never going beyond the ambivalence inherent in dualism. It becomes impossible to be finally pleased with the body.

We are alienated
from the body

The reason we dislike the body is not because of what it looks like, or how it is, but because *we are not connected to it,* not in touch with it. We are not in the feeling center; therefore, we are alienated from the body. Being alienated from and disliking the body, we think the fault is in the body, and we strive to change it. We are looking in the wrong direction. The fault is in our attitude toward the body. If this basic attitude is not corrected, we will never be happy with the body, no matter what it looks like.

When viewed from the feeling center, the body is no longer an object, owned like any other possession. In contrast, the body is experienced as the self. Even though the body corresponds to the Lower and not the Higher Self, the realization that the body is the self is powerful and meaningful. We transcend the tendency to think of the body as an object. We go beyond dualistic perception and experience the body as energy.

When we dislike and try to change the body because of the dislike, the body registers being rejected. It responds as anything or anyone will respond to rejection – by getting worse instead of better. The effect of diet and exercise is very much secondary to the emotional message we give the body. Of course, it is possible to bludgeon the body into shape to a certain extent, but it is an uphill fight, with impermanent results. Worse yet, we are left with the basic neurotic condition of being split against ourselves, of fighting ourselves, because the body is the self.

Alienation and the resulting dislike of the body come from a deep and unconscious place. We have been rejecting the body for long periods of time and have built strong, unconscious patterns that influence us. We have fallen into a vicious circle. We dislike the body, and because we handle the dislike improperly, we reject ourselves. The rejection registers in the subconscious, creating more negative conditions such as being overweight or poor health, and we reject ourselves further. The pattern builds, furthermore, over many lifetimes. It is not possible to uncover and purge all this negativity overnight. Indeed, learning to love ourselves is the work of a lifetime.

Hatred of the body
is often projected

We hate our body, and even ourselves, and suppress and project the hatred onto others. We hate them for no real reason except ones that we invent to justify our feelings. Or we feel that others hate us. Since we may experience a certain amount of rejection from others if our bodies are in bad shape, the projection is reinforced. We buy into the rejection, perceiving ourselves to be worse than we are. In contrast, if we genuinely loved the body as it is, imagine how different our experience would be. The healing power of love can bring about miraculous spontaneous changes. The body wants to balance itself and has the intelligence to do so. It is prevented from doing so because it is crippled by messages of rejection.

But even if you want to love yourself and your body, the question remains of how to do this. You cannot intellectually love yourself. You cannot simply think what you consider to be loving thoughts about yourself, or pamper yourself, and assume that you are loving yourself, although actions like these may result from loving yourself. Self-love is not a quality of the mind. Self-love comes about by developing the *feeling* capacity. You must learn how to accept and experience your feelings about your body, as they are, *even your hateful feelings*. This is what acceptance means. This is how you love yourself. This is what brings the catharsis.

When you learn how to accept and experience whatever hateful feelings you may have about yourself, you allow real transformation to begin – you learn the art of loving yourself. Resisting, denying, or being motivated by negative feelings to make external change results only in suppression. Learning to love yourself first involves understanding what love is. For now, turn to your body with a readiness and openness to *listen* rather than demand. Listening with the Heart, or feeling, will start you in the direction of self-love.

BREATH

In our work, we use breath techniques to help integrate and release suppressed material. In addition to supplying oxygen for respiration, the breath simultaneously draws in another quality, known as *prana*. Prana is the universal life force, the basic energy that sustains all living things. With proper techniques, the amount of prana that is taken in can be increased and directed to perform specific functions. Prana has an electrical quality and interacts with the energy body and the aura; the conscious direction of prana is effective in clearing energy blocks in the body.

Scientists have recognized the connection between breathing and the psychological condition. Fritz Perls, the founder of Gestalt therapy, stated, "Anxiety is the experience of breathing difficulty during any blocked excitement." We become unable to maintain proper breathing during the increased need for oxygen due to involuntary muscle clenching.

Inhibition of breath can be observed in ourselves. We encounter a challenging situation and respond by holding the breath, which is exactly what should not be done. You can learn to overcome the unconscious tendency to hold the breath simply by watching yourself and reminding yourself to breathe fully whenever you feel stressed.

Breathe into stress

"Breathing into" means the conscious and deliberate focusing of prana, the life energy, into whatever stressful condition is present. The type of condition could be "negative," such as an event that brings up fear, or "positive," such as being close to a loved one, because both negative and positive can be stressful and in need of integration. Stress may be defined as the inability to be in the feeling center with whatever is happening, regardless of the nature of the event; the feeling center is blocked. Thrown out of the feeling center, we fall into the mind, becoming separated from what is before us. Breathing into the blocked center activates it, allowing the energy to rebalance.

You breathe into the blocked center by breathing deeply as you hold the feelings or event in your consciousness. The prana that is taken in with the breath has an intelligence of its own, much like the cells of the body do, and will find and stabilize the energy imbalance. The stressful condition may be physical or emotional pain, confrontation with another person, essentially anything that you encounter and must contend with, including joy. When you don't breathe into an event – or worse, if you hold your breath – anxiety is created, and you inhibit the ability to respond creatively.

The unblocking of trapped energy is essentially a suppression-releasing function. Breath can be effective in performing this function, yet, as with bodywork, breath techniques by themselves cannot do the whole job. When the breath is incorporated with bodywork and a conscious psychological method for working on ourselves, satisfying progress with self-integration can be achieved.

During bodywork, you will cleanse suppressed energy. Various feelings will jump into your consciousness in the form of strong emotions, reliving past events, and so on. A major aid to the integration of this material is to breathe into it. Specific breath techniques are covered in Chapter 11.

*In my body are
my centers of
consciousness. As I
learn to feel in these
centers, I come into
contact with my real
self. If I avoid feeling
in these centers, I
block myself. My love
for myself grows as I
joyously enter these
centers and lovingly
behold what I find.*

5

The Centers of Consciousness

THE CHAKRAS

Before we begin discussing Integrative Processing itself, it would serve us well to become familiar with the Eastern psychophysiological system of the chakras. The chakra system fills a gap in contemporary psychology, giving us a matrix that can be used to classify energy needs that have been programmed into us as human beings. Using the chakra system supplies essential vocabulary and reference points, enabling us to recognize feelings within ourselves more easily. It provides insight into how blocks in the energy system come about, helping us deal with them more effectively. Awareness, the first step in processing, is facilitated.

The chakras are energy centers but also may be thought of as centers of consciousness, feeling, need, or experience. They are the "drives" to which psychology broadly refers. Each chakra, or center, as they are also known, provides a particular frame of reference through which our personal perception of the world comes to us. As we grow, we change our main focus from "lower" centers to "higher" ones. Our view of the world changes, our level of consciousness matures, we have a different experience. We develop the higher capacities of human potential.

Although there are many energy centers in the body, usually only seven are considered to be of major importance. However, in practice I have found it helpful to use a slightly more comprehensive schematic of the chakra system, giving a total of ten. The location of these additional centers was first suggested to me by the Taoist chakra system, but the psychological qualities I have assigned to them are based on my own observations.

Using the additional points clarifies the confusion and ambiguity that I previously found in working with qualities traditionally attributed to the Solar Plexus, Heart, and Throat chakras. The new points are the Power, Nurturing, and Creative centers. Each of the ten points corresponds to one of the ten planets, giving a useful correlation between the chakras and the astrological birth chart, which can be a useful tool for healing work.

The chakras are where
our blocks are located

We all have at least a minimum of activity in each of these centers, but certain ones will be strongly developed while others will not, depending on the person. Because of our personal history of suppression, we have conditioned ourselves to block energy from flowing harmoniously through the centers. Reconditioning ourselves to allow energy to flow easily through the centers is an important part of our inner work as well as that of any psychological therapy.

The chakras are located coincident with the physical body but are not part of the physical – that's why they have never been found by any scientist exploring the body. Being centers of energy, they are located in what we might term the energy body.

The energy body, also called the astral, emotional, or psychic body, may be considered to be an energy form identical to the physical body that coincides with it but is distinct from it, with different characteristics or "rules" of behavior, and which may even be separated from it under certain conditions, including sleep. It is where our emotional sense of "I" is located.

In normal waking consciousness, we do not usually sense the difference between the energy and physical bodies. Feelings and emotions that actually occur in the chakras of the energy body are felt as if in the physical body. For practical purposes, then, we combine the two bodies in our work, referring to them as the body function, the home of the feeling capacity. Hence, the emphasis on getting in touch with the body as the route to feeling.

Chakra is the Sanskrit word for "wheel." This name is appropriate because the chakras are actually in constant spinning motion. They are literally composed of energy and, to the psychic vision, have a definite shape and color. Because they are energy, the chakras should be thought of as being tangible in nature: more subtle than the physical, yet substantial enough to be considered not just "mental."

It is because of this tangibleness that I refer to the chakras as "psychophysiological." They represent states of consciousness, something that is often mistakenly considered to be only mental; but, having an energetic/physical basis, they can be worked with through the body, as in any of the bodywork techniques, yielding substantial results in stimulating and aligning consciousness. You should realize that these centers are of basic importance in influencing your everyday state of being: how you feel, what you feel, what you are preoccupied with, and so on.

The health of a center corresponds to its ability to receive and express universal energy into consciousness, through the function of feeling. Healthy chakras are vibrant. Unhealthy chakras are blocked and stagnant; the energy does not flow easily, leading to negative conditions such as depression, addiction, or poor health.

When the centers are stimulated with breath, bodywork, or processing, blocked energy is released. The resulting emotional cleansing can become an intense catharsis – it then becomes apparent how deeply the energy body influences our psychological con-

THE CHAKRAS

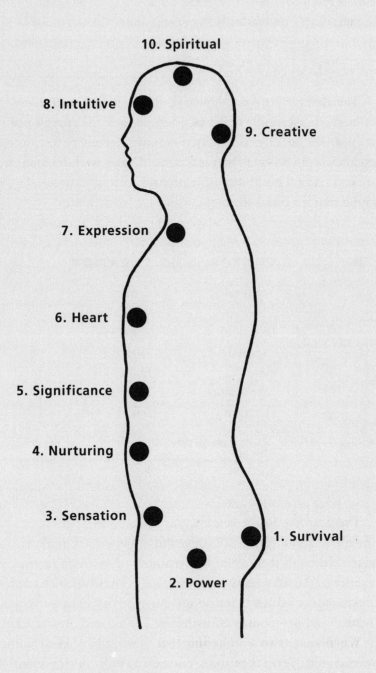

10. Spiritual

8. Intuitive

9. Creative

7. Expression

6. Heart

5. Significance

4. Nurturing

3. Sensation

1. Survival

2. Power

dition. Energy balancing also may be aided with quartz and other healing crystals. The atomic vibrational structure of crystals enables them to interact with the aura, energy body, and chakras, clearing blocks and stimulating energy flow.

The chakras are located in
precise places in the body

The chakras are spaced from the base of the spine to the top of the head, in ascending order of consciousness. Although not normally sensed directly, as you increase your sensitivity to your body, you will begin to feel the centers, as if they were located in the physical body. This ability is helpful for getting in touch with and stimulating the blocked energy.

	CHAKRA	LOCATION
10.	Spiritual	Crown
9.	Creative	Base of skull
8.	Intuitive	Third eye
7.	Expression	Throat
6.	Heart	Chest
5.	Significance	Solar plexus
4.	Nurturing	Navel
3.	Sensation	Lower abdomen
2.	Power	Perineum
1.	Survival	Root

The first five lower centers, Survival, Power, Sensation, Nurturing, and Significance, are active but unintegrated in most people today. Although these centers provide the raw force necessary to function in the material world, they are primarily selfish modes of consciousness, which manifest much negativity because they usually are holding suppressed material. The next center, the Heart, has the potential to be unselfish but is usually aligned with the lower centers. Love then has a possessive, selfish component. The last four centers, the Expression, Intuitive, Creative, and Spiritual, more clearly mark the beginning of selfless orientation and higher consciousness. These centers are only minimally active in most people today. Love, when aligned with these higher centers, becomes unselfish.

Why is it better to be unselfish than selfish? For a selfish reason: to be happy. But what is the cause of our selfishness? The problem begins with the lack of ability to feel. We are closed off to our own energies and are self-rejecting.

The Sense of Separation

Lack of contact with ourselves leads to the experience of *separation* from the world around us as well. The sense of separation is the basic cause of selfishness, anxiety, and unhappiness. We continually strive to overcome separation with self-defeating, often unconscious, behavior such as substance abuse, conformity, consumerism, mass entertainment, dependent love, selfless sacrifice, striving for recognition, and addiction in general, but such efforts provide only temporary relief at best. The sense of separation and isolation is what is meant by the Eastern concept of the ego.

When selfishness is spoken about in a spiritual context, it is the sense of separation from others that is being referred to. Sometimes we become confused about selfishness, equating it with a lack of generosity. It should be understood that going beyond selfishness means more than just cultivating a generous attitude toward others. Generosity, of course, may be a result of higher consciousness, but it is also possible to be generous for entirely selfish reasons, and spiritual seekers may choose to be giving only because it fits in with their spiritual self-image.

What is really meant by unselfishness is an altering of the basic perception that we are separate, isolated beings – a complete reversal of the normal premise. Until this change of consciousness occurs, there is no point in trying to fake unselfishness. We only become hypocritical, although perhaps some good may come from a simple, more considerate attitude.

*The lower centers
lead to isolation*

You can never go beyond selfishness and isolation while immersed in the first five lower centers – that is simply their nature. The viewpoint from the lower centers is self-centered, isolated, and unhappy, even when success is attained on these levels. The lower centers reinforce the isolation that is experienced from a lack of feeling in general. You can grow into selflessness and non-isolation by activating the higher centers, through intelligent work on yourself.

Moreover, in the lower centers, the law of duality is strongly invoked. No lasting satisfaction in any accomplishment or possession can be found because of the alternating perception of pleasure/pain. Pleasure becomes a transparent façade, never quite covering the barren, inner isolation; pain is perceived as the reality from which we cannot escape. When we realize that most of the world, while attempting to operate from the lower centers, is also suppressed and blocked on these same levels, we begin to get a picture of the real state of human affairs.

THE PLANES OF INDIVIDUALITY

The chakras should not be confused with the planes of individuality. In our work, we recognize four planes: the Intellectual, Mental, Body/Feeling, and Spiritual planes. A chakra forms the link among all the planes. Each plane corresponds to a step of processing.

An important concept to appreciate is that our degree of mental or intellectual ability has no correlation to our level of consciousness, which is determined by the chakra on which we predominantly operate. It is possible to be fixated in a lower chakra and bring impressive mental and intellectual capacities to the service of that center. Our abilities may be brilliant, and it may appear as if we are accomplishing with superb skill, but when we are focused primarily and compulsively on a lower center of consciousness, we are functioning on a self-centered, and ultimately self-defeating, level. We will never find happiness and fulfillment.

In addition, there is no correlation between capacities of the different planes. For example, we may be quite advanced intellectually but undeveloped emotionally. Unfortunately, in modern times, this is more common than not. We suffer more than we know from the misplaced emphasis on intellectual skills and superficial personality. If we are smart, it is assumed that nothing else is needed. All of our education and training is intellectual. There is hardly any comprehension of emotional growth, which occurs through the development of the feeling centers. As a result, we remain stunted, unable to reach to the higher potentials accessible only through feeling.

DEVELOPMENT

The spacing of the centers vertically in the body is symbolic of the relative levels of consciousness as well as the sequence of their development. Theoretically, the awakening of each center is preceded by the balanced functioning of the previous one. Centers do not always awaken in order, however, contributing to the energy imbalance and therefore the psychological imbalance that is experienced.

The awakening of the chakras is evolutionary. We, as individuals, are growing and maturing as time goes by. The evolutionary scheme becomes clearer when the concept of reincarnation is included. It then makes better sense why growth takes so long, why individuals are at such different levels, why it is never too late to start working on yourself and foolish not to. We grow slowly, from life to life. Moreover, life is individually designed to provide just the right conditions to stimulate that growth, although they may seem harsh at the time.

*Be careful about awakening
the Heart prematurely*

The chakras awaken step by step. Our global consciousness is now at the point of developing the Heart center. It is not possible to move forward into the Heart, however, by concentrating on the Heart alone and ignoring the suppression and chaos in the lower centers. These must be integrated before the Heart can truly function. Spiritual seekers often make the mistake of trying to integrate the Heart ahead of the lower centers. Efforts to awaken the Heart prematurely lead to confused and unstable experience in the Heart, mixed with the still-unreleased negativity of the lower centers.

As integration and clearing of the lower centers proceeds (which can be accomplished effectively through the techniques you are learning), the character of these centers will change. This change cannot be willed or manipulated but happens automatically as you work on yourself. When integrated, a center will start to behave differently, in a more mature manner. It will come under control; it will be less self-oriented. There will be less of a problem with dualistic manifestation, and the center will supply the power for the center above.

When a center is integrated, the next center above will spontaneously begin to function, gradually and naturally. The reason we don't gently progress into the Heart is because the lower centers are not integrated, even though they are active. When integrated, the lower centers become a dynamo of power, supporting the spontaneous awakening of the Heart. If we attempt to awaken the Heart without this support, it is likely we will not have the energy required.

INTEGRATION AND ADDICTION

A center is considered *integrated* when there is a balanced experience of the dualistic qualities of that center. This means we have learned to recognize and accept both the "positive" and "negative" poles of the duality, incorporating them into a basically positive experience. No large amount of avoidance and suppression is occurring, and previously suppressed energies have been cleared. If we cannot realistically say that we have learned to experience the negative pole in a harmonious way, at least we have learned how to accept it and work with it constructively – for example, through processing.

*We become addicted to the positive
because we are unwilling to face the negative*

Unintegrated, we become *addicted* at various levels of experience. We become addicted to the "positive" side of any one dualistic experience because we are not willing to face the "negative" side of its duality. We seek to escape to the positive side, often not even realizing that both sides are dependent on one another for their existence.

However, because of the nature of dualism, the more we try to experience the positive, the more we also generate the negative. We become frustrated. We attempt to suppress the intensifying negative with more experiences of the positive, and the addiction cycle builds. Addiction can occur not only at the Sensation or Nurturing levels, where it is normally recognized, but in all centers. We develop a deep hunger for a particular need, but no matter what we do to try to satisfy the hunger, it remains or even becomes worse. Addictive behavior is also known as "compulsive."

*Addiction requires
psychic energy*

Each addiction can be related to a certain center of consciousness. Addiction is the result of an energy imbalance in that particular center. The center is blocked and does not experience the normal energy flow of a healthy center. The center is blocked because of our suppression. Through the avoidance of feelings in the center, *we* create the block. To maintain the block requires energy, energy the addiction supplies. All addiction provides an extra supply of energy, taken either from external sources or from the body's internal reserves.

The cravings that arise for a particular object of addiction are learned. Through experience, we learn that energy can be obtained from a certain source and used to maintain the block. When the block begins to weaken, because the suppressing energy is getting low, we begin to get glimpses of exactly what we are suppressing, and we experience discomfort, anxiety, depression, and so on. We then seek the addictive experience once more, to gain the energy required to maintain the block to the feelings. The feelings are resuppressed, over and over. Because the suppressed feelings will continue to build, the suppressing energy also must keep increasing, resulting in the extraordinary means that must be used to provide the energy. We enter the expanding cycle of addiction.

Usually we are addicted to a center's complement to the negative experience. However, we also can escape to another, usually higher, center and draw energy from there. The higher center will suppress the pain of the lower center. Thus, if we experience anxiety from an unintegrated Survival center, we could attempt to suppress it by becoming compulsively addicted to wealth and security, but we also could suppress it by compulsive seeking in any higher center, such as sex, power, love, even creativity.

The first step in breaking addiction is to understand how it works. When you know why you act compulsively, you weaken the power of the addiction. You must stop yielding to the addictive experience. Process the addictive urge as well as *the feeling that you are suppressing* with the addiction. Self-processing can be the main approach, but other approaches, such as therapy, group support, or medical support in cases of chemical dependency, are helpful as well.

When you confront feelings related to addiction, you meet your demon head on. You must realize that you are clearing accumulated negativity; proceed patiently and gently as well as sensibly. You must not demand too much of yourself, nor should you yield too easily. The delicate balance, the sense of making steady progress, must be established. As you learn how to work on yourself, you will acquire new tools that will help you tremendously. You will be able to cleanse negativity that previously compelled you to act in addictive ways.

THE CENTERS OF CONSCIOUSNESS

1. Survival

The Survival center is the most basic center of consciousness to all life-forms. This energy center is located at the base of the spine. It is concerned with physical well-being, security, health, and, among humans, money. It is the home of the most primal fears, including the fear of death. Indeed, all Survival center concerns really are backed by the fear of death, but we are not usually conscious of this, thinking that we are concerned about more immediate and superficial issues.

Being focused but not integrated in the Survival center means the world is perceived as a jungle, where one must fight for survival. We are primarily selfish, concerned with our own needs. Addiction to anything that represents security is likely. Addiction means that no matter how much "security" is attained, feelings of insecurity and fear will continue or even increase, because of the strong dualistic nature of this center.

When fear is the motivation for pursuing and attaining material goals, that fear is not eliminated by the attainment of those goals. On the contrary, when we acquire more, we think we need more, and the cycle never ends. Of course, we have legitimate needs that must be met, but what's important is our sense of discrimination. Lack of integration means we will be unrealistic in determining what our real needs are and will never be satisfied, no matter how much we have.

Unintegrated, we project our fear continuously onto events, becoming suspicious, distrustful, and paranoid. We take care of one "need," and the fear seems to go away, but then it surfaces somewhere else, and we think we now have to take care of another need. We struggle to make more money so we can meet our bills and have a little extra, but then we get hit with more expenses that put us right back into financial distress. These expenses appear to be real and justified. We don't see that it is our suppressed fear that brings them to us. The cycle continues because we never confront and integrate fear itself, which is behind the compulsiveness of the Survival center. We confront fear directly in our work when we process it. The result is integration and clearing, not temporary suppression.

If we are unintegrated on the Survival level, the suppressed fear becomes known to us through the presence of constant anxiety. We become anxiety-ridden, trapped and preoccupied with Survival consciousness. Isolation is acute, because the first center is the most self-centered of all. We imagine that we would be happy and secure with one more possession, a better job, more money, or whatever. Such are the fantasies that result from being focused but unintegrated in this center. As you may have noticed, this is where most of the world is immersed today.

The feelings related to this center that are to be processed include: fear in general, but more specifically, fear resulting from the threat of material loss, lack, bodily injury, disease, death; general anxiety, nervousness, possessiveness, selfishness, insecurity, paranoia, vulnerability, rigidity, shyness; the sense of limitation or delay; having your physical or psychological boundaries invaded; the compulsive desire for protection, safety, and basic survival.

If you have integrated this center, your experience of it will be basically harmonious, with a vital, new sense of trust in life. You will understand that change is unavoidable and that clinging to any object or person out of fear keeps you locked into a cycle of dependency. If you accept that uncertainty is an inherent part of existence, you will not feel as if you must compulsively guard against lack. Placing your trust in the flow of life, you find yourself provided for. Acceptance of insecurity and uncertainty paradoxically brings about feelings of security and stability. The Survival center then serves as the foundation for a GROUNDED consciousness.

2. Power

The instinctive impulse to control our experience is governed by the second chakra, Power. Those already familiar with the chakra system will recognize that I have removed Power needs from their traditional placement in the Solar Plexus chakra. I feel that Power consciousness is genuinely contained in the perineum center. This reassignment allows the Power and Solar Plexus centers each to fully reflect its true nature instead of being hampered by the presence of the other. Although closely related to the Solar Plexus, Power needs are distinguished by the urgency *to control*. Power, along with the other three lower centers, is a nonindividuated aspect of our humanity that we experience before we begin developing our sense of personal self in the Solar Plexus, which results in the urgency *to be seen*.

Power needs are most basic to our sense of integrity. When we give away our power, by allowing some other force to control us, we are diminished and fulfillment is thwarted. Often, however, we do not realize that we have done this. Our only sign may be the feelings that keep returning: We feel used, controlled, dominated, intimidated, manipulated, helpless, powerless, resentful, angry. These are the feelings to be processed in this center. However, if we are repressed and out of touch with our feelings, as is quite common, we do not even realize that this is how we feel.

Giving away our power comes about through dependency – we are unable to activate true autonomy within ourselves. Even though we in the Western world live in a society based on freedom, we are very far from being able to assert our *emotional* freedom. We are emotionally dependent, or addicted, in countless ways that we do not suspect. Indeed, another apt definition of spiritual growth is the breaking of dependencies.

Emotional dependency means the inability to flourish without support from outside sources. The support is a form of *energy* that we take in. All forms of dependency, including emotional, are characterized by a one-way flow: We take, but we do not give. As we mature emotionally, we acquire the capacity for *mutually supportive* relationships, in which we give and take equally; this is a necessary, desirable, more enlightened step but still a form of dependency. As we develop in our spiritual selves – which results from the emotional work in which we are engaged – we are more and more able to access the same energy from inside that we previously found outside. As we become one with the inner energy source, we need less and less from others. It no longer seems that we are seeking and taking; there is only the sense of fulfillment and completion.

In the Power center, we experience forming *bonds* with others. Many of these bondings are an essential part of human development, such as the bonding between parent and child and the bonding between lovers. But they are still dependent bonds; we are meant to experience them, to grow from them, and to form our *individuated* selves. If we resist or are unable to grow beyond dependent bonding, our growth stops, and our life experience becomes difficult; our Karma will keep bringing us lessons designed to get us unstuck.

In dependent bonding, we form complex psychic networks that entangle us. On the psychic plane, these ties may be seen as tangible bindings of energy that connect people with each other or with groups and institutions. We do this as part of our evolutionary growth; I am not implying that it is wrong or that it can be avoided. However, an important aspect of our growth is the movement to individuality. Growth means transcending the instinctive impulse to bond dependently.

Dependency occurs in respect to any of the chakras, but the Power center is its psychological home. Our blind, instinctive, unintegrated tendency regarding dependencies is to control. Quite simply, we think if we can control the objects of our addictions, we will be OK. We do not realize that all attempts at control are ultimately self-defeating. Because of dualism, the more we control, the more things get out of control.

In order to break the control syndrome, you must first recognize that you have it. Then you must recognize the feelings that you are attempting to eliminate with the controlling. These are the feelings that you must process. As you work with the feelings directly and release their energy, you undo the suppressed pain that keeps you trapped in the futile attempt to control.

Before we break the bonds, we often question if we really need to do so. We may even vigorously deny that we are dependent. But when we succeed in transcending dependency, and when we experience the greater scope of consciousness and self-empowerment that growth brings, we know without doubt that we are heading in the right direction.

The Power center is located at the bottom of the torso, just above the place called the perineum. That it is located in such a prosaic, taboo place has had to do with the obscurity of this vital center and also accounts for its connection to the sexual force, which often is closely related to the tendency to control. As we bring the center into the light by processing the negative feelings that come up when the object of our dependency is unavailable, we prepare the ground for the positive expression of the Power center and for a noncoercive, mutually fulfilling sexual relationship.

When the Power center is integrated, we do not refrain from relationship with others, we simply modify the nature of our interaction. We work harmoniously with others, not out of dependency and compulsion but because of the joy of communion. An integrated Power center is the beginning of socialization and true COOPERATION.

3. Sensation

The Sensation center, located in the lower abdomen, is the next major center activated in our evolution. This is the center of sensuality and sexuality. The world becomes the source of *pleasure gratification* when viewed from the Sensation center, and others are viewed as objects to be used.

Although sex is the primary manifestation of sensation needs, they also can take the form of cravings for touch, entertainment, TV, music, luxury, or any other sensual pleasure. All these activities stimulate this center, and all can serve as the focus of addiction if the center is unintegrated. Cravings on the Sensation level are therefore somewhat interchangeable, and that is why if you are sexually frustrated, you can work off the energy with entertainment or food.

Sensation often serves as relief for the two centers below it. If you are unintegrated in Survival or Power, you can escape to Sensation. In functioning on the higher level, you forget your insecurities and feel as if you are in control for the time being. In our society, entertainment and sex are very important to keep anxiety and powerlessness suppressed.

Lack of integration here usually is concerned with sexual issues. There is a basic and unconscious rejection of the sexual impulse, resulting in sexual repression. This leads to sexual addiction, and as a result, satisfaction is impossible to achieve. Sexual addiction can take either of two forms. The first is that no matter how much sex we have, we do not find the release that we seek, and we continue to want more. Sexual needs become compulsive. We may even think that we have no sexual problem because of our capacity to engage in it. The second form of sexual addiction is the inability to engage in it because of self-blocking.

Feelings that are to be processed in this center include sexual longing, frustration, compulsiveness, violation, inhibition, revulsion; cravings and frustrated desires for sensuality, touch, enter-tainment, TV, and the corresponding physical sensations that such frustration may bring up.

When the Sensation center is integrated, sex is approached in a balanced and reasonable manner and naturally begins to tie in to the Heart, when sex blends with love. This center is also the social center, and we all need to play as well as participate in communal festivity and art, which can function on this level as well. Success-ful integration leads to a CULTURED society.

4. Nurturing

Located at the navel, the Nurturing center of consciousness has to do with the capacity for emotionally *receiving* and feeling in gen-eral. More specifically, it governs feelings related to being cared for, fed physically and emotionally, mothering and being a mother. Our hunger for these experiences, the pain of their absence or dys-function, including cravings for food, alcohol, drugs, and smok-ing, and a general sense of emotional neediness are the feelings that are to be processed to bring this center into integration.

Western psychology, in its attempts to explain the origin of emotional patterns, usually looks to childhood experience. If the child did not receive proper mothering, if the mother was emo-tionally unavailable, did not hold the child affectionately, did not accept and validate all the child's feelings, it would be presumed that the child would develop into an adult with emotional issues, seeking to attach dependently to a partner, usually unconsciously, for the care and nurturing not received in childhood. Many schools of psychology would include as "therapy" treatment that would make up for the absence of mothering in childhood. The thera-pist/surrogate mother would be especially caring and supportive, emotionally strong, warm, and present; guided meditations might be used to "reprogram" the child's experience to be positive.

Persons undergoing therapy will welcome this kind of treat-ment. It is, after all, what they have been striving for uncon-sciously. But this approach will produce limited results. The problem is not that the mother figure is or was absent but that the client does not have the *capacity* to open to nurturing, either as a child turning outward to parents or as an adult turning to a therapist or inwardly to access self-nurturing. What needs to be addressed is the capacity for nurturing, the lack of which resulted in the child attracting a parent with limited emotional skills.

Processing the pain of not being open to receive, not being nurtured, being hungry and emotionally needy is what brings the shift and is how the capacity for nurturing may be developed. This inner neediness is felt as a kind of psychic vacuum, and I believe it is related to the general experience of emptiness that we often are driven to satisfy. As the neediness and emptiness are welcomed, accepted, and experienced, we break the blocks to self-nurturing.

Self-nurturing is a key component of emotional maturity. When we do not possess this ability, usually we are not aware of its absence and that we are compulsively driven to obtain nurturing from others. But we are never able to be satisfied because even if we do find it, we cannot open to it. When we learn to nurture ourselves, we no longer frantically search outside; we are self-sustaining.

All these themes relate to the general experience of food compulsiveness. We eat compulsively in the attempt to satisfy the emotional neediness of this and other centers. If food compulsiveness is a problem for you, develop a practice of processing the feelings from which you attempt to escape through food. As you release the feelings in processing them, your compulsiveness for food will diminish. The feelings that you will process can pertain to this center, such as the general sense of emotional hunger or pain associated with mothering issues, or can be any other specific feeling that is part of your work.

When this center is integrated, we gain harmonious access to the archetypal inner female, with her qualities of receptivity, nurturing, softness, and empathy. We experience self-nurturing. Both men and women may be cut off from the inner female, but it is more urgent for men to make contact as part of their development since usually they are especially estranged. We gain access to the inner female when we process the negative aspects of this center. As we grow in this center, we activate our capacity for true FEELING.

5. Significance

The fifth chakra is Significance, located at the Solar Plexus. This center is the psychological home of the ego, having to do with needs for recognition, self-image, self-esteem, status, worth, authority, competence, and identity. The drive for Significance is very powerful and may be considered to be one of the three primary drives, along with Survival and Sex. In the lower manifestation of this center, we identify with possessions, people, talents, accomplishments, or anything that appears to enhance our importance.

If we are particularly unintegrated on the Significance level, we can be unaware of how much we crave recognition from others and the extent to which we push ourselves to get it. We become addicted to success or accomplishment in the thirst for recognition. However, actually no amount of recognition can satisfy us. We always feel the need for more and continue compulsively to pursue the nonattainable. This is the center where we must learn "we are enough," simply as we are.

In this center, typically we are driven by a diminished sense of self. We feel inadequate, worthless, insignificant, empty. We fall into the trap of thinking that we can remedy these feelings through accomplishment. Instead of being unconsciously motivated by insignificance, we must learn to work with and integrate the feeling. We must recognize that we all have feelings of inadequacy. To accept ourselves means to accept the feelings and not be driven by them any longer – to get past thinking that we need to prove something to anybody. The distorted need for significance can surface at any level of endeavor. Intellectuals, scientists, artists, even – and possibly especially – spiritual seekers can be unconsciously driven by hunger for significance: to be "more."

In the attempt to satisfy recognition needs, we actually feed on the energy of others. The *attention* they are forced or persuaded to give constitutes the actual transference of energy. Any performer or anyone who is up in front of an audience experiences this energy transfer vividly; it happens less dramatically in one-to-one encounters. The transference of energy becomes highly addictive. The problem with recognition addiction is that it must be experienced dualistically. The incredible highs are balanced by equally depressive lows. The amplitude of the swings, especially for people in front of an audience, becomes overwhelming. The addicted person usually does not understand what is happening and often develops other addictions to try to get through the lows, which furthers the downward spiral.

In working with Significance needs, it must be understood that I am not condemning accomplishment, success, possessions, or recognition that result from genuine contribution. I am just trying to point out the importance of bringing under control the compulsive and destructive impulse for recognition that results from the unintegrated Significance center. Most of us are driven by this more than we realize.

The Significance center corresponds to the archetypal male role. Men are driven intensely when there is a lack of integration here, because their masculine identity is threatened. If they can relate to a more androgynous sense of self, they can handle unintegrated Significance feelings more easily. Women need to develop this center to balance the inner male/female polarity. I do not mean that they should merely condition themselves to be more aggressive in achieving; rather they should integrate the feelings in the center, allowing a genuine, nondominating strength to emerge.

When we identify with projected Significance needs and then encounter frustration, we experience the emotion called anger. Anger is thought of as originating in the Significance center, although it appears to be felt and fed by all lower centers.

Integration of this center starts with awareness of the futility of trying to satisfy unintegrated Significance needs. By processing Significance impulses instead of being motivated by them, an integrated balance of self-affirmation and social purpose is attained. Feelings of this center that are to be integrated include: anger, aggressiveness, hostility, frustration; the sense of worthlessness, inadequacy, weakness, doubt; being blamed or mistreated; not getting the credit deserved; the desire for significance, importance, approval, recognition, and attention, and the pain of their absence; feelings related to the father and male side of the character in general; the pain of not having gotten the fathering needed.

Becoming more integrated in the Significance center, we see

that there is a genuine need for accomplishment, but it is such that we don't have to attach our name to the work to feel a sense of fulfillment. We are not looking primarily for recognition but for meaningful contribution. However, there will always be the human side that seeks and needs the recognition of others. We should not resist this aspect of ourselves, although we should not be motivated by it. In processing, attempt to change nothing. Accept yourself as you are, with whatever ego attachments you have, but don't act on them. Integration of the Significance center will lead to a balanced expression of SELFHOOD.

6. Heart

The Heart chakra is located in the center of the chest. The first of the higher centers, the Heart is where the potential for real humanity begins. We become aware of our deep, emotional connection to others.

The Heart is the center of unconditional love. Most of us would agree that unconditional love is highly desirable, but then we criticize ourselves for not being able to live up to such an ideal. The problem is not that we can't live up to the ideal, but that our concept of the ideal is incorrect. We must expand our understanding of unconditional love.

We assume that loving someone means liking them very much. Liking someone usually implies that we would not like them if certain conditions were not met. In relationships, we have a list of conditions that must be fulfilled, or we will no longer be "in love." This is called "dependent" love, because it is dependent on conditions, but also because we become psychologically dependent on the other. Dependent love is tied to the lower centers and is self-oriented. It is experienced dualistically, which is why it never lasts. In reality, we probably never outgrow having a certain amount of dependent love in our closest relationships, but as we grow, the dependency becomes less, and our dualistic swings also become less. We become conscious of ourselves and of how we approach relationships.

What, then, is real love? Love is acceptance, and unconditional love is unconditional acceptance. To love someone unconditionally means that you are able to accept them, and your actual feelings about them, even though you might not like the way you are presently perceiving them. To love yourself unconditionally means that you are able to accept your own feelings at any time, pleasant or unpleasant. Self-acceptance of feelings as they are leads to self-love and naturally extends to accepting and loving others. Self-acceptance is an ability that takes understanding and developing. It comes about as a result of higher consciousness but also can be cultivated and will lead to higher consciousness.

It may not even be apparent why you would want such a consciousness. All that can be said is that you must have the intuition that higher consciousness is possible and that it can provide the answer to the problems that you face. Higher consciousness can lead to a form of happiness that cannot really be imagined before you have arrived, but it does in reality exist. This is what poets and prophets have always been trying to communicate.

The Heart is a feminine center. Women feel and express the loving aspects of the higher Heart more easily than men. At the same time, they are perhaps more vulnerable to the lower aspects of the Heart, the dependency and emotionalism. Men must learn to activate and integrate this center as a most primary part of their work on themselves.

The Heart center is where we feel lonely. We must understand that loneliness is only the dualistic complement to the pleasant feeling we get from dependent love. If you can integrate loneliness, you will transcend the duality of dependent love/loneliness and be able to begin experiencing real love. If you cannot integrate loneliness, you remain attached to the addictive cycle of dependent love.

The feelings related to the Heart that can be processed include: loneliness, longing, sadness, shame, heartbreak, remorse, jealousy, rejection, resentment, embarrassment, despondency; grief over the loss of others; being abandoned, not receiving the love that is deserved; being hated or hating others; the desire for love, acceptance, belonging.

As you integrate the Heart, you experience unconditional self-acceptance. You are no longer dependent on others for their acceptance, you are whole within yourself. As love without dependency or external cause grows within, you realize the higher aspects of the Heart. Your love grows until you naturally feel the desire to help others. You give without attachment; you are not emotionally dependent on the results of giving. Others will sense that you do not give with conditions in mind. You awaken UNCONDITIONAL LOVE.

7. Expression

The Expression center is located in the throat. It is the center of communication, self-expression, and "putting out" into the universe. The fact that Expression comes after the Heart implies that genuine self-expression is possible only when the Heart has been integrated. Yet there are many people, in public life, for example, who have the skills of expression but who are not coming from the Heart. This is possible because the *lower* aspects of the Expression center still can be powerful. Unintegrated, Expression will serve the lower centers, particularly the Power and Significance centers. The result is expressive powers that are self-oriented.

When the Heart is active and integrated, the Expression center begins functioning in its higher capacity. When motivated by love, we act in a selfless manner. We are not doing for ourselves, not even for the subtle gain that can be felt from many "unselfish" acts. Being motivated by love transports us into a new relationship with the universe, and just because we are not doing for ourselves, what we do comes back to us multiplied. We gain, without expecting to. We activate the Law of Prosperity, the higher function of the Expression center. The Law of Prosperity states that what you put out returns to you increased.

To have true experience of Prosperity consciousness, first you must be integrated in the Heart, which means that you also have done substantial work on the lower centers, because the Heart cannot be integrated without the lower centers first coming into line. People hear about Prosperity and try to awaken it in themselves. The problem is that they are coming from fear and are trying only to satisfy addictions. They are not coming from the love of the integrated Heart, and Prosperity is not activated by fear but by love. Being a higher function of the Expression center, Prosperity cannot be used for personal gain, as many of the lower qualities can. This limitation is really for our own good. If we were able to use the principle behind Prosperity at our present level of growth, we would bring all kinds of misfortune to ourselves. We would be putting out mostly fear and other negativities, which is what would return to us magnified.

The feelings of this center that can be processed include not being able to express yourself or communicate effectively and not being heard. When you combine Expression with the Heart, you align yourself with the higher principles of the evolutionary force. When you come from lower centers such as Significance, you fall back into the dualistic experience of pleasure when you perceive that you are getting approval for your work and pain when your hunger for recognition is unsatisfied. You limit your capacity for true EXPRESSION.

8. Intuitive

The eighth center is known as the Intuitive, or Witness, center. It is located on the forehead, just above the eyebrows – the classic "Third Eye" point. Here, the capacity for intuitive knowledge is activated.

The Third Eye point represents the harmonious joining of left- and right-brain functions. The left-brain capacity is the logical, reasoning, rational mind that we normally use. The right brain is our intuitive, creative, feeling side, which is often dormant in our culture. We gain access to and awaken the right brain when it is activated by the functioning Third Eye. Reasoning continues to have a place in our lives, but we now use a *balanced* amount of thinking and feeling in confronting life. We don't try to reason where we should be intuitive. The negative feelings of this center that can be processed include airiness, disconnectedness, confusion, lack of groundedness.

The Witness capacity of this center is a special quality that marks the beginning of what might be called the "transcendental" consciousness of the Higher Self. Focusing on the Third Eye will awaken the Witness. In the Witness state, we go beyond the perception of ourselves as an isolated ego-self. We don't experience doing-to or being done-to, but just "doing." The doer and done-to become one. This may sound removed from any consciousness that you have experienced or may even care to, but the Witness center is actually the most important of them all in our work on ourselves. The Witness becomes our main vantage point; we awaken it first, before getting into the suppressed contents of the lower centers. Lower-center material is more easily integrated through the capacity of *nonidentification* and the healing power that is realized through the activated Witness center. We discuss awakening the Witness in detail in Chapter 11.

You will see that once you have become familiar with the principles involved, activation of the Witness is not a remote mystical possibility but a concrete, practical, accessible form of consciousness that can be used easily in everyday life. The activation of the Heart makes it possible for us to love ourselves, but the Witness marks the true beginning of TRANSCENDENCE.

9. Creative

The Creative center is located at the back of the skull. Activation of it awakens our powers of creativity, inventiveness, originality, radicalness, and rebellion.

If we are active but unintegrated in this center, we will tend to exhibit its lower qualities. We will be rebellious for the sake of rebellion, ungrounded and unrealistic in our foundational values, and even eccentric in our role relative to society. We will feel as if we are being held down and back by others. Our mind will be quick, unconventional, and nonconformist. We will feel misunderstood. People who are strong in this center are the seed-sowers of the race, awakening humanity's potential for the future. As such, they are bound to be misunderstood and even ridiculed by the noncomprehending bulk of society.

If, however, you can recognize that these difficult possibilities are only the negative dualistic side of the special function and privilege that this center confers, and if you can accept that you must process this negative experience as a form of "paying your dues," you will integrate the center and be able to manifest the extraordinary power that it brings. The power can find expression in innovative intellectual thought in any avenue of life: the arts, social change, industry, healing, education, business, and so on.

A particularly difficult negative manifestation of this center is the critical voice. The critical voice is simply the inherent negative side to that part of ourselves that would break free and soar. It is there to keep us in balance. When we reject and suppress the critical voice, it starts to act up, and we appear to be endlessly critical of ourselves or others. When the level of suppression builds to a certain point, we attract people to us who harshly criticize us, whether we deserve it or not.

To deal with the critical voice, recognize that its beginnings are within, despite whatever direction you experience it from, inner or outer. Take responsibility for it, and process it. Hear it and feel it without yielding to it; recognize that its severity is only the result of an imbalance.

The ultimate key to effective use of the Creative center lies in its consecration to serve. It is the center of the ideal of selfless service, which is a tool for cultivation of higher consciousness and also the result of higher consciousness. In its fulfilled realization, this center brings the gift of true RENEWAL for society.

10. Spiritual

The Spiritual, or Crown, chakra, as it is also known, is located at the top of the head, just outside the body. It is the center of cosmic consciousness, where the individual self realizes its oneness with the Universal Self. The vision that this center brings is what great spiritual leaders and artists have always tried to communicate.

To approach the Spiritual, you must be integrated in all the centers below and be living completely in the moment. Any desire is enough to bring you out of the moment and back into your time-based existence. The negative sides of the center to be integrated are isolation, separateness, chaos, and depression in general.

You are fortunate if you can experience cosmic consciousness for even a brief period. It is in the future for the majority of us. To attempt to describe this essentially indescribable experience would be a misplaced effort. It is enough to know that such a consciousness exists and that it is the culmination of human evolution, the experience of ONENESS.

part

Integrative Processing

2

THE STEPS OF INTEGRATIVE PROCESSING

I. Awareness

- Focus on the Present

- Do Not Seek Understanding

- Maintain Inner Awareness

- Identify Your Feelings

- Identify the Dualistic Pattern

- Own Your Experience

- Affirm that You are Processing

II. Acceptance

- Accept Yourself

- Accept Your Feelings

- Accept the External

- Be Nonreactive

- Identify Self-Rejection

- Activate Your Heart Center

III. Direct Experience

- Process the Feeling

- Use Breath and Bodywork

- Integrate Feelings Behind
  the Addiction

- Process Feelings During
  Meditation

- Bring Up Unresolved Issues
  from the Past

- Accept Resistance

- Bring Your Feelings to
  a Crisis

- Observe Your Toleration
  Point

IV. Transformation

- Activate the Witness Center

- Bring in Healing Energy

- Allow Psychic Energies
  to Balance

- Open Yourself to
  Transformation

- Trust

- Understand Psychic
  Cleansing

- Recognize the Hindrances

- Take Part in Group Work

I enter complete awareness of my feelings. I realize that many of my feelings are negative and painful. I take responsibility for my feelings, understanding that the purpose of the events of my life is only to make me conscious of these feelings that I carry in my subconscious. I choose to work with these feelings as they come up and not to suppress them again.

6

Awareness

*A*wareness is the capacity beyond the mind that can observe both thoughts and feelings. Awareness, the first of the four steps of Integrative Processing, belongs to that level of individuality called the intellect.

Many people confuse the functions of the mind and the intellect, making no real distinction. The mind is that part of us which thinks and reasons in a somewhat impersonal manner, almost like a machine. The intellect is that part of us which knows. The intellect is closer to our real identity, although it would be a mistake to consider either of these functions the real person.

Awareness is not an end unto itself, as some may believe. You may be aware of your real feelings, but if you do not know how to handle this awareness, you still may be immersed in self-rejection and suppression, not allowing the feelings to complete their cycle and be released. Awareness is only an intellectual function. The intellect does not connect to life's experiences. It does not have the capacity to be "in the moment," perceiving and responding spontaneously. Nevertheless, you can make no real progress on yourself until you become aware. It is the first step.

FOCUS ON THE PRESENT

Much of the focus of traditional psychotherapy involves going back into the past to try to uncover suppressed feelings, but in our work, probing the past becomes secondary to working with the present. Our present feelings are, in fact, formed by the past. Our past subconscious conditioning is what determines how we perceive what happens to us and what kinds of events and people we attract. Through the mechanism of projection, suppressed emotions are attributed to present situations. Therefore, looking at the present is also looking into the subconscious.

When you realize this deeply, the world will become fascinating, because you understand that your subconscious programming is right here – this very moment – right in front of you. There is no need to attempt to push into the subconscious. On the contrary, you cannot avoid it. Your interactions with the world, and even with yourself, serve as the stimulus for bringing up your blocks. You experience your energy patterns in the present. Even though the blocks were formed in the past, it is not necessary to trace back to the original circumstances. Processing is a *present-centered* self-therapy. However, this does not mean that we never work with memories of the past. Especially when they spontaneously come forward, we will process them as well, recognizing that we are working with present feelings about a past event.

Do Not Seek Understanding

At one time, psychology believed that understanding the cause of blocks in the personality was the key to the elimination of those blocks. Acceptance was considered essential in resolving the condition, but it was assumed that one had to understand before one could accept. The psychological schools of analysis were founded, and years were spent investigating the subconscious. People caught up in analysis became intellectual, articulate, and knowledgeable about their blocks, but remained blocked because they avoided functioning on the feeling level, where integration takes place. Indeed, both analyst and patient became characterized as lifeless and nonspontaneous.

Understanding is not required
for awareness or acceptance

Contemporary psychology has evolved into what are called the humanistic and transpersonal schools. These schools deal much less with analysis, although there may be some, and focus primarily on other forms of therapy that bring about the surfacing and experience of suppressed emotion, without necessarily elaborating on its cause or origin. Understanding the cause is not considered essential for the acceptance and releasing of emotions. You might think you understand why you are unable to love, based on childhood conditioning, for example, but that does nothing to solve the problem. Integration with the hostile, hating self within will bring about the catharsis and enable you to go beyond being blocked at the love/hate level.

Yet many people still mistakenly feel that in order to work on themselves, they must go into the past – either remote or recent – and understand what happened. The urge to understand is popular in our culture because of the misplaced emphasis on the intellect and lack of comprehension concerning the feeling side. Even seasoned spiritual travelers can be unclear about the proper role of understanding.

Do not confuse understanding with awareness. Awareness means being conscious of a feeling; it does not imply that the origin and history of the feeling are known. Understanding is not to be considered valueless, only that it is not essential for integration and healing. Integration occurs as a result of acceptance, not understanding. Understanding is likely to occur spontaneously, without effort, at the proper time, as a *result* of integration, which often will be accompanied by a catharsis of blocked energy. Insights will flash into awareness, connections will be apparent, and the emotion that accompanies catharsis will show that suppressed energy has been released. Understanding then can be used to make any required changes or to ensure that past mistakes are not repeated.

Therefore, you should not expect integration to come from understanding, nor should you seek understanding directly. The very effort keeps the mind preoccupied so that integration cannot take place. The mind takes on a tremendous and futile burden when it insists on understanding. Moreover, when you try to understand, your biases keep you from clear perceptions. Suppose you try to understand the cause of any current psychological condition within yourself. You may go back to childhood; but since you are searching for a specific link, you will choose from all your childhood experiences the ones that seem to provide the causal connection. You probably had many other strong experiences that did not "result" in a current condition. Why did you react traumatically to certain ones? You ignore the possibility of the condition being latent and the event merely activating it.

If causes are to be traced to a past existence, which is usually not part of conscious memory, you can appreciate the difficulties involved in relying on understanding original causes. Your current feelings are exactly the same as the ones you suppressed sometime in the past, probably extending into past lives. They reappear, in apparently different circumstances, but the suppressed energy that is attempting to clear is the same. There is no need to go into the past to analyze, search, or understand what happened. If you are in touch with your feelings *now,* you have all the information you need to begin healing, which will happen if you just accept and experience those feelings.

Maintain Inner Awareness

In working on ourselves, our main focus is on our feelings. Inner awareness is the ability to be in touch with your feelings, to be conscious of *what is* in your inner world as you function in the outer world. It is the recognition of feelings as they occur. Inner awareness may seem a simple matter, but in fact it is a difficult step for many people. This is one of the places where the insightfulness of a therapist can be helpful.

Self-awareness
must be a priority

A main reason why we ignore feelings is because of cultural conditioning. Men are trained to be "manly" – having tender feelings or giving them any importance is considered to be a sign of weakness. Women are trained to invalidate feelings as well, often in the name of cooperation and getting things done, or simply if the feelings are seemingly too wild or too much for the people around them to contend with.

Another reason for difficulty with inner awareness is our sense of priorities. The lifestyle of the average person is such that little time is available for self-awareness. Our lives seem to be incessantly busy because we are caught up in the endless quest to satisfy addictions, which requires time, energy, and money. Or we may feel that we have legitimate responsibilities, such as a family. Either way, even though it seems that we are acting to satisfy needs, we become goal-oriented.

Preoccupation with goals necessarily makes us less conscious of inner events; self-awareness becomes secondary. You may think it is possible to maintain goal orientation and still be aware of your feelings, but the subtle priority of goals over feelings conditions you. In the long run, the ability to feel what you are experiencing is diminished. Feelings simply do not enter the threshold of conscious awareness. You become unaware of your inner condition because it does not matter; you become engulfed in the rush for results.

Feelings become repressed. They occur, but there is no awareness of them. The result is stress. We must change our priorities and become more sensitive to inner feelings. Many times we learn to do this only after a breakdown related to burnout, heart attack or other health crisis, or alcohol and drug addiction, which results from this kind of inner neglect. Then we finally get the message. As we turn our attention to feelings, giving them the priority they deserve, we discover much more than was suspected and that the underlying emotional entanglement goes deep.

It's not goal orientation alone that makes us insensitive to feelings. The simple and often involuntary habit of avoiding unpleasantness gradually erodes both the willingness and the ability to be in touch with ourselves. Another reason that we allow insensitivity to ourselves to build is that we don't know what to do with negative feelings when we do become aware of them. We may think that we are handling them by ignoring them or by escaping into various diversions, but instead we suppress.

Some people think they are being selfish if they take their own feelings into consideration and may, in fact, consciously or unconsciously pride themselves on their "unselfishness" when they pay no attention to their own feelings. A parent, for example, may put children or spouse first and not consider their own feelings equally valid. This kind of martyrdom is sometimes an unconscious power maneuver, calculated to instill guilt in others, but not always. It may simply be another way of avoiding one's feelings.

*Do not deny your
real feelings*

Denial is common and is one of the first hurdles to therapy and emotional growth, whether you are working alone or with a therapist. In denial, you simply do not know that you have certain feelings. The feelings are repressed and do not come within conscious view. You must be very careful that you do not deny your real feelings. Becoming aware of your feelings is a skill that will develop as it is exercised, but you must begin to exercise it.

You must expect that as you look within, pain and chaos will be encountered. However, knowing how to handle this turmoil will bring you confidence to face it with courage instead of doubt.

As the pain emerges and you clear it instead of again suppressing, you will experience the elation that comes from the release of buried and traumatic tensions.

What needs to be emphasized is a sense of *priority*. When you give priority to inner feelings, you begin integration; you become feeling oriented instead of goal oriented. This shift in values may be thought of as the beginning of spiritual life and the turning away from materialistic life. You learn that what is within is most important; that you can dissolve the compulsion and pain that has been suppressed in the past but has not been eliminated from your life.

IDENTIFY YOUR FEELINGS

Throughout the book, I have been broadly referring to any inner, psychic event as a "feeling." Let's now look more closely at the different kinds of feelings that we experience:

CORE FEELINGS

EMOTIONS

MOODS

ATTITUDES

IMPULSES

DESIRES

ADDICTIVE COMPULSIONS

BODY SENSATIONS

SENTIMENTS

CORE FEELINGS are dualistically occurring, pure feelings that are not filtered through the personal belief system and may be physical, physiological, or psychological. You may be tired or alert, hungry or filled; you may encounter loss or gain, rejection or approval; you may experience hate or love, futility or fulfillment.

Core feelings are not emotions; they are matter-of-fact feeling reactions to objective/subjective experience. If you are aware of, accept, and are open to a core feeling, there is no need to process; you are already in the moment with your experience, and you will not undergo stress. If you are not open to your core feelings, they become suppressed, and the uncovering of them forms the basis of psychological work undertaken to restore emotional stability.

EMOTIONS result when core feelings are filtered through incorrect beliefs. Emotions always indicate a body/mind conflict. The beliefs held in the mind conflict with the feeling experience as it is happening in the body. A feeling may be a completely natural part of life, but because it does not fit in with our concepts about how things should be, we believe it is wrong, and we resist it. The resistance interferes with the flow of psychic energy through the chakras; a "block" is set up. The result is what we call an emotion. Because you believe you should not be tired, you become discouraged; because you believe you should not be rejected, you become jealous and hurt; because you believe you should not be restricted, you become angry. The same blocking that creates the emotion also prevents it from being adequately experienced, and it becomes suppressed along with the original feeling.

Emotions indicate a significant underlying belief when they recur with forcefulness. They may be clarified by relating them to the center of consciousness that produces them. If it is possible for you to see how you create emotions by filtering core feelings through beliefs and then resisting the feelings, it will help you integrate your emotions. At the right time, this insight occurs spontaneously; however, normally it is not profitable to pursue this line of inquiry in a program of emotional healing, and I do not recommend going out of your way to attempt it.

Beliefs are stuck deep in the subconscious. The probing that is required to uncover them takes you out of the feeling center, impeding integration. Even if a belief is discovered, the suppressed energy that maintains it still must be released through processing. In our work, we do not attempt to confront and change beliefs intellectually. Instead, we integrate the emotion produced by the belief. Integrating the emotion brings about a clearing of the suppressed negative energy that is responsible for the continuing existence of the belief, and the belief is let go of in an unforced way. As this happens, you may or may not become aware of the belief.

MOODS are vague feelings of discomfort or distress that are not severe enough to be thought of as major problems but stay with us as repeating themes. You may have the feeling that you don't look good, that you are never comfortable, are unsure of yourself, not at ease with others, hate to spend money, are abnormally hungry, nervous, never satisfied, and so on. Seemingly innocuous moods represent other, more basic energy patterns. Moods should not be dismissed. Generally they can be traced back to the lower energy centers and will relate to unconscious issues such as insecurity, sexual imbalance, low self-esteem, loneliness, and the like. Working with moods probably will contribute as much to self-integration as working with the intense emotional events in your life. Meditation is the best time for working with recurrent moods.

ATTITUDES are energy-based and so may be processed. Attitudes represent our defenses, opinions, and, in general, suppressed patterns. They are largely unconscious, but as you continue working on yourself, they will come more and more into awareness.

IMPULSES AND DESIRES relate to motivation; they are the inner urgings to satisfy perceived needs. Rather than acting on it and running after the illusion of satisfaction, you can release the energy of an impulse or desire by processing it. Impulses are generally more irrational than desires. With desires, we think we understand why we need something, even though many of our desires are compulsive and can never really be satisfied. For example, we may experience the impulse to buy something for which we have no need or to be with a person whom we may dislike. With desires, we have no doubts about why we want something, or why we want to be with a certain person or achieve a certain goal; we expect to be fulfilled.

ADDICTIVE COMPULSIONS are impulses concerning addictions. We are compelled to seek out the object of addiction to avoid other feelings, but processing gives us an alternative. Processing *the feeling behind the compulsion* can provide a release without having to yield to the addictive pattern. This is our basic approach in dealing with addiction. For example, if you experience chronic anxiety when you are alone, which leads to the impulse to be with other people, you may decide the impulse is compulsive and an addiction. If you process the anxiety itself, instead of being motivated by it, eventually you will be freed of the addiction.

BODY SENSATIONS form a class of feelings by themselves. They may be thought of as physical, but actually they occur in the energy body. Hence, body sensations indicate energy status, and a recurring sensation indicates energy blockage. When we have a severe sensation, we call it a "symptom." It is important to recognize that body sensations are opportunities to clear the energy body, which will occur if we just sit with and process the sensations. Processing will lead to an unexpected amount of emotional clearing as well.

Body awareness is central to certain spiritual disciplines, where practice consists of sitting and witnessing body sensations. Working with body sensations is very helpful in developing the capacity for feeling, since feeling occurs in the body. As you become more sensitive, you will discover that emotions and body sensations occur together. The beginning of a pattern is noticed first in either the emotions or the body. Focusing on whichever of the two you are aware of will bring the other to light.

For example, the Navel chakra rules the experience of poor digestion, food cravings, and general emotional neediness. The awareness and processing of any of these will lead to the others and to a healing of all. The Throat chakra rules thwarted self-expression, which may first come into awareness as a continual pain in the back of the neck.

Other sensations or pains may occur in any part of the body and be linked to specific trapped emotions. A logical connection between them is not always apparent.

SENTIMENTS are the only class of feelings that will not generally benefit from processing, although no harm will be caused. Sentiments are *emotional judgments* to other, more primary feelings and do not represent suppressed negativity. We are pleased or disgusted, concerned or apathetic, enchanted or distressed, amused or bored, about our experience. Sentiments also tie into *emotional idealism.* We value heroism over cowardice, reverence over desecration, grandeur over the mundane, care over indifference.

Although sentiments have an important place in our inner lives, they become a problem when we equate them with ultimate happiness. We become attached to the positive sentiment, rejecting the negative, and fall into the dualistic trap once again. It must be understood that sentiments are the result of unconscious concepts, values, and beliefs and do not represent intrinsic qualities in themselves that must be attained at all costs. We must allow a place for the negative side of any sentiment to coexist with the positive. Most important, we must process the feeling that is behind the sentiment.

Distinguish between thoughts and feelings

Feelings are not always accompanied by outer events. A feeling may be accompanied by only a thought, and sometimes we may purposely use a certain thought to bring up a feeling for processing. The thought serves as stimulus for the feeling, just as an outer event can. Even so, it is not primarily the thought that is being processed but the feeling. It is helpful to distinguish between thoughts and feelings and to understand that we are working with energy, as it manifests in feelings. A thought that has no charged feeling associated with it would not even hold our interest. Feelings are energy-based. They occur in the chakras and get blocked in the chakras. The ultimate purpose of all growth therapy is to loosen the energy blocks. For example, these are expressions of thoughts:

I have bills that I can't pay.
There are no employment opportunities around here.
I feel that people look down on me.

These are expressions of feelings:

I am afraid of not having enough money.
I am discouraged about not finding work.
I feel worthless.

Identify and locate the feeling

After you have isolated the feelings with which you are working, you should identify them in the simplest terms possible, along with the chakras or other areas of the body involved, and when the feelings come up. At first you may not be able to detect feelings in a specific part of the body, but after some practice, you will develop this sensitivity. Remember, do not search for an explanation, just maintain awareness: I feel anger in the Solar Plexus when I talk to my boss. I feel lonely in the Heart when my partner is not there for me. I feel anxiety about money in the Survival center and a clogged feeling in the throat when new expenses present themselves. I feel sexual impulses and frustration in the Sensation center and a tension in the back when I think of a certain person, or even all the time. Try to clarify the feeling or sensation and link it to the apparent triggering stimulus if there is one – that is, the external event or inner thought. Look for the feeling *behind* the event.

Any event that occurs with emotional impact should be given priority. Sometimes you may become aware of a feeling but then dismiss it, thinking it insignificant. As you start getting into yourself, you will find that these feelings, which you probably have had for long periods, are really problems calling out for attention. You just never realized their significance. If you don't stop to experience and integrate the feelings, you suppress.

Most of our feelings represent attempts of the subconscious to clear. There are no insignificant feelings. When feelings come up, try to condition yourself to automatically stop and recognize that something worthy of your attention is happening. Processing doesn't necessarily require a lot of time; you can learn to handle feelings quickly so they are not suppressed.

A therapist may be helpful at the beginning to assist you in sorting out your feelings and to guide you in learning how to process, but there is definitely no need to be tied to one for any length of time. You learn to view *life* as the therapist, and life is designed with absolute precision to bring up exactly what needs to be surfaced from your subconscious. This is the purpose of life on the Earth plane. All you need learn is how to use your circumstances to facilitate a therapeutic result.

CHAKRAS AND FEELINGS

In processing, we start with whatever feelings we are aware of. These are usually what we call *first-level feelings*. First-level feelings are those that are most superficial and apparent; they may or may not be part of the suppressed subconscious. They are important to include in our process but may not represent our ultimate issues. As we work with first-level feelings, we will be led to our *core feelings*. Core feelings are the ones that are trapped deep in the subconscious, the ones that must be released. Core feelings are where the energy begins; they correspond to our issues and patterns.

Usually, first-level feelings are more emotional than the feelings behind them. Sometimes first-level feelings may represent our resistance to core feelings. The most important of the first-level feelings will be suppressed emotions, and that is why they are emphasized in our work, but first-level feelings also may include moods, attitudes, impulses, desires, addictive compulsions, and body sensations. It is important to realize that we are interested in more than releasing just these first-level feelings; the driving core feelings behind them eventually must be engaged.

Identify first-level and core feelings

The following table will help you identify your first-level and core-level feelings and relate them to the chakras. I have presented core feelings with their dualistic complements to help you identify positive feelings to which you may be addicted in the unconscious effort to avoid the negative. The table lists the positive feelings on the left and the negative feelings on the right. Within each center, any negative dualistic core feeling can produce any of the associated first-level emotions when resisted. There is some overlap between centers; a feeling in one center may produce an emotion in another center, depending on personal history.

*An emotion occurs
when a feeling is resisted*

Understanding how emotions originate is important. For example, let's look at the Survival center, the first in the table. We may experience the *first-level emotion* of fear when we resist the *core feeling* of lack, insecurity, or vulnerability. Can you see that it is perfectly possible and reasonable to experience lack, insecurity, or vulnerability and not be frightened by it? It is only when we resist and reject the feeling, according to our unconscious beliefs, that fear arises. To clear all the feelings in this complex, we would start with processing the fear, which is the first-level emotion.

After clearing some of the fear, the core feeling dualism in which we are trapped will become evident: We resist lack and are addicted to abundance; we resist insecurity and are addicted to security; we resist vulnerability and are addicted to safety. Now we must process the negative feeling itself, instead of yielding to it by compulsively chasing after its complement. If we can integrate the feeling as a result of processing it, meaning that we get to the point where we find a position for it in our inner and outer lives without rejecting it, we will not experience fear.

Use the table to make yourself familiar with potential feelings and emotions; it can be an important step to finding them in yourself. You also may want to use the table to try to identify your important issues, as best as you can. For example, if you have a Nurturing *issue*, you may have an *emotion* of general emotional neediness based on a *feeling* of an absence of mother love as a child. Or if you have a Heart issue, you may have the emotion of loneliness because you do not accept your aloneness. Or if you have a Significance issue, you may experience the emotion of worthlessness because you reject your feeling of failure. But do not try too hard to dig deeply at this point. Let yourself be guided to recognize only whatever is easily apparent. Most of our issues are unconscious. They will be revealed as you continue working.

CHAKRAS AND FEELINGS

1. Survival (Base of Spine/Saturn)

Key First-Level Negative Emotions: **fear,** panic, anxiety, nervousness, paranoia, rigidity

Dualistic Core Feelings:

Positive	and	Negative
Abundance		Lack
Security		Insecurity
Safety		Vulnerability
Health		Sickness
Gain		Loss
Comfort		Pain
Boundaries		Invasion
Life		Death
Infinite		Limited

2. Power (Perineum/Pluto)

Key First-Level Negative Emotions: **futility,** despondency, anger, rage, contempt, powerlessness

Dualistic Core Feelings:

Capable	and	Helpless
Dominant		Subordinate
Respected		Used
Controlling		Controlled
Self-determination		Manipulation
Freedom		Coercion
Energetic		Fatigued
Independent		Dependent
Unbound		Restricted by authority

3. Sensation (Lower Abdomen/Mars)

Key First-Level Negative Emotions: **frustration,** lust, humiliation

Dualistic Core Feelings concerning sex, touch, sensuality, entertainment, TV, luxury:

Satisfaction	and	Craving
Indulgence		Abstinence

4. Nurturing (Navel/Moon)

Key First-Level Negative Emotions: emotional **hunger** for food, drugs, smoking; general emotional neediness

Dualistic Core Feelings:

Nurtured	and	Starved
Supported		Engulfed
Life-giving		Life-withholding
Receptive		Demanding
Mother love present		Mother absent as child

5. Significance (Solar Plexus/Sun)

Key First-Level Negative Emotions: **worthlessness,** anger, intimidation, emptiness, envy

Dualistic Core Feelings:

Competence	and	Inadequacy
Significance		Unimportance
Superiority		Inferiority
Recognition		Invalidation
Success		Failure
Honor		Scorn
Identity		Conformist
Strength		Weakness
Approval of authority		Disapproval
Father guidance present		Father absent as child

6. Heart (Chest/Venus)

Key First-Level Negative Emotions: **loneliness, longing, sadness,** hurt, possessiveness, resentment, shame, jealousy, heartbreak, remorse, embarrassment

Dualistic Core Feelings:

Acceptance	and	Rejection
Togetherness		Aloneness
Compassion		Indifference
Care		Abuse
Belonging		Excluding
Loyalty		Betrayal
Cherished		Abandoned
Dependent Love		Dependent Hate

7. Expression (Throat/Mercury)
Key First-Level Negative Emotions: **dullness,** blocked expressiveness, boredom
Dualistic Core Feelings:

Expressing	and	Keeping in
Being heard		Being ignored

8. Intuitive (Third Eye/Neptune)
Key First-Level Negative Emotions: **doubt,** airiness, disconnectedness, lack of groundedness
Dualistic Core Feelings:

Connect to inner self	and	Connect to outer world
Intuitive guidance		Dependence on reason

9. Creative (Base of Skull/Uranus)
Key First-Level Negative Emotions: **self-criticism**
Dualistic Core Feelings:

Creative flow	and	Creative blocking
Individualism		Conformism

10. Spiritual (Crown/Jupiter)
Key First-Level Negative Emotions: **isolation,** despair, selfishness, unfulfillment
Dualistic Core Feelings:

Realization of oneness	and	Self-orientation
Peace		Chaos
Clarity		Confusion
Unconditional love		Conditional love

IDENTIFY THE DUALISTIC PATTERN

The basis of emotional stress is lack of integration. We become addicted to one side of any dualistic core feeling in an effort to avoid the other side, establishing a *pattern*. Patterns tend to function on an unconscious level. Nevertheless, they influence us tremendously, distorting our perception of reality and generally leading us to act in self-limiting ways.

When feelings related to any issue are processed, two results are achieved. First, the suppressed negative energy that has been manifesting as an emotion is cleared. Second, the dualistic core feeling pattern that produces the emotion is usually revealed. This will happen spontaneously, as clearing proceeds, and does not need to be pursued actively. In fact, searching for the pattern can be used as an escape from having the feeling.

Identification of patterns is helpful but not essential

Although you have just examined the table of core feelings and emotions, it is likely that you have not spotted some of your major patterns. This is because they are unconscious. After you have worked with your feelings, you will become aware of some of your patterns and possibly the underlying beliefs. However, identification of patterns is not necessary for processing to be effective and actually may not come until a fair amount of clearing has taken place.

For example, suppose a man has a problem with authority. He continually finds himself in situations where he is in conflict with various authority figures, because he unconsciously seeks out or attracts these situations and even unconsciously creates them. He will do things such as park in no-parking areas, becoming indignant when ticketed. More serious signs would include periodically recurring conflict on the job, such as becoming resentful whenever the opportunity arose, thinking that he was being controlled, restricted, and used. Such is the power of the mind to project the conditions held in the subconscious that many times the conflict will have an objective basis.

The conflict with authority is a Power center affliction. The unconscious and irrational belief at the bottom of the conflict might be that yielding to authority signifies weakness, which must be avoided at all costs or else he will be taken advantage of. The belief results in his resistance to the core feelings of being controlled, restricted, and used. In the attempt to avoid the feelings, he falls into the dualistic pattern of addiction to rebellious self-determination. He tries to escape into "freedom," rejecting any and all authority. A more integrated perception of this duality would be reasonable self-autonomy balanced with respect for authority as representation of the cooperative nature of society.

His first-level emotions are rage that his life is being controlled by others, coupled with contempt for authority. Normally he would not have the insight or background to understand the basis of the conflict, and he may easily go through his entire life unconscious of the source of his pain. Much anger has probably been suppressed, resulting in a chronic condition. Anger, by the way, may be caused by other patterns; the chronic presence of this emotion does not necessarily imply an authority problem.

If he is taught an effective method to clear the suppressed emotions, he can realize therapeutic benefits without understanding the source pattern that is causing them. Not until a certain point is reached in clearing will the knowledge of the authority conflict have any significance for him. He may have been exposed to this information previously, with no comprehension. Awareness of the pattern is reached naturally, as long as processing therapy continues. When recognition of the pattern occurs, he does not automatically gain sudden freedom from it. Clearing therapy must continue, although now it is likely to proceed at a faster rate, because the pattern itself can be addressed.

You should handle your self-awareness similarly. As you process whatever feelings you are aware of, you are making real progress in your work on yourself. When the time is right, the underlying dualistic core pattern will become evident, as eventually will the belief behind the pattern.

When you are aware of them, patterns of behavior may be meditated upon. You will increase your knowledge of the pattern and release suppressed energy. Other linked emotions will come up, to be integrated. You can go deeper into the awareness of how the pattern influences your behavior and weaken its influence through acceptance.

When you start to become aware of your patterns, you will be able to sense an emotion coming before it builds. The awareness will enable you to neutralize the emotion, if you want to, by not resisting the feeling. Processing becomes unnecessary, because no energy builds up, and suppressed emotion is not called up or already has been cleared. Still, you must be careful not to become too intellectual, thinking that you are controlling your emotional reactions because you know your patterns. It is better to process any feeling that starts to come up rather than to assume it has been neutralized because the pattern has been recognized.

Patterns are reflected by the astrological birth chart

Although astrology is not usually taken seriously by the psychotherapeutic community, we should remember that Jung himself considered it valid and sought for a way to include it in psychological work. I have found astrology to be quite compatible with processing. Because I have a strong background in astrology, when I am consulting with a client, I often use the client's birth chart to assist in identifying patterns that need to be integrated. The relationship between the planets at the time of birth represents the energy potentials of the inner self and corresponds to the energy relationships between the chakras. Blocks in the chakras can be immediately identified and worked with directly through breath, bodywork, and precise processing. Transits and progressions to the chart will show when in our lives important issues will come up – these are the times to work with those issues.

An exploration of the chart contains insights about personality type, motivation, basic psychological makeup, and most important for our work, the specific feelings that are likely to be suppressed in the subconscious. The chart also substantiates one's experience. If one has potential for sexual compulsiveness, or fear issues, or anger, or a certain type of relationship experience, or even a potential for substance abuse, for example, the psychological interpretation of the chart clearly shows this. This capability of astrology is invaluable in helping us take responsibility for ourselves instead of believing that others or our childhood "caused" our condition. It is obvious that we came into life with those patterns in place.

Even so, astrology does not provide the solution; it only identifies the problem – processing provides the solution. Before I had a working knowledge of the principles of processing, I approached

astrology as a system to warn me about what was troublesome

about my own or another person's character that had to be avoided; I had no concept of acceptance. The result was suppression of feelings and experience. In using astrology, we must remember that integration of patterns, not avoidance, is our central purpose. However, astrology is by no means essential; processing therapy can proceed quite well without it. The patterns will emerge soon enough. I recommend using it only if you have an interest. When it is not used, you begin by working with the emotional energy that is felt.

We come into life with but a few major patterns. Our life's work is the integration of these patterns that cause us so much pain. We must understand that progress will proceed slowly. Slow but steady progress is actually the most powerful kind of transformation, because when we get overnight results, the results go as quickly as they come.

OWN YOUR EXPERIENCE

One of the most important principles of processing is the need to "own" experience. Because of suppression in the past, we have created our Karma, the subconscious reservoir of negative energies, which we project outward and then experience as being directed toward us from other persons or circumstances. These outside agencies act like mirrors, reflecting back our negativities. They are actors in the play we are directing. They function precisely to bring up the suppressed feelings we carry inside. That is the purpose we unconsciously assign to them.

To understand this, and take responsibility for whatever negativity you are faced with, is to own your experience. You will go nowhere in transforming any feeling or condition until you own it. Granted, this can be challenging and difficult. You may think you are being treated unfairly; you may feel anger, bitterness, or heartbreak, but if you do not take responsibility, you miss the point. You must assume that you have created your negative experience through projection of suppressed energies.

Realize that you are projecting

The realization that you are projecting is the most important aspect of awareness. Until then you are asleep. You react to your projections blindly. When you become aware, you stop reacting. You own experience instead of rejecting it and being driven by it.

When you are in this first step of processing, generally you will not be able to do any more than make the assumption of owning – you will not feel it on a gut level because you are still in the intellect, and your sense of owning will necessarily be no more than an intellectual assumption, but this is enough. You must understand the theory behind owning thoroughly so that you will be able to proceed on faith, especially during times of emotional stress, when it is not easy to keep a clear perspective.

Whenever you begin to process, assume that you are responsible for what you see before you. In other words, do not blame any other person, thing, or situation. Also, *do not blame yourself.* Because owning is essential to self-work, let's take a detailed look at exactly how we create, through projection, the negativity we encounter. There are five different kinds of projection.

Dualistic Projection

In simple dualistic experience, there is no subconscious Karma at work. The perceived negative is an inherent part of the perceived positive; both must be experienced. For example, pleasure soon loses its glitter. It does not last and seems to bring with it other negative aspects that were not anticipated. We create the other aspects, assigning negative values to them to balance the interaction.

Experience will always contain the negative together with the positive, even when we have done substantial work in clearing the personal subconscious. Integrative Processing may be thought of as having two levels of application: The first is the *healing* level – to release built-up, suppressed feelings that keep us dysfunctional and in acute distress. When we have done this, we bring ourselves into balance, meaning a balanced experience of duality. Being in balance does not mean that we will be free from the negative. We continue to encounter it as part of the normal, dualistic experience of life. Processing techniques then serve us in their second level of application, that of integrating balanced dualities. We still work with the negative, but successful work now results in the final integration and transcending of the dualism. When we reach this stage, we are not so much concerned with healing as with advancement of consciousness.

Shadow Projection

Because we have cut ourselves off from parts of our inner self by rejecting certain feelings, we then become more sensitive to and even attracted to qualities in others that remind us of those suppressed emotional parts we are missing. This is what is meant when it is said that *you see yourself in others.* However, because we have essentially condemned those inner qualities – through the act of suppression, forming our personal shadow – we then usually condemn the outer reflection. We become judgmental, intolerant; we condemn the mirror.

For example, we are sexually suppressed, and then we condemn sexuality outside of ourselves. We suppress anger within and then condemn and punish those of us who commit violent acts instead of treating them with compassion. At the same time, we are fascinated by whatever we have suppressed and projected – just look at sex and violence on TV. We find ourselves in the impossible position of resisting and suppressing vital parts of ourselves, recognizing and being attracted to those same qualities in others, and at the same time condemning those qualities.

Clearing Projection

The next stage of projection is when we start having strong feelings and think that some situation or person is making us feel that way. We assign responsibility for our feelings to others. Not only are we more sensitive to outside stimuli, but we overlay simple reality with the suppressed inner; we see things that are not really there. We perceive what we carry inside – what we unconsciously project in order to clear.

Our partner has to work late one night, and we think we're being abandoned. All of our abandonment fears and issues come up; we feel helpless, angry, alone. We blame our partner, we have a confrontation and make demands. We don't see that the event is merely triggering the feelings that we are holding within. We don't see the real world, we filter it through our layers of suppressed energy and think the cause of our feelings is outside. Understanding this point is important and basic to our work. Your levels of realization of how you have been buying into these kinds of projections will continue to deepen and amaze you.

These feelings are being cleared because they were previously suppressed. They come to the surface *when conditions are right* – when there is an event or the negative side of a dualistic experience that will support the projection. Inevitably, your reaction is out of proportion. You overreact.

In more advanced cases, we unconsciously provoke others and then react to their reaction. You made an unreasonable demand of your partner and then react with resentment and despair when refused. You set yourself up to fall. Cases such as these can be difficult to recognize as they are happening. That is why you always must assume, whenever difficulty arises, that you are projecting and clearing negative emotions.

This level of projection is generally recognized and understood by Western psychology. The next level is not fully understood by the West but is by the East.

Manifestation Projection

This level of projection occurs when the amount of subconsciously suppressed energy builds to the point where we attract events and people that correspond to the energy. We actually create the conditions we encounter in the seemingly "outside" world. If we continually suppress emotions that come up in the previous stages, we will come to this stage, as most of us have in many areas.

We attract someone who really does abandon us, starting with our mother or father, continuing into our first and second marriages. And even when we become aware of the pattern, we seem to be unable to break it. We take great care, we scrutinize relationships that we enter, but we seem to keep getting into the same situation; we just don't recognize it at first. We've fallen into what's called *compulsive repetition.* We can't break the pattern because we haven't released the feeling energy that keeps attracting this kind of person or situation to us.

In our work, we recognize *compulsive repetition* as a form of projection. We keep attracting the same situation in order to bring up that feeling energy from within for clearing. We could say that our Higher Self keeps bringing us these situations for our ultimate good, or we could say that the feeling energy goes out and attracts similar energies on the unconscious inner planes. In the East, this is the phenomenon that has been known for centuries and is called Karma.

The condition of manifestation projection is much talked about in the New Age field. I'm sure you have heard the phrase "You are what you think" or "Change your thinking and your life will change." Our beliefs create our world. The problem, however, is that most of what we believe remains on the subconscious level and is not easily seen and changed, even with whatever reprogramming techniques you may have heard about.

It is not the beliefs themselves, but the suppressed subconscious energies that result from the beliefs which go out into the world, form our experience, and come back at us. We attract the very same energy we suppress, in order to clear it. A very angry person may suppress anger to the point where they will be the victim of someone else's irrational outburst, violent assault, or even a seemingly impersonal car accident. The fact that suppressed energy is carried over from past lives will help to explain why an apparently innocent person will suffer such calamities.

This is the essence of the Karma theory as it relates to events that come to us for no apparent reason. Being born into poverty, enduring hardship, loneliness, bad luck, and so on – all these conditions result from energies that have not been released properly but have been carried inside.

Relationships are particularly susceptible to Karmic carryover.   **113**

It can be assumed that major difficulties we undergo with another are due to incomplete exchanges with that same person in a previous life. We maintain our connection because we are attached, through dualistic love/hate, tending to repeat the dynamics of a particular relationship until its energy is properly released. Certain psychotherapists are now, in fact, practicing past-life therapy. Its premise is that reexperiencing the suppressed pain in the context of the past life will cause the unblocking.

Past-life therapy is logical and effective, but my feeling is that you don't necessarily have to go back into the past, whether your childhood past or past lives, to release suppressed emotions. The past has formed the present, and the problems and feelings that you face now are the very same ones you faced then. The point is to release the energies through acceptance and experience of them and to cease the self-rejection that prevents the release. This can be done quite effectively by working with negative feelings as you perceive them today. In contrast, you can go back to a past life, maintain self-rejection, and still not release or integrate feelings. What is important, whether in a past or the present life, is to take responsibility for your experience as the first step to clearing it.

Spontaneous Clearing

The final way we create our experience comes about through no external interaction but occurs during meditation, bodywork, breathwork, or anytime. Once we begin to work on ourselves, we set the stage for spontaneous clearings.

Spontaneous clearing will take the form of negative emotions coming up for no particular reason. Sadness, anger, depression, sexual feelings, moods, whatever – these feelings may even temporarily get worse than before you started working on yourself. This is common once deep inner work is begun. It should be interpreted positively, knowing that your psychic garbage is being released. When it is released, you have to experience it; if you resist, you only suppress it again.

How long does clearing continue? Once you understand what you have been doing to yourself – probably for your entire life as well as previous lives – and you make the shift to a spiritual, or feeling, orientation, you can no longer be the same person. You become unsettled in the world, because the old, materialistic goals do not attract you, yet you are under siege from the release of psychic toxins from within. Furthermore, you have no real grasp of what life will be like in the future, when your higher consciousness is developed. This awakening is, indeed, a very fragile period, and you must be gentle and caring about yourself. How long? For as long as you need.

AFFIRM THAT YOU ARE PROCESSING

The intellect is the home of the decision-making capacity. An important function of the intellect is making the conscious decision to go ahead with processing and not fall back into unawareness and self-rejection, which makes integration impossible.

When you affirm that you are proceeding with processing, you automatically call into operation the skills you have learned. Thinking about what to do next is not necessary; you simply watch as problems take on the new perspective that leads to integration.

I accept myself, my feelings, and my life circumstances as they are. I blame no one, understanding that I have created what I perceive. In no longer trying to avoid my experience, I make possible the eventual transformation. My love for myself grows because of the courage I show in accepting and facing myself as I am.

7

Acceptance

*A**cceptance** is the second step in Integrative Processing. At this point, we have become aware of a negative feeling or condition and have made the intellectual assumption that we are responsible for it. We may not yet understand its full depth and significance; still, we are aware of something painful that needs to be resolved.

The painful feelings have not cleared; they remain strong because we have habitually rejected them. Rejection of feelings is self-rejection, because on a certain level we *are* our feelings. We find ourselves in an endless cycle of pain and self-rejection, the opposite of self-love. Rejection of feelings is also suppression. Pain stays suppressed, and whenever it breaks into awareness we again suppress it through self-rejection. In this chapter we will explore how we self-reject, even when we don't want to. Self-rejection is a critical issue, and we will examine it in detail.

There is something almost automatic in us that tends to self-reject, or suppress. Trying to fathom the reason for this is futile, but it seems a part of human nature. Suppression is a requirement of existence as we know it. If we didn't have our Karma, our suppressed subconscious, there would be no reason for the world to exist, in the metaphysical model. The world is our projection, and projection has to have suppressed contents. This perspective has proven helpful to me; it makes it easier to maintain equanimity and not get discouraged because there is so much in the subconscious to go through.

Self-rejection is a function of the mind

The mind is the gate that opens or closes, thereby allowing or preventing direct experience. Any action of the mind that blocks direct experience is self-rejecting; conversely, any action of the mind that allows direct experience is self-accepting.

Self-acceptance is more of a passive quality than an active or aggressive quality. It comes into being when the mechanical mind reaction of self-rejection has ceased. Accordingly, there is nothing really to do, only to stop doing. We are conditioned to be aggressive in pursuing goals in the world. Often we turn toward inner growth with the same kind of aggressiveness and impatience for results. This very attitude is self-rejecting. Acceptance happens when there is no active seeking, when there is no expectation or striving, when the mind has come to rest.

When something is accepted, the barriers of the mind to direct experience – to the *feeling* of the event – are taken down. When you are feeling, you are not suppressing; you are in the moment. Whether you intellectually prefer the moment to be as it is has nothing to do with your acceptance of it. If you are self-accepting, your mind does not block your feelings. The intellect remains free to have any preference it might. You don't have to like something to accept it. Your preference that the event be different may take the form of actively initiating change, but your preference does not influence your acceptance.

ACCEPT YOURSELF

When I first became interested in working on myself, I was attracted to teachers and methods that seemed to offer an approach to help me change myself into a better person, without the "faults" I found objectionable. I also tried to develop skills that would help me acquire what I thought would make me happy. I was attracted to growth therapies as a means of self-improvement. I am still attracted to growth therapies, but my motive is different. I now seek to accept and integrate, not to change. In accepting, I become aware of parts of myself previously unrecognized; my individuality expands and is enhanced; patterns become balanced; growth occurs.

I hope I have been able to communicate that trying to avoid or change the perceived negative, trying to be better, even more loving, is, in the end, all self-defeating. You may attempt to change yourself, but you only strengthen the negative when you fight it. In fighting the negative, you fight yourself, and you cannot win. You only suppress negative energies through self-rejection. Unconscious conflicts are not resolved, and conditions recur, in a different time and place. Of course, we are not justified in continuing to *act on* negativities; we simply do not attempt to force change.

Growth occurs through integration, not change. You cannot seek growth directly. You cannot seek to change yourself directly. Integration happens after you truly accept who and what you are *right now, without seeking to change* any part of yourself. Seeking to change is the subtle state of mind that self-rejects.

ACCEPT YOUR FEELINGS

To become integrated and to grow, you must accept and experience your feelings as they are, whatever they may be. If you have failed at something and are disappointed, you must accept and experience your disappointment. If you are fearful of something, you must accept and experience your fear. If you are compulsive, you must accept and experience the compulsiveness. Note that I am not saying you should act on or be motivated by any of these emotions; I am just saying that you must not resist feeling the emotion.

*Self-rejection does not come about because
you have negative feelings – Self-rejection
occurs when you reject the feelings*

In other words, feelings are never self-rejecting or accepting, even feelings of hatred toward yourself. It is the attitude toward the feelings that is accepting or rejecting. If you discover subconscious feelings of disapproval, resentment, or hatred toward yourself, you must handle them carefully. Such feelings certainly might be thought of as self-rejecting; paradoxically, this is not so if you can accept the feelings. It is when you reject the feelings and become motivated by or against them that you self-reject. Feelings of self-hatred are what we project onto the world. We hate ourselves, we suppress and then project. We perceive others as hating us, or we hate them.

Self-condemnation represents stored negative energy, just as other negative emotions do. It must be cleared somehow. When you consciously accept and experience the energy, clearing can take place. Allow feelings of self-hatred to exist without guilt. Bring them into consciousness, allowing them to work out their energy cycles. As you accept the feelings, entering into direct experience of them, they will clear. You will have a catharsis of the trapped energy that has been affecting you adversely. You will spontaneously understand the history and how the patterns behind the hatred formed, possibly even going into past-life circumstances. But this happens only when you start with acceptance.

*Acceptance means allowing that
you will be unhappy some of the time*

Unhappiness is easier to accept if you can grasp the dualistic nature of existence. Dualism means that happiness and unhappiness always go together. If you can accept both dualistic happiness and unhappiness, you open the door to real transformation. You begin to grow, to transcend the issue. Paradoxically, you start to experience a different, nondualistic kind of happiness, a happiness that does not depend on circumstances. Happiness becomes *unconditional.*

This is the pattern for real change. Real, and lasting, transformation occurs when you integrate the dualistic experience within. You no longer cling to one side of any duality and resist and suppress the other side, rejecting yourself. You release suppressed energies, establishing balance.

Jung was probably the first to incorporate the concept of integration of duality into contemporary psychology. His formulation was that we must accept the *shadow* side of ourselves, the dark and negative aspect that we suppress because of its painful nature. According to Jung, we all have such a nature. Making peace with it was one of the central aspects of his work. Processing is an approach that will enable you to do this.

If you are to accept your negative side – your misery, if you will – how can you be sure that it will be resolved? Asking the question implies the motive of avoidance. This motive will impede acceptance and integration. Such is the fragile nature of acceptance. You can't accept to get rid of; you have to accept to make part of yourself.

Surrender to what is

Acceptance is a more modern term for what is called *surrender* in classical terminology. Surrender is a complex subject, and I have encountered people who have, in my opinion, a distorted understanding. Does surrender mean blind obedience to the guru, complete submission to external events and persons, resignation to personal circumstances, the attempt to destroy the personal ego through renunciation, or simply indifference? Or does it mean total compliance with your own impulses? It is none of the above, but these are some of the traps that are available.

Surrender is a personal concept that will grow and change as you engage in an active spiritual practice such as processing. It is basically *ceasing resistance to what is,* in terms of both inner feelings and outer events. We harbor resistance on deep levels, for no rational reason.

I have found it easiest to begin cultivation of surrender on the body level. Becoming aware of physical sensation, which is really energy sensation, and accepting without choice teaches us how to accept emotions.

Surrendering to emotions gradually will become easier as you continue working on yourself. In my own work, I remember coming to the point of acknowledging and accepting the inevitability of painful experiences. As I surrendered to the eventuality of my anger, which was what I was working on, I released my resistance on a deeper level, and the judging, analytical, protective ego loosened up. I no longer feared my anger. I didn't care as much if I was angry or not, and I saw that the attainment of a perfect state of nonconcern would be liberation. The anger would not necessarily have disappeared, but in not caring about it, I was no longer bound to it. I set up the proper condition for a possible final cleansing, but I was not relying on this, as I knew that it might never happen.

The final condition of surrender is when there is no resistance at all to inner or outer experience as it happens. All concepts that dictate how things should be have been dropped; there is no critical self that evaluates life as it happens, trying to avoid certain parts and cling to other parts. Of course, we still have a personal identity and preferences, but our feelings are not inhibited – we allow them to be as they may, without having to act on them. We are *real*.

Being real is an important part of emotional self-acceptance. It means tactfully allowing your true feelings to show when appropriate – being what you are, instead of trying to be what you or others might prefer or expect. Being real becomes possible only when you have taken responsibility for your feelings. Until then, others will become alienated or threatened when you show negative feelings, sensing that you blame them or circumstances outside yourself for your condition. When you take responsibility for your feelings, others will not be threatened but will welcome and appreciate your honesty. You don't have to broadcast the fact that you have taken responsibility either. Others will sense this as well.

Accept the External

Experience can be divided into two broad classes: inner and outer. Often experience consists of both elements. It may appear that the outer causes the inner. Something happens, and we seem to respond with an emotion. However, we know that we create our experience through the mechanisms of projection; the outer is only the trigger. Because we project onto appropriate screens, there is always an element of what we have projected in the person or circumstance that serves as the screen. We don't try to sort this out before processing; it would be difficult in our subjective state and would impede integration, keeping us in the mind. Therefore, we assume we have projected all of our perception. Later, after integration has occurred, we will gain a more objective understanding of what each party has brought to the event.

Acceptance of the external is self-acceptance

Since what we perceive in the external is our creation through projection, accepting it results in self-acceptance. For example, when you perceive qualities in others that you dislike, you are largely projecting those qualities, as a form of *shadow projection.* If you can accept the qualities without trying to change them or your feelings about them, you are self-accepting. To do this, you may have to accept your dislike.

In other words, don't try to force yourself to like something in order to accept it. Remember, acceptance means opening to your feelings, whatever they are. Accept your feelings as they are, accept your dislike, but don't act on it. Since your dislike is the result of your projection, do not hold another person responsible for the dislike. If you can take responsibility for your dislike, you will be able to relate to the other person constructively, going beyond the dislike.

Similarly, with any actual happening or circumstance that affects you, you accept yourself if you accept the event. Do not blame anyone else or take refuge in thinking it just "happened" to you. Your unconscious psychic forces mold circumstances to fit your needs exactly. You project your suppressed energy onto the world and perceive it as coming to you from the outside. It follows that if you resist what is happening or, simply, *what is,* you are self-rejecting. If you fight the event, you fight yourself.

Understanding this puts all our struggles into a different perspective. If we have created the event through projection, fighting it has a certain self-defeating aspect to it. When we struggle against ourselves, who can win?

Acceptance does not imply complacency

You should not be complacent about confronting conditions that call for creative response. Acceptance means only that you accept conditions *now;* acceptance has no bearing on the future. Accept responsibility for conditions, accept the pain associated with them, but also take action to improve or change conditions, if necessary.

Much of our Karma is such that confrontation and change are necessary. We are presented with real problems, and we must deal with them in constructive ways. The difficulty is that if we have not cleared the subconscious, we will go on to create or attract the same conditions all over again when we take action. If the problem is approached through acceptance, the required change will take place without struggle. You must therefore strike a reasonable balance between action and acceptance, with the emphasis on acceptance.

I would like to emphasize a point about acceptance that many people misunderstand. They think that to be accepting, they have to resign themselves to negative circumstances and then try to force themselves to like the circumstances. This is wrong. Intellectually, you are free to have preferences. What you need to accept are your *feelings, as they are,* about the circumstances.

If you accept painful feelings associated with a certain event, you eliminate self-rejection, even though you might prefer not to have the feelings. You may continue to dislike the actual event, and this would, of course, be appropriate under many circumstances. However, if you accept your feelings concerning an external event, you also accept the event in a certain way, and this will lead to the eventual integration of the event. You arrive at the paradox of both accepting and disliking an event at the same time. You dislike on the intellectual level; you accept on the mental level; you feel on the body level; but you also take steps to make necessary changes. This highly practical metaphysical position should be the point you eventually come to in your self-acceptance regarding events that are clearly destructive.

For example, if you suffered abuse as a child, you should *not* try to accept the abuse intellectually. Instead, you have to accept your feelings about being abused. You felt pain, outrage, humiliation, abandonment, sadness – these are the feelings you must accept. The feelings were already hidden within your subconscious, and the purpose of your experience was only to bring them into consciousness in order to clear. If you process the feelings, you can release them.

With events not blatantly destructive, but just annoying or bothersome, you will find that accepting the feelings that come up will change your opinion about the events. You will no longer think of them as problems. Your opinion will change naturally, coinciding with the release of negative energies through your self-work; it is not something you can do directly.

In other words, whether you like something or not has nothing to do with your acceptance of your feelings. Liking or disliking is irrelevant to feeling. Accepting your feelings, as they are, is what self-acceptance is all about.

BE NONREACTIVE

Nonreactiveness is the necessary complement to acceptance. You cannot accept negative feelings and then think that you are free to act on the feelings, or to extend them into the universe in any way. This would be a serious mistake. Acceptance makes sense only when you become nonreactive.

Nonreactiveness means that you do not react to, that you are *not motivated* by negative feelings. It does *not* mean that you should try to resist, limit, control, or not have the feelings in the first place. Feelings come up spontaneously, and the attempt to control them is suppression. You should allow feelings to come up as well as any accompanying physical expression that is part of the inner release – such as laughing or crying – but then you should not react to the feelings.

Nonreactiveness does not result in suppression because the feeling is allowed to express itself fully in your consciousness when you enter direct experience. Direct experience of the feeling is all that is required to eliminate suppression. You do not have to act on or act out the feeling to avoid suppression. When feelings come up, you are in a precarious position. You have not yet released through processing any of the tension that accompanies difficult feelings. The temptation is to act on the feeling to relieve tension.

Don't act. Don't be motivated by the feeling. Don't extend the negativity into the universe by doing or expressing anything that probably would be self-destructive in the long run. You are learning sophisticated techniques that will enable you to dissolve negative feelings without having to act on them, but you must exercise willpower and self-discipline. Will is an important function of the intellect, which must be used now.

Nonreactiveness is essential in regard to active emotions, such as anger, possessiveness, jealousy, or lust, but it is also needed in working with the more passive emotions, such as fear, sadness, or loneliness. When we give in to negative emotion, when we are motivated by it, we reinforce its power over us and strengthen the negative pattern. By not reacting or being motivated by it, we loosen the pattern.

Not reacting is most difficult when you are under attack and have to defend yourself. If you have been practicing nonreactiveness at other, more meditative times, you will gain the ability to maintain it during stressful times. You can defend your rights much more effectively, because your emotions are not in the way, even though you are still feeling them.

Nonreactiveness does not mean that you become passive to anyone else's aggression; it just means that you do not blame them. Although it may not be apparent now, you have created or attracted what appears to be coming to you through the other person. You should acknowledge this intellectually, but do not refrain from defending your rights.

Thus, if another person appears to block you, it is you who block yourself. You will feel anger because the Power center is frustrated, but do not think the other has made you angry. Take responsibility for your anger, and dissolve it through processing. Then you can go on to work with the other person to make the necessary creative changes regarding the situation. You will be immensely more effective at implementing change because you are not coming at the other out of anger. The situation is likely to have changed automatically anyway, because of your processing.

Contain the feeling

Reactiveness always coincides with the attempt to get rid of the energy of a feeling. We resist it, we act it out, we blamefully express, we are motivated by it, and so on. It feels as if we are releasing the energy, but this is not so. We are just spreading it out, suppressing it, dumping it on others. We do not use the experience for growth.

In contrast, when we are nonreactive, we do not attempt to get rid of or turn away from the energy through any of the self-rejecting mechanisms that we are about to discuss. The feeling is *contained;* it is not dissipated. The feeling is held in place, in the body, in a pure and concentrated form, ready for direct experience. This is what makes it possible to process the feeling and what allows the experience to be used for clearing and growth.

Blameful expression does not release negativity

Psychologists generally agree that unrestrained blameful expression of negative emotions is counterproductive to the release of the emotions. By blameful expression, I mean confronting others, arguing, accusing and blaming them, yelling at them, vindictively trying to get even, and so on. Considering the overall effects of unrestrained blameful expression, there is no question that it is self-destructive.

First, it reinforces the misbelief that the other is responsible; you condition yourself into victim consciousness. Second, what you put out comes back to you, usually intensified; there are plenty of unconscious people around who are just looking for someone to exchange negative energy with. Third, it doesn't really do anything to dissolve the emotion, which still sits with you in a more agitated state. Fourth, in attacking others, you hurt them; they become alienated from you, sometimes irreparably.

I would even question the value of energetic "releasing" in therapy sessions, where the client acts out emotions by beating on pillows, and so on. In the case of resentment toward parents, for example, it is usually not made clear that the parents are not ultimately responsible for the hurts the child has suffered; the child chooses the conditions that will activate its character in accordance with the suppressed subconscious. This therapy may serve only to condition and reinforce the sense of blame, which may be the primary reason that the suppressed resentment cannot be released. Still, after an energetic therapy session in which catharsis has been achieved, blame has dissolved as well. But how often is real catharsis achieved, and which comes first, the catharsis or the dropping of blame?

Do not confuse spontaneity
with emotionality

The first step in avoiding the problems inherent in unrestrained expression comes with nonreactiveness. It is totally erroneous to think that you are becoming less spontaneous or more inhibited by becoming nonreactive. To be spontaneous means to be able to respond in a positive and creative manner to whatever is happening, not to be chained to any predetermined emotional response, like a robot that jumps when its buttons are pushed. To be so lost in your drama that you have no control over the outward expression of negative emotions is nothing but unconscious emotionalism. When you practice nonreactiveness, you train yourself to become the kind of person you want to be. When you fail to maintain nonreactiveness, you self-reject.

IDENTIFY SELF-REJECTION

Often we find ourselves aware of a particular feeling, or confronted with a recurrent event, but we are at a loss to resolve the issue. We linger with emotions, dwelling on them perhaps for years. We don't know how to get rid of them. These feelings and events stay with us because they are not cleared. When we have direct experience of something, we clear it. The cycle of energy is released and finished. Direct experience means staying with a feeling long enough, and in the right way, so clearing can take place. However, self-rejection prevents direct experience, and the feeling never clears. We "wallow" in our misery and self-rejection. The feeling comes up again and again and is suppressed again and again.

You must watch your mind carefully

Self-rejection takes place because of the activity of the mind. We mentally react to our feelings instead of staying nonreactive. Of course, not all activity of the mind leads to suppression, but we often misuse our mental powers in the unconscious intent to avoid feelings. Since self-rejection is a product of the mind, the intellect – a higher function – can identify it and make the decision to stop doing it by exercising its discretionary power. We stop self-rejection simply by making the conscious decision to do so.

But to stop self-rejection, you must first become aware of how it works and what it does to you. You must become very attentive to how your mind works. This is the "mindfulness" of Buddhism. Self-rejection is part of our basic conditioning and can be changed through education and awareness. When we become aware of how we self-reject, that actual awareness begins the freeing and outgrowing of the self-rejecting mechanism.

The principles we are about to discuss concerning self-rejection have always been central on the traditional path to enlightenment. In contemporary society, the principles remain the same, but the emphasis may be different from what might have been appropriate in previous times. Still, one problem remains constant: the appearance of the principles as being negative in nature.

Pointing out exactly how we reject ourselves can become tedious. Moreover, when we fall into habitual self-rejection, we tend to become dependent on the mental conditioning that keeps us suppressed. When the conditioning is challenged, we become anxious, possibly enough to make us turn a deaf ear. We resist hearing because our basic ego formations are being threatened. We remain in denial. It makes no difference that we are miserable with ourselves, because we cling to our misery. We fear that we will be nothing when our self-destructive conditioning is taken away.

This is not entirely irrational. Our self-rejecting habits support us; they limit us, yet they get us through. When they are removed, we have no suppressive mechanism to defend ourselves from the possibly overwhelming negativity that lies close in the subconscious. We feel like our supports are breaking under us, our anchors are no longer holding, and we become temporarily lost until new frames of reference are established.

Maintain the spirit to gently break through self-rejection

Resistance to the loosening of self-rejecting mind-sets becomes a secondary problem when you begin inner work. If you are working with a therapist, the therapist takes it for granted that resistance will be encountered; handling it is part of a therapist's skill. You may become defensive and resentful toward the therapist or toward anyone who points out your self-rejection. If you are working by yourself, you must remember that unconscious resistance can keep you from making progress and that you must maintain your intention to cut through self-rejecting conditioning. Once you understand that self-rejecting habits keep you in misery, you will gain the "warrior" spirit necessary to advance in the inner quest.

It's possible you may feel that our discussion of self-rejecting modes of behavior has no relevance to the work you would like to do on yourself. You may feel that you need depth work of a particular type. You may be justified in thinking this, but you also may be putting up just another type of resistance. Modes of behavior, while mundane in a certain respect, affect us deeply. The *attitude* behind the behavior is what influences us, and we are apt to overlook the attitude, thinking it insignificant. We miss the forest because of the trees.

We don't see that we reject ourselves almost every minute of the day, from the moment we get out of bed. We are conditioned, and we keep reconditioning ourselves to self-reject, and we don't understand why we are miserable. You may think that a particular attitude you have is not a problem, that you can live with it, that you're only human, but remember: You cannot accept self-rejection.

Self-acceptance does not mean that you may yield to self-rejection

Self-rejection must be understood and changed with gentleness and love. Self-rejecting supports must be broken, and often real pain occurs in the breaking. You must understand what is happening and be neither too reluctant to give up your supports nor too hard on yourself as you look at your behavior patterns. You must be gentle with yourself as well as with others. Even though we may discuss self-rejection in detail, sometimes it is difficult to be objective about ourselves. This is another area where a qualified therapist or even a sensitive friend can be helpful.

So when we discuss self-rejection, please remember that we are not being negative, even though we are discussing negative behavior patterns. Many of the concepts may be challenging for you. As you continue to entertain these ideas, eventually the logic will become clear.

THE WAYS OF SELF-REJECTION

Repression

Repression is unconscious suppression. In suppression, part of us always is aware that we are suppressing. Chronic suppression lapses into repression, where awareness is lost of both feelings and the act of avoiding them. Repression is the most serious type of self-rejection because we become totally out of touch with ourselves. Eventually the buildup of negativity results in neurotic behavior and self-destructiveness, such as chronic depression or hostility, illness, or physical calamity, such as accident or assault.

Most of us engage in a certain amount of repression, especially if we lead active lives. I feel there is no cause for alarm, however, as long as we begin to work on ourselves. When we start address-

ing the issues and feelings that are conscious, we gradually change
our threshold of awareness, and previously repressed material will
come into view to be integrated.

Resistance

The first way we consciously suppress is by resisting feelings.
Because aversion to pain is instinctual, it's not hard to see why we
want to avoid negative experience. We assume pain can be avoided
by turning away from it. Resistance is probably the basic cause of
suppression, resulting in the creation of the subconscious. It is one
of Nature's traps, having us create our Karma in order to project
the world.

We simply have to be aware of the implications of resisting our
feelings. Even so, you do not have to be constantly ill at ease, waiting anxiously for the next moment when you will suppress. You
should just remain aware of the tendency to resist and gradually
condition yourself to confront, accept, and experience fully your
feelings regarding the more important issues that come up.

As you condition yourself to confront feelings rather than
resisting, your personal boundaries will grow. When you accept
pain instead of avoiding it, its nature will change, and it will
become neutralized. By raising your threshold for pain, you effectively lower the amount of pain in your life. If you run from pain,
you lower the threshold, and you can never get away from it.

Blame

Blame is the next most common way of rejecting ourselves. We
blame because we want to avoid responsibility. When we blame
any person, object, or circumstance for our experience, we essentially become blind to reality. Self-acceptance is impossible, and we
simmer in self-rejection. This includes blaming ourselves, which is
called guilt, a special form of self-rejection. Blame is essentially
the same as complaining.

Blame is so common that it is seldom questioned. It is almost a
form of bonding ritual among certain people to blame somebody
for something every time they speak. If you want to support your

friend, you support their blame. People blame their job, various authority figures, the government, the economy – the list is endless. Blame can be the common element that binds spouses, lovers, or partners together. When I encounter a person who is heavily into blame, I almost feel as if I am watching a stand-up comic routine.

People who are intelligent and educated believe that their spouses do things that make them furious. Or their children. Or their employees or boss. These are all cases of projected emotion. There is no reason to assume that whatever triggered your emotion was the cause. You just took that opportunity to bring up your feelings.

Self-work is not possible when blame exists

In Eastern philosophy, a person is considered unconscious when into blame, becoming conscious when moving past blame and understanding the true cause of the problem. As we have discussed at length, *the person* is the cause. Understanding this does not eliminate the problem; it just means that work can begin.

When we take responsibility for our feelings, we begin to make significant headway toward inner healing, but the difficulty is that even when we intellectually own our experience, we continue to *unconsciously* blame. We remain stuck in self-rejection, preventing true acceptance, integration, and release of negativity. One of the essential challenges of any therapy is getting past unconscious blame.

You may try to enter into direct experience of your feelings, thinking you are past blame, but energies are not released because you are still blaming on a deeper level. The free flow of energy is inhibited. Instead of integrating, you are stewing in your negativity. I suggest that you be particularly aware of this possibility when working with feelings concerning relationships. Occasionally, I'll find that I've gotten nowhere with processing until I finally become aware and deliberately let go of the blame that is holding back the energies. However, dropping blame becomes easier as integration proceeds.

Unconscious blame is not part of our subconscious Karma as are suppressed energies. Blame is a conditioning of the mind, not an energy-based feeling. Therefore, make sure you are not trying to accept or process blame to get past it; doing so will reinforce the blame instead of releasing it. Blame is handled by being deliberately dropped. However, the feelings behind the blame are definitely Karmic and will need to be processed. Unconscious blame must be brought into awareness, because it influences how we perceive reality, creating a blame-suppression cycle: We perceive a feeling, we unconsciously blame, self-acceptance is not possible, and we self-reject. We suppress the feeling and also our blame. The same scenario exists for guilt. It is largely unconscious, making it hard to get at.

These are sensitive and difficult issues to address in psychotherapy. In traditional therapy, it is assumed that blame eventually will go away as therapy proceeds. I know of therapists who do not confront clients with the notion that they should take responsibility for their feelings and their experience, because the client would resist and resent this. Instead, forgiveness is suggested.

Forgiveness is the realization that blame is a mistake

Forgiveness is, of course, a very desirable quality, but often we misunderstand what it means. Forgiveness means finally seeing that the other person was not really responsible for what we thought came from them. Sometimes we try to force ourselves to forgive, thinking we are being spiritual or loving, or simply in the attempt to avoid pain. We continue to believe that the other is responsible for what has happened to us, but now we have pardoned them for their behavior.

Such "forgiveness" is intellectual, pseudo, and self-deceptive. It puts us more out of touch with our inner experience. It can even inflate the ego, because we think we are generous enough to forgive. True forgiveness means understanding that the original blame was wrong; it is not the granting of a pardon for what we mistakenly believe someone has done to us.

Blame is particularly relevant in parent/child dynamics, which traditional therapy focuses on heavily. We are encouraged to forgive our parents, often without understanding that we should own our past. This kind of therapy can work in the long run, but the question is, would another, more realistic approach work more effectively? We choose our parents and early environment to serve as a catalyst for our character. The events of childhood merely activate contents latent in the child's subconscious, a viewpoint being discussed and supported by transpersonal psychologists today.

Often we don't want to let go of blame because of nothing more than pride. Unconsciously we understand the truth that we are responsible for our experience. The conscious ego, however, wants to blame because it is defending itself. It does not want to feel that it could be stupid enough to cause harm to itself. The nature of the ego, and of highly egocentric people in particular, is always to be right, and blame is usually how self-righteousness is maintained.

Guilt

Self-blame, or guilt, is a variation of the basic blame dynamic. It is a self-serving mechanism calculated to avoid owning and feeling on a deeper level. By blaming ourselves, we protect ourselves just as blaming others will protect the ego from the realization of its responsibility for its experience.

Self-blame is not the same as taking responsibility

Spiritual seekers, when first realizing that they are responsible for their experience, may fall into the trap of blaming themselves rather than others. The result is still self-rejection, preventing them from going further in their work. You must realize that your Karma has been formed out of ignorance, not deliberate intention; it is simply the result of where you are on the evolutionary journey.

If you feel self-blame because you think you are responsible for someone else's condition, you should realize that you are reacting inappropriately. Relationships are always mutual, meaning there is mutual consent. Others also have their Karma and have chosen the relationship to bring their experience to themselves. Of course, this does not condone deliberate mistreatment of others.

Guilt may start because we want to blame someone else, but that may not be possible. Having no other outlet, the blame is redirected to the self. In Gestalt, this is called "retroflection," and can occur with other aggressive impulses as well. For example, if a child is unloved, the child may feel guilt about not being lovable enough for the parents. The belief "It's my fault" is activated. In addition, the child feels frustration about not being loved and wants to blame the parents for this. However, it is too threatening to blame the parents, because the parents might become angry and withdraw life support. The child redirects the blame back to itself, creating more guilt.

Guilt is unconsciously created by the child as a shield from the deeper realization that it does not feel love for others. Instead, the child is locked into a previous-life Karmic pattern of dependency/ resentment. The resentment is unconscious because it has been suppressed, but it is one of the factors that originally brought the child into a relationship with these particular parents. The child projects the unconscious resentment onto the parents and experiences them as unloving or even hating.

As an individual coming into birth with this Karma, the Karma is harder to accept than the idea that the parents don't offer their love. If the child can feel that the parents hate the child, the ego is protected from the realization that the hatred is coming from within; the awareness of the hatred within remains suppressed. The child's ego grabs at the idea that the parents will not provide love, choosing parents who will comply or else behaving so as to invoke their disapproval. The child projects their nonlove and then avoids responsibility by feeling guilt. The same pattern extends to adult relationships.

Intellectual therapies, in particular, take a long time to resolve unconscious blame or guilt. How should this be handled in processing? The guilt of the mind needs to be *reconditioned,* not accepted. The principle of affirmation, which is discussed in Chapter 13, can be used effectively here.

The final, and possibly most important realization about blame is that, when we are blaming, we give up our right to autonomy. We are slaves to the other if the other is really responsible for what we are feeling; we have no self-determination in the most vital sense. When we finally take responsibility for our feelings and what happens to us, we are obviously no longer being controlled by agencies outside ourselves. We cease giving our power away to others. Taking responsibility means that we control our own destiny. We are no longer the victim.

Blameful Expression

Unrestrained blameful expression does not release negative feelings. Although the act of expressing and returning our hurt back to the source from which it apparently came seems to be a natural impulse, this is only because of the unconsciousness from which we are emerging. When we finally understand that the other is not responsible for our experience, it becomes obvious that taking out our emotion on them is completely inappropriate. You may have felt that someone was "making" you angry, but now that you have a better understanding of what actually happens, I hope it is clear that blame is a distortion of the truth and that blameful recrimination is nothing less than ridiculous. In our passion, however, we often lose objectivity.

Confronting, yelling at someone else, acting
out your emotion as if others are to blame
is totally wrong and will get you nowhere

Blameful expression won't even give you the pleasure of venting. Trying to vent by confronting someone emotionally does give some movement to the energies, and so may appear to provide temporary relief, but the eventual result of unrestrained expression is further suppression, not release of the energies. You may have verified this in yourself or others by observing that emotional outbursts only become worse once they begin, even if you "express yourself" in a quiet, calm manner. In addition, damage to the relationship, and ultimately to yourself, results.

When you express negativity in a blameful and accusing manner, you undermine the trust that exists in any close relationship. The other person is hurt, sometimes deeply. They may have no choice but to back off, if your expression is continually blameful and harsh. They may be able to see what you can't: that you are creating and reacting to your own distorted perception of reality. You end by driving away the ones you love.

Moreover, when you release negative energy into the universe by expressing it, you set up conditions for it to come back to you, which it will do, magnified. The actual physical expression is what starts the cycle. Before it is expressed, negativity is in a more potential form and may be handled more easily. Blameful expression *affirms* the negativity. If the person at whom you have expressed negativity happens to be unconscious and vindictive, the negativity will return through that person. If the person is not vindictive, the energy will find another path back to you, often surprisingly quickly. This has been called "instant Karma."

Of course, you may share your feelings in a nonblaming way with someone who will be understanding enough not to become threatened and defensive, but this is much different from active, blameful expression. Blameful expression is a vindictive attack. On the psychic level, hostile energy is sent out to penetrate the aura of the attacked person. This is why anger, for example, is so painful to contend with. What we don't realize is that to hurt someone in blameful attack, we must first hurt ourselves. The attack is as debilitating to the sender as to the receiver, and vindictive people end up destroying themselves.

Still, blameful expression may appear easier than nonreactiveness, because when we express, we avoid really facing and experiencing our feelings – we suppress them. This is the real motive behind blameful expression and why "expressing" can feel like feelings are relieved. However, the negative energy is only driven deeper into the subconscious. If you can observe how this works in yourself, you will take important steps to gain control of your emotions.

When strong emotions are felt, there is movement of energy in the energy body; this is what an emotion is. If expression of negativity is ultimately self-defeating, how is the surge of energy to be handled?

Strong emotions are to be
released by processing

By using breath and bodywork, entering into direct experience of the energy; by not avoiding it but simply feeling it, any emotion that comes up can be cleared instead of suppressed. There are times when this is not easy, but these are the times when the most may be gained: when deep subconscious pain is surfacing. Significant change can take place now.

One point is critical: If you continue to mentally blame, even though you may refrain from blamefully expressing your emotion, you will still suppress instead of clear. You will be locked into blame, and self-work will not be possible, even though the ability to restrain the impulse for blameful expression indicates a more advanced consciousness. It is when you can see past blame and understand the destructive results of blameful expression that self-acceptance occurs.

Acting Out

Acting out means that negative energies are extended into the universe by being included in our personal behavior. Instead of being aware of, accepting, and not reacting to negativities, we affirm them and their power to influence us by acting them out. We remain unaware, self-rejecting, and reactive.

For example, if you act out fear, you will go to unnecessary extremes such as installing extensive security systems, not going out after dark, being highly suspicious, and so on. You project fear needlessly, becoming fearful of the objects onto which you have projected. You react to those objects, not perceiving that you are reacting to yourself.

Awareness would help you recognize that the fear comes from inside you and that you unconsciously project it. Acceptance would help you not try to avoid the fear by running from it. Non-reactiveness would further your capacity for integration and the eventual desensitization and clearing of the fear.

Motivation/Acting On

Motivation covers a wide range of human needs, mostly originating in the lower centers. In motivation, we act on negative impulses, trying to satisfy them, instead of confronting and dissolving them. Motivation is a large area for investigation, made difficult because most motivation is unconscious. However, we can become aware of our motivation if we watch ourselves carefully, starting with whatever is conscious. As we process impulses that we are aware of, we begin to uncover other, deeper motivation.

What all motivation has in common is that we are coming from a sense of *lack*. We feel that something is missing, and we go out to get it. The assumption is that a sense of balance, or happiness, will be achieved when the missing something is found. Taken to its logical conclusion, this orientation has resulted in the consumer society. Motivation based on a sense of lack is not questioned; nor is whether our needs are valid or not. Of course, we do have valid, basic needs that must be met, but as I have pointed out, many of our needs have grown to the point of being artificial and compulsive.

The sense of lack can never be satisfied, but only transcended

How does motivation relate to acceptance? This is subtle and may have to sit with you awhile before it sinks in. When you are motivated to satisfy any desire that comes from a sense of lack, you are essentially rejecting yourself because you are attempting to avoid the feeling of lack. The nature of the dualistic experience is such that no amount of "satisfaction" will be effective, and the lack is affirmed and perpetuated, instead of being finally transcended.

Often the attempt to escape from lack through satisfying it in one form or another is not apparent to us. We assume we act normally, we think we have needs, we rationalize our behavior, but the truth is that we are attempting to avoid feelings, rejecting ourselves. After blame, wrong motivation is the next largest area of blindness that keeps us in suppression.

This type of motivation is referred to in the classical literature as the problem of desire. Most desires are considered as keeping us in bondage. Release from desire, not the satisfaction of desire, is a major part of liberation. Release from desire comes about by processing the desire impulse and whatever negative feelings may be behind it instead of being motivated by them.

For example, suppose you are lonely. If your habitual response to this feeling is to suppress it by constantly being with people, you are being motivated by your loneliness or by your perceived lack of relationship. In seeking to avoid loneliness, you are rejecting it and rejecting yourself. Integration of the feeling is not possible, and you will not get rid of the loneliness, except perhaps temporarily. If you were to face the loneliness and begin integrating it, it would gradually come into balance. It wouldn't go away immediately, because you are likely to have a lot of suppressed feelings needing to be cleared.

The same logic can be applied to all the centers of consciousness. We seek to avoid insecurity by grasping for psychological and material objects. We seek to avoid helplessness by going for power. We seek to avoid sexual tension by mindlessly chasing after sex. We seek to avoid feelings of inadequacy by going for approval and prestige. Our efforts are all self-defeating because they affirm and perpetuate the very thing we are trying to avoid. We are trying to avoid one side of dualistic experience by escaping into the other.

When we are motivated by the desire to be rid of body sensations that we classify as "pain," we also self-reject, although this may be more difficult to comprehend. Our physical sensations and symptoms correspond to our psychic imbalances as well as to our emotional imbalances. If you accept physical sensations, by accepting and experiencing the pain to whatever extent reasonable, you do the most possible to integrate the psychic imbalance. When you resist the pain, you strengthen it by feeding additional energy to it.

We also self-reject when motivated by moods of uncertainty, restlessness, irritation, and the like. We become motivated into all kinds of evasive, self-destructive behavior. Simply be aware of your negative moods; accept and experience them. Let them dissolve by neither opposing nor being motivated by them.

If you understand that you cannot avoid the negative, you will cease to be motivated by it. You will accept it and end its compulsive influence.

Worry

Worry is the condition of thinking about feelings instead of feeling the feelings. Often, there is a strong component of blame present.

Worry consumes much psychic energy, draining us and encouraging addictive tendencies to replace the energy.

You can cease worrying by first becoming aware of your worry, then consciously dropping the thoughts and blame about the feelings. Embrace and enter the feelings, no matter how difficult this may be. When you stop thinking about your feelings, you stop rejecting yourself because the thinking prevents direct experience.

Activity/Excitement

We need a balanced amount of activity, including physical exercise, to keep our energy from becoming lethargic, but sometimes we engage in activity for no other purpose than avoiding ourselves, resulting in self-rejection and suppression. The simple act of constantly doing something draws the attention outward, away from inner awareness. Since no real goal is involved, "keeping busy" becomes compulsive. Or else unnecessary goals are created; workaholism prevails. We immerse ourselves in activity, and when the newness wears off, we assume we need a new activity. We run from one diversion to another, but we are really running from ourselves. In our culture, shopping and spending money have become major lifestyle activities to suppress feelings.

Excitement also draws us from inner awareness. We become thrill seekers. Because of the suppressive power of excitement, our pain or anxiety is made to disappear. We vibrate with the thrill. Excitement can become an addictive cycle. We oscillate between the up of the thrill and the down of having exhausted our energy, trying to get out of the down through more excitement. Since the old is no longer exciting, we are forced to find something new; we become desperate in our search. We become addicted to loud rock music, dangerous sports, violent entertainment, and so on. We put ourselves into perilous situations for the thrill of it, becoming self-destructive.

As we survey modern life, it is hard to escape the conclusion that much of the frenetic pace that is common fits these descriptions. We have actually lost the ability to just sit and do nothing, which is what meditation is. Trying to be still brings up anxiety or other feelings, often masked by boredom. Confronting these feelings is the first obstacle to any spiritual journey, and most people never get past it.

If compulsive activity or excitement is a problem for you, you must realize that the feelings you attempt to avoid are the result of past suppression. Continued suppression will result in eventual stagnation, and no amount of activity or excitement will do any good. There is no other way to regain contact with yourself except to begin to confront these feelings, through accepting and experiencing them.

Ambition

Ambition is one of the most common attributes of the isolated ego. The pain of isolation is felt, and it is assumed that release will come when personal success, wealth, possessions, or fame is acquired. This is the essence of materialism and the still-popular American dream. Ambition is very much socially acceptable. We become conditioned from childhood to reject ourselves and our present condition, whatever it may be, and to want more. We enter the race to nowhere, sometimes never waking up from the madness.

Ambition is one of the more acute forms of self-rejection and eventual self-undoing, because a great deal of energy is mobilized to achieve goals. The same energy then serves to form the suppressing shields around feelings. We become highly goal-oriented and out of touch with ourselves. Note that it is not the actual working toward goals that comprises ambition; we must achieve certain goals to survive. Ambition is the addiction of the ego to the attainment of goals. The ego thinks it enlarges itself when it achieves. Goals become nonhumanistic. We become selfish and isolated. Yet ambition seems to be part of growing up.

We may delude ourselves that we have gone beyond ambition when we have merely shifted objectives. We stop being ambitious about materialistic things, becoming ambitious about artistic expression, recognition, or spiritual growth – another common trap for the spiritual seeker. Ambition for any of these has the same self-rejecting effect. Dropping ambition means learning to be happy as you are, in the moment, with no projections into the future.

Impatience

Impatience is another form of self-rejection that goes almost unnoticed. Impatience implies rejection of what is happening right now. Because *what is* is our projection, self-rejection is the result. Impatience is the same as *rushing*. Realizing that most of our lives are spent rushing to achieve goals gives us another perspective on the level of self-rejection that is common. When we are constantly rushing to get somewhere, we lose the ability to be in the moment, which is where direct experience takes place.

Loss of ability to enjoy the moment especially shows up in our attitudes toward work. The idea of enjoying work is almost nonexistent today. Enjoying work is made difficult by the pressures we face; but then, how many of these pressures are our own creation? Behind the impatience and rushing lie suppressed feelings of fear, dissatisfaction, or frustration. We are compelled by such feelings, unconsciously assuming we can avoid them if we hurry, but we inevitably learn this is not possible.

Second Reaction/Overly Emotional

If you observe yourself carefully whenever a negative feeling comes up, you will notice something that might be called the "second reaction." The first reaction is the feeling you are working with – your subconscious material, your Karma – coming to the surface, triggered by circumstances. You have no control over the first reaction and should not attempt to resist it. The first reaction is of the body; it originates in the blocked chakras.

The "second reaction" is of the mind. You become upset about the feelings that are coming up. If you are feeling angry, you will become more angry and impatient about having to take time to deal with the first anger or situation. You become angry about the anger, but you could also become depressed or vindictive. Similarly, you become fearful about fear, sad about sadness, and so on. With the second reaction, you inwardly react to your feelings and reject yourself.

When you allow yourself to react to your feelings, you self-reject because you don't permit free expression of the feelings into consciousness. Clearing will not occur. When the mind becomes agitated by the feelings it is perceiving, it is judging and decides that it doesn't like what it sees. The mind is resisting, not allowing the feeling to pass into direct experience. Moreover, when you become angry and then angry about the anger, the second anger is directed at yourself. You are angry with yourself for allowing yourself to become angry. You falsely believe that you can and should control your feelings and that anger is bad because it is painful.

Processing is based on the premise that we have no real control over our feelings. They come and go spontaneously as we unconsciously project and create our world. Surrendering to the inability to control feelings while maintaining nonreactiveness is an essential part of your self-acceptance.

I want to be sure you understand that the second reaction refers to your reaction to your feelings, not to the original feelings themselves. I am not suggesting that you have no feeling responses to the events of your life. Feelings are what you are learning to integrate. Being nonreactive means letting your feelings come and go spontaneously, without reacting to them. Accept your feelings without choice, and witness them impassively in direct experience. Learn to distinguish between the initial feeling and the second reaction. Since the second reaction is induced by the mind, you can control and eliminate it consciously, and no suppression is involved. This technique by itself can be enough to teach self-acceptance.

If you find that you cannot drop the second reaction easily – for example, if you continue to be angry at yourself for becoming angry – then process the second reaction as well. Doing so will effectively integrate the second reaction, because you are now aware of the dynamics of what you are doing to yourself. Allowing yourself to be influenced by the second reaction is also known as "beating yourself up." If you cultivate the ability to not react to your feelings and just allow them to be as they are, integration will begin. You open the door to direct experience of feelings and eventual transformation.

Habitual indulgence of the second reaction contributes to the chronic condition of being "overly emotional." We think we are in touch with feelings, but instead we are merely allowing ourselves to react emotionally to them. We do not get to our core feelings; we remain blocked by our reaction.

The second reaction is also related to the *sentiments*. We cherish a positive feeling and condemn a negative feeling, instead of accepting both and processing the negative.

Drama

We dramatize when we are overly emotional and then express that emotion into the world. Dramatizing may be thought of as *acting out emotionally*. It may appear to others, and ourselves, that we are "expressing" our feelings, but this is not the case. We are just indulging ourselves in the drama because it shields us from the deeper, inner experience of our true feelings. We become trapped in the drama and eventually are not able to find our real feelings because they are obscured by the habit of dramatizing. We become more and more out of touch with ourselves.

For example, if your spouse tries to criticize you tactfully for the way you have just handled the children, you may feel hurt. If you respond by indignantly and passionately citing all the good things you have done for the children, the sacrifices you have made, how they mean more than anything to you, and that you just can't understand why your spouse doesn't appreciate this and know that you would never, ever do anything except what is the absolute best for them, you are dramatizing your hurt instead of containing it and taking it through the steps of processing.

People who have developed the capacity for dramatizing often are perceived as powerful and emotional, and can easily intimidate others who have not cultivated this personality trait. Yet they are trapped, tragic victims of themselves. Maintained by the illusion that they are expressing themselves, they do not see any need to look within. They remain cut off from their real feelings, isolated and in despair.

Whenever you feel the impulse to dramatize, ask yourself what is the feeling that you are covering over. Take responsibility for it, and learn to sit with it in quiet processing. If you are especially prone to drama, you especially need to learn to go within.

Control

Control can become a central issue for some people. We feel that we like to be in control of whatever our needs depend on. When things get out of control, we become anxious. The areas that we would like to control may be divided roughly into inner feelings and outer circumstances. Control of the outer is what most people focus on, but it is the inner that they are attempting to influence.

Outwardly, we attempt to control whatever does not fit in with our mental concepts of how things should be. This amounts to self-rejection because perception of the external is always our projection; rejecting our projection is rejecting ourselves. People who need a high degree of control over their environment are suppressed, becoming threatened when events reveal their suppression.

Inwardly, it is difficult to accept that we have no real control over emotions, moods, or desires. We try to control our feelings because they are painful or don't fit in with our belief systems, concepts, self-image, and goals, all of which are conditioned mindsets keeping us from the experience of ourselves as we are. We reject ourselves when we attempt to control or edit our feelings, thinking that we should or shouldn't be having a certain feeling, or else attempt actually to control outside circumstances or people.

Addictions result in the need to exercise control over dependencies. Addictions may happen only in certain specific areas. It is easy to fool yourself or others into thinking that you have no dependencies when you may be completely dependent on one thing: a particular possession, person, or self-image, for example. Many times we are unaware of the dependency because of its sheer magnitude.

Judging

It is normal to filter perceptions and feelings through a kind of evaluation grid. Something is presumed to be good and some other thing bad. Whenever we categorize things as good or bad, we essentially reject ourselves because the very activity of the mind in making the classification blocks off direct experience. It does not matter that something has been judged as "good"; direct experience is still inhibited. Moreover, when we judge something as good, whether it is an internal feeling or an external event, we affirm its dualistic nature and set ourselves up for the complementary "bad" experience.

Judging, evaluating, and comparing are all based on the sense of the isolated self. In judging, we affirm and reinforce the isolated self – we judge for our own benefit. In our present stage of consciousness, this is unquestioned, but we can avoid reinforcing our isolation by enlarging our sense of "I" to include others. The sense of the isolated self is the basic misconception that spiritual practice addresses.

Concepts/Expectations

Concepts and expectations come into effect whenever we have an idea about how something should be rather than accepting it as it is. This usually applies to conditions in the external world, but we maintain concepts about our inner life as well. We feel we should always be happy, and we reject ourselves when we are not.

Our concepts, instead of helping us, actually form our limitations. We shut out reality because it does not match preconceived notions. Life is spontaneous and ever changing; our concepts can never keep up, and we reject life, simply because it does not fit in with what we know or expect. Thus, if we are heavily into concepts, we become rigid in our behavior. We become narrow; we are not interesting to be with because we are always analyzing everything to see whether it will be good or bad for us. We are self-centered instead of reality-centered.

Concepts are always based on addictions. For example, if you are addicted to Survival issues, your concepts will concern security. You will feel that you have to possess certain objects to serve as protection. Your security is bound to the objects. You become anxious about losing the objects and obsessive about them.

Self-Image

Concepts concerning the Significance center form the special category of *self-image*. Self-image is a basic ego concept, made somewhat difficult to recognize because it is often unconscious. We form mental pictures about ourselves and how we should be and reject any part of ourselves that does not match. Self-image leads to the "masks" that we put on.

The influence of self-image can be felt on the most basic levels. We picture ourselves as strong and reject ourselves for being weak. Feelings of weakness are then suppressed and not allowed to exist and find an integrated balance. We create the neurotic need to be strong, to balance the suppressed, but still unconsciously felt weakness. Moreover, self-image defines exactly what strong and weak behavior is, which varies according to individual and culture. Self-image can be especially limiting when we try to establish personal growth goals. We think we should always be happy and successful, and we suppress perceived unhappiness and failure. The free flow of energies is inhibited. Our perception of *what is* becomes limited.

A trap for the spiritual seeker is the self-image "I should always be loving." When we are not loving, we feel as if we have failed. "Love" becomes a forced sentimentality, which later rebounds as the complement is experienced. The problem is that our idea of love is just another concept constructed by the mind; it is not real love. I am not saying you should express resentment if that is what you are feeling. It's just that, as a spiritual seeker, it is easy to fall into the self-rejecting habit of judging your feelings and becoming upset when you discover negativities you think you should not have. This is nothing less than suppression, and I have seen "spiritual" people who continue to reject themselves even though they have been in spiritual circles for years. As a result, they make no progress and become hypocritical, thinking they are "loving," when they are constantly giving out messages from their suppressed subconscious of exactly the opposite. They are trying to make themselves conform to a spiritual ideal that they have acquired.

Whenever you want to be like anything or anyone, no matter how beautiful or exalted, you reject yourself. You are trying to mold yourself in the image of another, and this never works. If the person whom you admire is a great person, they didn't become so by trying to emulate someone else but by being themselves. Being "yourself" is what we are talking about – not trying to force yourself to conform to a concept of the mind.

The task becomes one of recognizing what you really are instead of what your concepts superimpose on you. This is yet another way of describing the nature of the spiritual quest. Self-image concepts are part of our unconscious mental conditioning. As you go further into understanding what you are not, other conditioning will surface to be released. By processing whatever negative feelings you are aware of, you will gradually discover the underlying concepts. You may pick up the thread at any point, and eventually the complete pattern will become clear.

Identification

Identification refers to the attempt to lose oneself by merging with something outside of oneself. This can be almost anything – an organization, another person, an idea, purpose, career, role, creation, or possession. Although most of us probably are familiar with the concept of identification, it is still one of the most common ways of self-rejection. We identify with something because we want to escape from ourselves. We try to avoid the pain that we are feeling, such as the pain of isolation or emptiness.

When we attach to something outside ourselves, we feel larger than we were. We are no longer just our small selves, with our pain. I believe that an energy transfer takes place, and we feed dependently off the object, even if it is an object we have created. Examples would be attachment to corporations, groups, or a small business of our own, all of which have their own existence as entities with energy potentials and boundaries.

Identification builds a false sense of importance and relates to the Significance center. We attempt to find significance in the identification syndrome but never succeed. We say, "my" wife or husband, "my" career, "my" home, "my" knowledge. Anything that threatens these objects is perceived as a personal attack: If our work is criticized, we feel that we are criticized; if the work fails, we have failed.

A particularly insidious form of identification is when we identify with our self-rejecting patterns themselves. For example, if we have a lot of suppressed anger that, through projection, results in a constant battle with authority, we identify with that battle. We see ourselves as a crusader; we believe it is our destiny to bring about reform; it gives us a reason to get out of bed in the morning. We miss the point that we are completely identified with and enslaved by the role we have taken on in the unconscious attempt to defend against our projection.

Identification results in self-rejection because whenever we identify with something, we avoid ourselves in merging with the object. We also disidentify with and reject everything outside of the object. Since we usually project heavily onto whatever is excluded, we reject ourselves. This can result in extreme behavior such as racism, where suppressed negativities are projected onto the group that is perceived as the "other."

In the initial stages of identification, it is possible to feel an elation that can obscure objective awareness of the addiction. The elation is all the more heightened if one has been leading an aimless existence, because it will appear that finally something has been found that gives meaning to life. The dualistic experience that awaits is not sensed. For this is the problem with identification: In the end, it is strongly dualistic. We are addicted to and dependent on the object. We will create our negative experience, as we have created the positive. We will soon crash.

Once you are aware of the mechanics of identification, you will be able to see it in yourself. At that point, it must be treated like an addiction. Breaking the identification will entail pain, because you will feel as if you are losing a part of yourself. You will feel lost and empty. Previous negative feelings that were sup-

pressed by the identification will come to the surface. All this has
to be processed, and eventually equilibrium will be found.

The term "identification" also describes the tendency to think
of ourselves as the same as our emotions, both positive and negative. The aim of spiritual practice or therapy always has been to
break emotional identification. Paradoxically, we then own our
feelings but do not identify with them. Feelings are seen to be of
the Lower Self, while our sense of identity is transferred to the
Higher Self.

Future Orientation/Hope

Our culture always has encouraged holding and working toward
hopes, ideals, and goals. At times, there is a real need to improve
conditions, but when we are continually dreaming about the
future, it becomes obvious that we are attempting to avoid the
present. The unpleasant present is avoided by fantasizing about
the future, even if we are being motivated by what we might think
are the highest of ideals. It is also possible to fantasize about how
dreadful the future may be, giving full play to our fear. The point is
that we live in the future in order to escape from the present,
which consists of all our feelings, as they are.

*Hope takes you out
of the moment*

A certain kind of strength can be drawn from fantasies and
hopes about the future. If you have a strong goal before you, you
can endure hardships that normally would be incapacitating
because you think you are working for something that will bring
you, or even someone else with whom you are attached and identified, happiness in the future. The hope keeps you going. However,
the strength that comes from hope is a false strength. It is more of
a strength from *tension* than from being centered.

Becoming accustomed to using this kind of energy results in
chronic future orientation and the inability to be happy now. You
become "time-bound" – conditioned to look to the future for fulfillment. You become restless and incessantly addicted to activity,

thinking that fulfillment will always be around the corner; but future orientation never allows you really to experience the pleasure (or pain) of the moment. When you finally get to the future, you are still thinking about another future goal, and you again miss the present.

Attachment to future goals, ideals, and hopes is so pervasive that it becomes an area of continual self-discovery. We think everything will be all right when we get our college degree, when we find the right person, when we make enough money, when we get to therapy, and so on. We keep finding new areas of attachment that we did not see before. Nevertheless, at times we may need to rely on hope to get us through; taking away all hope from ourselves or others may be pointless or even cruel. In dealing with self-rejection, gentleness and judgment are called for, and we must not exceed our toleration point.

Past Orientation/Idealizing

Living in the past, thinking about how good or bad things were, becoming attached to people or situations in the past are all ways that are used to block awareness of the present. The exception is when a past event is reexperienced in order to integrate it. In this case, we work with present feelings about the past event, which are usually the same feelings that were suppressed at the time of the event.

If we are continually thinking about pleasant times in the past, we are avoiding the present; but sometimes the motivation may be even more subtle. Usually the pleasantness of the past was of a dualistic nature. At the time of the experience, the negative component was suppressed. The suppressed negativity remains and keeps surfacing in thoughts that draw us back to the episode in question. We don't recognize that the subconscious is trying to clear, and we persist in dwelling on the positive parts of the experience, which were a projection to begin with. The suppression is held in place. This happens when we idealize someone from the past: a parent, spouse, or child whom we have "sanctified." We become attached to the projection and avoid confronting our real feelings.

Trauma

Occasionally we find that we can't let go of negative, traumatic events of the past. We dwell on them, sometimes to the extent that our spontaneity is inhibited by the recurring thoughts of the event. This may happen with victims of crime, abuse, assault, war, and severe psychological shock or pain.

Trauma is actually suppression in which feelings are involuntarily rejected, blocking release of the energies. This mechanism seems to be part of the instinctive defenses. Treating traumatic reactions always has been the focus of much of traditional psychotherapy. Trauma arises because the pain involved in the event has not been faced and experienced so that it could clear. Instead, we remain in the mind, constantly thinking about the event. Ironically, our thoughts become the shield from our feelings. Even though we constantly think about the event, we still do not integrate the feelings, which continue to haunt us.

There is no way to clear traumatic feelings except by ending resistance to them and experiencing them, as was not done when the event occurred. You must carefully watch how you reject and resist the feelings. Enter meditation, activate the Witness, and drop resistance; allow the feelings just to be. Allow them to work out their own cycle and eventually dissolve. Try to distinguish your thoughts from your feelings. Often there is a strong component of blame present in thoughts. This is all that is needed to prevent acceptance. You then remain unable to clear the feelings that are trapped in the energy body.

Seeking Understanding/Searching/
Analyzing/Rationalizing

Searching for understanding results in the incessant mental activity known as thinking, which prevents direct experience of feelings and therefore can be considered self-rejecting. Excessive thinking has always been considered to be a hindrance on the path to spiritual enlightenment, or mental and emotional health, whichever way you prefer to look at it.

The primary aim of spiritual disciplines is to quiet the mind, not to provide intellectual answers. When the mind is quieted, the answers will come, but they will not be of the mind. The mind can never go beyond the known, and the known will not provide what is needed. When the mind is quiet, direct experience can occur. We move into the moment, and the answer comes spontaneously.

Still, certain things must be understood. The key is proper use, not abuse, of the mind and intellect. We need to understand how our energy systems work, which includes understanding their limitations. Eventually we need to become aware of our patterns, our beliefs, and our motivations. We need to know how to approach our problems, how to work on ourselves.

We misuse the mind when we search for the answer that will make everything right. There is no such answer, and everything will never be right. This is what must be accepted. Then integration will occur. Excessive searching is a defense and an escape.

Rationalizing is when we misuse thinking to try to talk ourselves out of our feelings. We say to ourselves that we were not really hurt by that person, that it does not matter to us that we lost something that was precious, that we are above needing recognition, and so on. We remain in denial of our true feeling selves.

Escapist Behavior/Boredom

When you immerse yourself in activity with the conscious or unconscious intent to avoid feelings, you are attempting to escape. Anything can be used as an escape. The most obvious is entertainment: the television, film, news, radio, publishing, and music industries that form such a huge business in our culture. You can escape into work, sex, relationships, humanistic pursuits, art, anything. It is not the activity that is the escape but how it is used. Of course, from time to time there is a legitimate need for escape from the pressures of daily routine. When escape into diversion is conscious and moderate, no harm is done. Self-rejection begins when escape from our feeling reality is excessive and compulsive.

Boredom is one of the feelings from which we commonly try to escape. Boredom is the mask for any number of negative feelings that are hiding just behind: anxiety, depression, sexual frustration, fears of all kinds, for example. When you react to boredom by trying to escape from it, you self-reject. You continue to suppress the negative feelings lying just behind the boredom. Boredom is a sign that a large amount of suppression is taking place.

Boredom often comes up in meditation or breathwork practices. It means you are disturbing suppressed energies and are unconsciously defending yourself with the boredom. Do not be defeated by boredom but transform it. Processing boredom can be fruitful; it will lead to the feelings being covered over. You don't have to become compulsive about this either, thinking that you can never turn to any kind of activity because you will be escaping. Keep a balanced and moderate frame of reference.

A good rule of thumb is to ask yourself whether you are engaging in any activity to find happiness or to express the happiness you feel within. Usually there is very little we do that is expressive of happiness. We remain trapped in the dualistic world, oblivious to the spiritual reality that happiness must come from within, through the reconciliation and transcendence of dualities.

Substance Addiction

Substance addiction, whether to drugs, alcohol, smoking, or food, is a form of escape. The addictive cycle provides psychic energy that is used to maintain suppression as well as to provide energy to simply function. This condition is reached because of the habitual behavior of escaping. The constant turning away from ourselves builds the blocks that cut us off from our natural, inner energy resources, resulting in extreme self-rejection and real dependence on the substance.

The energy to which we gain access in the addictive cycle is of two basic types: that which comes from within and that which comes from without. In all substance abuse, we gain access to energy within. What we tap into, however, is a form of reserve energy. We use up our reserves, and the eventual end is complete psychic and physical exhaustion. Addiction to alcohol as well as to illegal and prescription drugs is rampant in our culture, although many people think they are not addicted because their level of consumption is no more than normal. They become "social" drinkers or drug users. If you must have one or more drinks every evening after coming home from work, you may want to take a hard look at whether this constitutes addiction. In other forms of addiction, we tap into energy outside of ourselves. This happens in power or sexual addictions, for example, when others are involved.

All addictions have the same deceptive quality. We think we are benefiting from the addiction because we feel more relaxed or function better when we are on the peak. We forget that the valleys between the peaks are also created by the addictive cycle.

Food addictions
can be important

Food is a vital part of the program for emotional healing. Most of us today are aware of how critical proper nutrition is. As part of the focus on the body that we have been discussing, therefore, you must be careful to maintain a decent food intake free from contaminants and harmful foods. A simple diet high in vegetables, whole grains, and beans with occasional chicken or fish is all you need.

What most of us don't realize, however, is the role that food addictions play in maintaining suppressed feelings. There is a reason why it can be so difficult to give up red meat, dairy, sugar, wheat, grease, soft drinks, fast foods, junk foods, caffeine, and nicotine. All these foods become addictions, and probably certain foods suppress certain specific feelings. When we attempt to give up the food, the feeling comes up like a dragon rearing its head, and we are driven to the food.

You must handle food addictions like any other addiction. As you work with the feelings involved, you will ease up on the compulsiveness for the food. The purity of the diet you are able to maintain is another measure of your inner psychological and emotional condition.

Relationships

Relationship dependence is a special kind of addiction, where we seek in the other the energy of the qualities we have blocked off in ourselves. Romantic relationships can be an effective form of self-rejection. It is possible to escape from ourselves into the newness and excitement of the romance, leaving it when the excitement wears off. This form of self-rejection and the longing for it are epidemic in our culture. Of course, I am not saying that one should not enter into relationships. The need for relationships of all types is genuine. It is when the relationship is used for escape that it becomes self-rejecting. We will discuss relationships in more depth later.

AFFIRMATIONS

An aid in breaking self-rejection cycles is the use of *affirmations*. To explain how affirmations work, let me first summarize our approach to self-therapy: Processing is a technique for the uncovering, integrating, and controlled releasing of traumatic and negative feelings that have been suppressed in the past and continue to plague us. Suppressed feelings are composed of *energies* that are kept locked in the body, in latent form.

Self-rejection, however, is not an energy-based feeling; it is of the *mind*, not the body. Self-rejection is a conditioning of the mind, a means of shutting out experience. Processing techniques that release emotions therefore will not help to change conditioned mind-sets, such as blame or guilt. In fact, trying to process blame or guilt will not work, and holding blame or guilt in your consciousness as you do feelings during processing will only reinforce the blame or guilt.

Conditioned mind-sets can be changed through the use of affirmations. However, affirmations cannot be used to integrate or change suppressed feelings. No matter how many times you tell yourself you are feeling great, you will stay depressed if this is the feeling that is surfacing. If the affirmation has any effect at all, it will serve only to *suppress* the negative feeling. Feelings must be experienced. We will study the proper use of affirmations in Chapter 13 and explore reconditioning the subconscious mind to be self-accepting. For now, remember: Processing integrates feelings; affirmations recondition the mind.

ACTIVATE YOUR HEART CENTER

All of us suffer from many forms of self-rejection. Sometimes we will be clear in most areas but completely self-rejecting in another area. This area is where we defend ourselves from ourselves. It is what prevents us from breaking out of our self-enclosed ways.

You must approach acceptance slowly. Work on one aspect at a time. Be careful that as you become self-accepting in one area, you do not transfer your self-rejection to other areas. Stopping self-rejection requires courage of the highest type. You are, indeed, approaching the work of a lifetime, and it will require all your fortitude. You now know, however, that accepting yourself is the work that you are to do.

The courage to face your real feelings will bring the first light of self-love, the birth of true self-esteem. Self-love is of the Heart center, and you can activate it further by concentrating on and breathing into the Heart as you accept yourself and your feelings. Know that self-love is not dependent on any object. It is dependent on your acceptance of yourself and of others as reflections of you.

Self-love can help you face any negative condition. Moreover, self-love will come into being *as you face* those conditions. You will know that what you are doing has real value, value that will stay with you forever. You are building the spiritual body, which is the only thing you take when you leave this earth.

As your respect for yourself grows because of the courage you demonstrate in facing yourself, your respect for others will grow also, because this is an extension of your respect for yourself. So too, as your self-love grows, your love for others – real love – will come into existence. Real love cannot be thought, persuaded, or imagined into being; it comes about through your acceptance.

I enter the direct experience of my feelings. I understand that I must confront fully what I have avoided in the past, in order to bring myself into balance. I experience the feelings behind my addictions and compulsions. I enter my feelings during meditation, observing my toleration point.

8

Direct Experience

When you drop self-rejection, you end the mental activity that interferes with the clear perception of both inner and outer events. You become self-accepting, and your mind assumes a transparent quality; it is still there, but as it is quiet, you can see through it. Perception is not colored by the mind. You enter *direct experience*. What can now be experienced directly and clearly is of the nature of energy – what we have been calling feelings and emotions. Energy patterns and exchanges make up existence. When you open yourself to energy, you open yourself to life.

Direct experience is possible because you have entered "the moment." This is the state that comes about when the mind has ceased its self-rejecting activity. Until then there is always a sense of time, either looking forward or backward. The mind is the creator of time. Entering the moment means that the mind is no longer attached to time consciousness and is content to encounter life as it manifests now. There is no resistance or desire to escape from *what is.*

This is when integration begins. Integration means the mind has accepted, and you are in the moment with, your feelings and experiences. Being in the moment is the end point of all psychological, spiritual, or true religious teachings. It has been called peak experience, cosmic consciousness, self-realization, or God consciousness, but all these names refer to the experience of the eternal "Now."

The moment is completely simple, and that is why it is so easy to miss. You can enter the moment at any time, by dropping the self-rejecting mental activity that searches, judges, clings, and avoids. The moment is a state of consciousness, a new feeling, and does not imply that you should cease preparing for the future, only that you don't live in the future. Be careful as well that you don't confuse living in the moment with living *for* the moment. Such confusion could possibly lead to becoming irresponsible, self-indulgent, or unconcerned with the rights of others.

EXPERIENCE, NOT EXPRESSION

Integrative Processing is a therapy based on a new paradigm of psychological thought. It has been recognized since Freud that suppressed feelings must be released. Perhaps because it has seemed obvious, it has been presumed that the antidote to suppression was expression; that instead of holding the feeling in, it must be let out, that we must get the feeling "off our chest." As various schools of psychotherapy emerged over time, they were distinguished by the inventiveness and methodology of how the trapped feelings were to be let out.

Freud himself proposed free association. Reich introduced the radical idea of working with the body, an idea taken up and expanded by Bioenergetics with its pounding on pillows. Gestalt incorporated psychodrama with the patient acting out roles. Primal therapy brought the patient to the point where the deeply held pain was expressed through a spontaneous, soul-wrenching scream. In humanistic psychology, the client is encouraged simply to talk about feelings, supported by the therapist.

Of course, success has been achieved in these various approaches, all based on the idea of "expression." However catharsis may be induced, it will release feelings. Still, it is time for a new paradigm that is more in line with the evolving nature of society and even more effective in maximizing psychological benefits.

Do not think you must "express" a feeling to release it

What has not been realized, I would venture, is the dualistic nature of suppression/expression. Expression is the dualistic complement to suppression, but it is not its antidote. When we indulge in "expression," we are simply pursuing the positive dualistic pole in the effort to avoid the negative, just as with any other dualistic manifestation. We do not satisfy the suppression; in fact, according to the principles of dualism that we have established, expression may serve only to further the amount of suppression that we hold. We remain trapped in the dualistic syndrome, not achieving true release of the feeling energy and increasing our compulsiveness to express.

What is needed is to *experience* our lost feelings, not express them. Feelings originally became suppressed because they were not properly allowed into consciousness – not experienced when they occurred – not because they were not "expressed."

Experience, not expression, is the antidote to suppression

When a feeling is allowed to enter consciousness without resistance, it begins clearing. The feeling does not have to be expressed verbally or acted out in any way to be released. Release will sometimes be accompanied by sounds, movements of the body, or weeping, which is perfectly fine, but do not think that you must express feelings outwardly to release them. Bringing suppressed feelings into consciousness, *with complete acceptance,* is all the expression that is required for their release.

I find it unfortunate that many psychologists still create the impression that to release suppressed feelings, they must somehow be "expressed" outwardly. Often we get no additional explanation about exactly what it means to "express" a feeling. Should we be more emotional? Should we lash out, should we hurt the people who hurt us? Should we always be out front with all our feelings, communicating exactly what we feel? Should we continuously vent our feelings? Should we work off the feelings through physical activity? Should we always follow what our feelings tell us to do? All these alternatives are counterproductive, as we have discussed.

When the emphasis of therapy shifts to experience, not expression, as the guiding paradigm, there may still be a place for therapeutic technique based on expression. What these techniques will accomplish is to stir up feelings – to bring them into awareness. If it is understood that the feelings will then need to be processed for completion, the technique is providing a helpful function. However, it is not necessary to incorporate any of these techniques, such as psychodrama or beating on pillows. In Integrative Processing we use breath, body, meditative techniques including alpha-state induction, and the events of our lives to bring feelings into awareness, at which point they are processed – accepted and experienced – and released.

Sharing is another type of outward expression. Of course, I am not against the sharing of feelings with either a therapist or a close friend. Sharing can be helpful at the right time, but don't think that you have to share in order for integration to occur. Sharing can be abused and become another dependency and a way to avoid feelings.

Feelings must be experienced,
not changed by modifying thoughts

It is crucial to recognize that feelings must be experienced and not addressed by any "rational" or "cognitive" approach, in which the attempt is made to change, avoid, or reprogram the feeling by changing your thinking, or though mental "anchoring." In my opinion, all these approaches are naive and dangerous – feelings only become suppressed by them. If you try one of these approaches and it seems to work, you are deluding yourself. You are cutting yourself off from your soul and real healing and eventually will be brought back by your Karma to address the continuing buildup of the suppressed subconscious.

PROCESS THE FEELING

Feelings are processed by keeping them in consciousness without resistance, experiencing them fully, *witnessing them,* without acting on them. The natural flow of the energy of the feelings is permitted to occur. If feelings are avoided or resisted, they are suppressed. By simply staying in the moment with feelings, allowing them *to be* for as long as necessary, the emotional charge is dissolved.

Allowing feelings to exist without resistance eventually results in their cycle of energy being completed. Stay with the experience of processing the feeling until you sense a change, a shift in the energy – the feeling will no longer have the same urgency about it. Have faith that facing the feeling will result in the eventual integration and transcendence of the issue.

If the feeling with which you are working is associated with an outer event, such as an interaction with another person, keep the event in your consciousness along with the feeling. Drop all forms of self-rejection, such as blame. Simply hold the scene before you in your imagination, opening to and experiencing fully the feelings that come up.

Process in activity or meditation

Feelings may be processed either during activity or in meditation. Both times are valuable. Feelings tend to come up strongly in activity when triggered by a certain stimulus – the interaction with another person, for example. If you can process then, you make the most of the opportunity. The ideal would be to complete the interaction tactfully and then get away and sit down by yourself, to work inwardly with the feelings that are strong and fresh.

If you can't get away, you may try to process during the interaction. This is not easy, however, and you probably will not be able to do it until you have gained some facility with processing skills through practicing by yourself. The alternative to processing during the interaction is to *contain* the feeling, through nonreactiveness, for later processing in your personal practice time. When you sit for your practice, bring the event before you to activate the feelings and process.

Identify what type of feeling you are processing

The actual feeling that you are processing may be any of the different types that we covered in detail in Chapter 6. You might be working with a very active first-level emotion that you may or may not be able to relate to any core feeling pattern, or you may have started with the emotion, and it linked into the core feeling or another emotion. You may be working with a mood or simply a body sensation or "symptom." You may be working with an addictive compulsion. Do not try to control what types of feelings come up; surrender to the flow and *be with* whatever you are guided to receive.

Look for the feeling behind the event

Feelings usually occur in relation to an event or circumstance in our lives. Any recurring or strong feeling signifies that suppressed material is coming up and that processing is appropriate. Always take care to identify the feelings *behind* the event.

For example, if you are encountering hardship, you must integrate the feelings that the hardship brings up in you. You may be feeling the pain of not having certain necessities, but behind this is the emotion of fear. Both the feeling of lack and the emotion of fear are to be processed. If you have failed in your work, you may be experiencing the emotion of worthlessness along with the core feeling of failure. Both must be processed.

Go into the body experience of the feeling, in the moment

As you process any feeling, maintain awareness of the body, where feelings originate. With an accepting mind, you will be able to sense your body with a clarity and sensitivity that was never possible when you were self-rejecting. Accept the feeling in the body. Open yourself to it. Experience it without resistance. Witness it. Allow yourself to simply *be with* it. Become *choiceless* about whether you want to have the feeling or not.

Feelings can occur in the chakras as well as in any other part of the body. Try to focus on the physical area where the feeling is occurring. If you cannot associate the feeling with a specific place, go into your body in general. Feelings can be complex and can be the result of the interaction of two or more chakras; it may be hard to pinpoint a specific feeling. Eventually your sensitivity will increase, and you will be able to relate different feelings to their body locations.

Keep scanning the body, making sure it is relaxed. Often when we are contending with strong feelings, our inclination is to tense the body. Keep aware of the body, and consciously relax any part that has become tensed. At the same time, breathe into the part of the body that is holding any tension, or where the feelings may seem to originate. This need not necessarily be a chakra; it can be any part of the body.

Allow feelings to link

When you start processing first-level feelings concerning an event, as the feelings become integrated usually other *linked* feelings will emerge – another emotion will come up that you did not know you were holding; another core feeling will jump out into awareness. It is important to allow linking to occur and to keep tracing back to all the linked feelings behind any event or condition; this is the process of growth and the uncovering of the subconscious. However, linked feelings usually cannot be uncovered intellectually. They must be allowed to reveal themselves sequentially as you process.

For example, if you have an argument with someone, you may be impatient and angry, but behind these feelings are other, more basic ones. Your sense of personal worth may have been challenged – the feeling of inadequacy emerges to be processed. Then you find that the emotion of sadness comes up. As you stay with this, you may uncover a core feeling related to the sadness. Perhaps it is related to the loss of your father and even other, more basic feelings.

While it is possible for feelings to link quickly within a single processing session, it is more likely that linking will take place over a period of time – a few weeks, months, even years. There is no particular sequence to the emergence of feelings as they are processed. It is different for everyone. Simply surrender to your flow, stay with your experience as it is, be patient and trust in the guidance you are receiving.

Do not try to analyze the feeling

Remember that you are not entering the feeling with the intention of analyzing and understanding it. Don't try to understand why the event happened, why you did or felt what you did, and so on. These insights will come spontaneously *as a result* of the integration that direct experience will bring. For now, just fully experience the feelings of the event. If you persist in trying to analyze, integration is inhibited.

Keep a clear distinction between feelings and self-rejecting thoughts

Even though you dropped self-rejecting thoughts in the second step of acceptance, you are still likely to oscillate between self-rejection and acceptance. For example, suppose you are integrating a painful feeling that you had previously rejected because you blamed someone for causing it. As you work with the feeling, you probably will tend to fall in and out of blame.

As long as you are holding blame in your mind, you are not in direct experience. You have fallen back into self-rejection. You are trying to process the blame along with the feeling, but remember, self-rejection such as blame cannot be processed. Processing applies only to suppressed energy. Self-rejection is a function of the mind, not of the energy body, and is to be simply put aside.

When you catch yourself falling back into self-rejection, you must deliberately shift again to focusing on the feeling and away from the self-rejecting thoughts. Keep bringing your attention from the blame back to the feeling whenever necessary. Keep separating the blame from the feeling. You could focus your attention on either one, but when you focus on the feeling, the blame will not be present in your consciousness. You can develop this ability with a minimum of practice and will be able to stay with the actual experience being integrated, avoiding the self-rejection.

PROCESS FEELINGS BEHIND THE ADDICTION

Confronting addiction is central to inner work.

First, you must realize that you actually have an addiction. You may think you only have needs, but there is a subtle distinction between needs and addictions. Addictions are compulsive; you are attached to the object. You escape into the object and become anxious when denied it, whether it is a person, possession, substance, or mode of behavior. True needs are more in line with the natural cycles of being and may be thought of as originating in the body, not the mind. Addictions usually develop in relation to the lower centers. Let's summarize the most common types:

1. SURVIVAL: Anything that represents security and serves to mask fear or anxiety: wealth, material possessions.

2. POWER: The impulse to control other people or situations to maintain dependencies.

3. SENSATION: Tactile and sensual sensations, including sex, luxury, entertainment.

4. NURTURING: Substances, including alcohol, drugs, tranquilizers, smoking, food.

5. SIGNIFICANCE: Status, self-image, significance, influence, importance, accomplishment, approval.

6. HEART: Relationship dependency.

If you have any such addiction, there will be many times when you will be compelled to satisfy it. This is the time when you can set yourself free. Unfortunately, there is no other way to proceed except to confront the pain and anxiety that will come up now. Use the principles we have been discussing. Use your knowledge to accept the anxiety, depression, and pain. Refuse to reject yourself any longer by rejecting these feelings. Enter them, and experience them as they integrate and dissolve. Use witnessing techniques to absorb the negativity, instead of yielding to it and being motivated by it into the addiction.

Distinguish between the impulse to satisfy an addiction and the feeling behind the addiction

Suppose you have a food addiction. The food cravings are the impulse to satisfy the addiction. Behind the addiction are the feelings that you are suppressing with the addiction. You may not even be conscious of those feelings. You may have unconscious fear that you keep suppressed with the food addiction.

Begin by working with the impulse to satisfy the addiction. This impulse is a form of energy tension, which will respond to the techniques you are learning. Strong concentration on the impulse will reduce it without your having to act on it. In the case of food or any other kind of cravings, allow the cravings to be without acting on them. Do not fight having the feelings; fighting gives more power to the cravings. Do not try to escape from the cravings by ignoring them or distracting yourself from them. Confront and integrate the cravings, using the powerful help of breath and bodywork. You can beat cravings with acceptance. Cravings are cyclical. If you can face them for a short period, they will retreat until the next time. The time between attacks will become longer, and you will start gaining the upper hand.

If the impulse is too strong to resist, practice accepting the impulse for a while before giving in to it, gradually increasing the direct experience time. Substitute something harmless for the addictive substance. If you have a severe addiction problem, a support group will be invaluable, but in the end, confrontation in some form is what it comes down to. The feelings must be faced.

Eventually, you will become aware of the feelings you are suppressing with the addiction, and you can start working with them.

When you get to this point, you are making real progress. Sometimes just becoming aware of these feelings can provide the catharsis necessary to break the hold of the addiction, but usually further integration of the feelings will be needed. Confronting your addiction is no easy task, but remember, this is essential work. You are working on your evolution into higher consciousness.

USE BREATH AND BODYWORK

If you are working on integrating a serious issue, you will want to set aside some time for incorporating breath and bodywork. We have not discussed these topics since Chapter 4, but that does not mean that they are of secondary usefulness; in fact, they can be instrumental in bringing about integration.

Working with the body brings us into closer rapport with the feelings

Feelings are composed of energy and occur in the body. When the energy gets stuck in the body, in the chakras, we experience emotional problems. Working with the body can be instrumental in loosening the stuck energy and quieting the self-rejection of the mind. You may use any body approach with which you are comfortable, as long as it encourages you to *relax into* the body. Sports, exercise, and working out in the gym do not qualify. Bodywork techniques involving a practitioner might be added if you are so inclined, but I do not consider this essential.

I would recommend a basic routine of yoga postures as an effective and convenient approach for working with the body. Certain yoga postures will work on unblocking certain chakras, and if you can identify the chakra, you can hold the appropriate postures while experiencing feelings, increasing the cleansing effectiveness. A yoga session can last anywhere from ten minutes to an hour or two, but even a short session will be invaluable to get you into your body.

After loosening the energy flow with bodywork, conscious breath will be helpful in breaking energy blocks. Breathing into the feeling or chakra is the basic strategy, but it may be combined with any of the breath techniques that we explore in Chapter 11. As you are breathing, continue to integrate the event by being with it without resistance. The prana that you are generating through the breath goes directly into the energy block. This serves two purposes: First, correct breathing will bring suppressed issues into consciousness, allowing you to become aware of them and begin conscious integration. Second, breath will implement the integration of the issue, which may not always happen quickly with acceptance alone.

PROCESS FEELINGS DURING MEDITATION

Many of us are, unfortunately, allergic to the word "meditation." Perhaps you have tried it and didn't get anywhere, or possibly you aren't attracted to the peripherals that may accompany it. A large part of the problem, as I see it, is that meditation often is incorrectly explained. We are led to expect unrealistic results, and we become discouraged when we do not get them.

Meditation, to me, means sitting and doing nothing. It is not another form of activity but *inactivity*. I am not referring primarily to physical activity but *mental* activity. Usually we think we need to do something with our minds in order to meditate. We become preoccupied with doing and again ensnare ourselves in thought. If you can just flop down into your favorite chair, stop all activity of the mind, and let yourself drift into your feelings, you are meditating. However, we are so bound to the mind, its activity, and its self-rejection, that we have lost the capacity to drift or to even have an appreciation for the state.

The need for meditation comes about because we are incessantly active in our minds: doing, striving, asking, planning, thinking, seeking, evaluating, worrying, perhaps even praying. The mind simply needs some time off. Cultivating this capacity is an essential part of inner growth. When you enter the state of *nondoing*, you allow the mind time to recharge and to cleanse, both of which are essential for optimal inner health. If you develop this state and enter it regularly, it will easily become your favorite part of the day. If you don't practice meditation, the sole alternative for cleansing is the projection mechanism, which results in a distorted perception of the world.

Use a focus point

Remembering that meditation means doing nothing – stopping mind activity – will help you to enter the state. Sometimes, however, a *focus point* may be useful to help stop mind activity. You may watch the breath, or mentally repeat the word "om" or any another word, or inwardly watch a visual symbol. The focus point is not a requirement of meditation and need not be used all the time; it is only a tool to train the mind. Focus your attention on the point you have chosen as you sit to meditate. Soon, the mind will begin to drift to other thoughts. Keep gently bringing yourself back to your focus point.

The focus point is not to have any content. If you are watching the breath, make sure you do not alter the breath; only observe it in its completely natural form. If you use a word, take care that you do not focus on what the word represents, such as "love" or "peace." Doing so amounts to attempting to condition the mind and feelings according to a dualistic concept instead of allowing them to be revealed as they are, which is the basis of processing. It is better to use a word that has no intellectual meaning, that is simply an abstract sound on which you focus. Similarly, any visual symbol should not have emotional content or meaning at this stage of the meditation. Later you may bring emotionally charged symbols before you in order to bring up certain feelings. In this initial stage, we are setting up conditions for entering alpha and allowing *nondirective* emptying of the subconscious.

Witness feelings in meditation

There is one more vital requirement for meditation. When you are entering the state of *nondoing* with the mind, or when you are using a focus point, you must maintain the *sense of self*. This means a sense of "I," a sense that you are awake, attentive, and present within the meditation. When you lose the sense of "I," you lose yourself in the meditation. You become identified with your thoughts and even drowsy. The state you enter becomes not much different from sleep. In contrast, when you maintain the sense of "I," at certain stages of meditation your body may fall asleep, meaning you lose awareness of it, but you will be totally awake, even more awake than in normal consciousness, and functioning on planes of being beyond the physical. The first of which would be the emotional, or astral, plane. When you maintain the sense of "I" during dreaming, it is referred to as a *lucid* dream.

This sense of "I" is the same as the Witness. In witnessing, you are detached, aware, awake, focused. Witnessing is a basic requirement for meditation and processing.

Allow suppressed feelings to emerge

In meditation, brainwave frequency slows down to the alpha level of activity or lower, inducing relaxation and healing. If you work on yourself in alpha, you have a tremendous advantage. Integration proceeds almost by itself, and the Witness is easily activated. Direct experience of feelings can be best accomplished in alpha during meditation (although it also can be done in activity, when the event is taking place). When you first sit to meditate, you may not be aware of feelings that are affecting you because they are suppressed. When you allow yourself to enter the state of meditation as I described, suppressed feelings will spontaneously begin to jump into your awareness as the subconscious cleanses. Just sitting still gives the subconscious the opportunity to bring its suppressed contents to consciousness.

Two things happen when you sit quietly. The first is that your mind starts to go back into gear: doing, striving, planning, thinking, worrying. Usually no particularly intense feeling is associated with this kind of superficial activity. When you detect this superficial wandering of the mind, you are to gently stop such activity by reminding yourself that you are supposed to be doing nothing or by coming back to your focus point.

The second is that a suppressed feeling will come up. This occurrence is distinguished by the emergence of strong emotion. This is what you want. Recognize that clearing is happening. Do not turn from the feeling or go back to your focus point. Stay with the feeling and with any associated thoughts or images, such as the interaction with another person. Move into a processing mode – own, accept, experience, witness. Allow the feeling to remain in your consciousness until you feel a shift – until the feeling starts to link to another related feeling or diminishes.

Do not resuppress feelings that come up in meditation

When feelings come up in meditation, they must be handled properly if cleansing is to be effective. When I first began to meditate, I didn't understand this. My intention in meditation was to calm the mind, expand my consciousness, and enter more blissful states – in other words, to escape.

Whenever disturbing emotions came up, I assumed I was having a bad meditation. I tried to avoid the feelings by bringing my attention back to my focus point. I became upset and would get angry about the anger, fearful about the fear, and so on. Meditation became a fight to try to control my thoughts and feelings. What I was doing, I understand now, was resuppressing negative energies that came up for clearing. I had no concept of integration, as we have been discussing. I thought that eventually I would get past the negative intrusions, but I never did, and I became pessimistic about meditation. I was unknowingly practicing what is called "suppressive meditation."

Eventually I came to understand that the problem was in my approach. This single insight had much to do with my decision to write this book, because I feel other people probably make the same mistake. By emphasizing integration and clearing, perhaps the pitfall of suppressive meditation can be avoided. When negative material comes up, in activity as well as in meditation, the subconscious is trying to clear itself. You must take time to accept and experience whatever is surfacing. Even though I have been practicing meditation for most of my life, I have benefited most in recent years when I understood cleansing and did not resist being with negative feelings. Much, if not most, of my meditation time is still spent working with negative feelings.

When I sit to meditate now, I first enter alpha and the Witness. I go into my body. I start gentle breathing and watch for whatever body sensations may occur. I assume that any discomfort that appears in the body is just negative energies releasing themselves. I witness these. If I feel an emotion, I go into the corresponding center, breathing into the center to free the energy. I let the emotion or feeling build without reacting to it – I simply watch and feel. Soon that particular feeling will have dissipated and something else may come up. After a while, feelings and emotions will have spent themselves. I begin to lose awareness of the body and enter other stages of meditation. There is no fighting, no controlling, no intention, no expectation. I am fine with whatever happens.

BRING UP PAST UNRESOLVED ISSUES

Even though our main focus is on present feelings as they occur in response to our current life experiences, sometimes it is helpful to work with feelings about past events. Many painful, unresolved issues have a past-time reference. We have sustained hurt and loss in the past, and these feelings must be cleared. Actually, we are still dealing with present feelings, but since they have a connection to the past, the feelings can be precipitated by going into the past. This is simply a therapeutic technique and does not mean that you are living in the past.

You can go back to any painful incident, recent or remote, and bring it into your field of awareness as you sit in meditation. See it before you. Allow the story to be told. Relive the incident from the Witness vantage point. Bring persons before you, in your meditation, who are important. Visualize emotionally charged scenes in your mind. The trapped subconscious pain will be triggered. As feelings come up, welcome them. If there are certain issues that you consider too painful to go into, they are obviously the very ones that need attention. They are likely to be influencing you in ways you do not suspect. Other important areas of the past will become apparent to you. You will spontaneously see how past incidents connect with current problems.

Remember that you are not going back into the past to try to understand. You are bringing up feelings for acceptance, ex-perience, and integration. Allow understanding to come as a *result* of integration. Searching for understanding during meditation will prevent you from going into meditation, alpha, and the Witness. Remember to stay aware of the distinction between the feeling and the self-rejection that originally suppressed it. Deliberately drop the self-rejection. Don't sit and resuppress the feeling by reliving the self-rejection.

Do not question if memories are "true"

You may question whether going back into the past is pertinent to living your life now. It is, because the past becomes *symbolic* of the present. In a sense, it does not matter if your memory is accurate or not, and usually it will not be; you are recalling your own subjective view, which may be very different from someone else's. Such recall is still effective because your memory is a symbolic drama, a metaphor, that triggers the subconscious.

You are doing therapy to yourself with this technique. Don't be afraid of going deep into traumatic issues. Past events are the most common format in which feelings come up during meditation. Don't resist memories that recur – it means that something is crying out for release. Accept the memory, no matter how painful, and stay with it until all negativity is cleared. You can assume this has happened when there is no longer an emotional charge associated with the memory. If something is especially hard to face, it is a major issue for you and represents much more than you probably realize. Working with it will integrate more than you expect.

In therapy, this kind of approach is similar to *desensitization,* which is used with phobias, obsessions, and compulsions. Gradually and gently increase your exposure to the threatening issue, and open to whatever feelings come up.

Work with the inner child

As we have discussed, parents should not be held ultimately responsible for childhood trauma. Even so, reliving events from childhood can serve as a valuable door for bringing up suppressed feelings, if you feel so inclined. Working with the wounded inner child, for example, can be an important part of self-healing for some people, although it is by no means essential.

Find the child within that is still holding the painful feelings. Do not try to change or reprogram the child's feelings, but just *be with* the child as it experiences the feelings. Help the child to drop the self-rejection that originally suppressed the feeling and to understand that it's OK to have the feeling, and that it is not the child's fault.

ACCEPT BLOCKING

Sometimes, when we are trying to move into direct experience of a feeling, we get stuck and it seems that we can go no further. When this happens, usually we are coming face to face with our inner blocks themselves. Blocking occurs unconsciously; therefore it is difficult to undo it deliberately. At this point, we must move to *acceptance* of the blocking.

We allow ourselves to remain where we are as we sit in meditation – stuck. We accept being stuck. We watch it. We witness it. We process it. We do not turn from it or become upset about it. We do not wish that we were somewhere else in our process.

Acceptance of the blocking is crucial to its releasing. Striving to overcome it only strengthens it, exactly like any other obstacle that we meet. When we accept, we lay the ground for the eventual loosening of the blocking. As we get to know the blocking more intimately, by allowing it to come more and more into consciousness, eventually it will open, without our asking, and we will move to direct experience of the feelings that have been hidden.

BRING YOUR FEELINGS TO A CRISIS

If you enter the experience of a negative emotion and do not give in to outwardly expressing it or in any other way try to avoid the feeling, it may build within you. You may begin to tremble, feeling the energy as it moves around your body. You may become lost in emotion; your sense of identity may alter; you may begin weeping. In not avoiding the emotion, by accepting it, you permit it to build to the point of crisis. This is the *healing crisis*. Crisis should not be pursued too actively, but if it happens, you should know what to do.

Allowing your feelings to come to a crisis does *not* mean you are not "letting your feelings out." Of course, feelings must be released and not allowed to accumulate in the energy body. Often, however, whatever method we choose for letting feelings out involves self-rejection. The feelings are resuppressed and not really let out at all.

When feelings are accepted, they are not suppressed. The very act of keeping them in consciousness means they are being cleared. If they can be kept in consciousness to the extent that a crisis builds, a catharsis and healing will follow. Allowing a crisis to build calls for the warrior spirit. Try it if the opportunity arises. You will push back some of your personal boundaries, I can assure you.

Meditation is the best format for entering a crisis. Do not prolong the crisis beyond the period of meditation, but you may break from the sitting pose to assume any spontaneous posture that the body needs. Alternate between sitting and the posture. Breath control becomes important. Use the Integrating breath, which we study in Chapter 11. The breath will keep the energies manageable. Breath will allow easier access to the Witness, which provides a calm vantage point to observe the crisis that is happening, usually in the lower chakras. The breath need not necessarily be fast or deep, just steady.

The crisis will always pass, and any shaking or trembling will cease. You will know that you have cleared a considerable amount of negativity from your subconscious because of how you feel. I have never been hurt from allowing my feelings to build to a crisis, nor have I known anyone who has. Our fears of emotional crisis are usually unfounded, but you will have to decide if this kind of intense work is appropriate for you. If you have a history of pronounced mental or emotional instability, allowing a crisis to build would probably *not* be advisable, and you should consult with a therapist before proceeding. You also might want to be cautious in allowing an inner emotional crisis to build when working with active emotions, such as anger. Anger produces adrenaline, making the body ready for fight or flight. Physical release like beating pillows, sports, manual labor, may be helpful if you have not yet fully developed the capacity for inward releasing.

However, I have found that active emotions are not deeply

affected through physical "releasing," but only the most superficial aspects of the energy are touched. I have been able to accomplish more of a physical/emotional release with yoga postures. I have devoted considerable time to passively allowing anger to build to a crisis in meditation and have achieved substantial clearings. The adrenaline always has been able to dissipate and has even aided, I believe, in breaking up the congested energy in the Solar Plexus chakra. Other, more passive emotions, such as fear, sexual impulses, loneliness, and addictive impulses, do not have the same motive power as anger and may be safely brought to an inner crisis.

OBSERVE YOUR TOLERATION POINT

Even though a healing crisis can provide integration, you should also be aware of your own personal toleration point.

As you drop self-rejecting habits, you open to the possibility of real growth, but growth does not come without a certain stress. When you look inside, you are likely to become aware of chaos. Fear, anger, sexual frustration, loneliness, all of which have been suppressed, are now coming to the surface for integration. You may even think you are getting worse instead of better; this is common on the path to healing and growth. You are not getting worse but are just noticing what has been hiding in the subconscious. You cannot return to the blissful state of ignorance about yourself; you must go forward, through the negativity that is surfacing.

When you stop self-rejection, you are left confronting the negativity that normally would be suppressed through the self-rejection. You are learning to integrate this negativity, but because you are still learning, it may not be possible to integrate as fast as necessary to handle all that is coming up. You reach the condition of *overload*. Overload is stressful, and to find an escape from the stress, you will self-reject, possibly in a different manner from what you have just dropped.

Do not exchange one kind of self-rejection for another

For example, after you become conscious of how you have been self-rejecting through blaming others, you might shift to blaming yourself to resuppress the excess energies that cannot be integrated. Or you could shift to escape through excessive activity or entertainment, such as movies and novels. Shifting methods of self-rejection is common and often unconscious. You exceed your toleration point for integration and compensate by creating new habits of self-rejection to take the place of the old.

Being aware of this syndrome will help you to avoid it. You should try to get a sense of when you are approaching your toleration point and not exceed it. You may have to stop inner work and fall back into old habits of self-rejection, but this is better than unconsciously creating new habits of self-rejection. Just being aware of the self-rejecting pattern will, in itself, help to loosen it. Gradually your ability to integrate will increase. Do not feel any impatience with yourself for having such a limitation. If you accept the limitation and work within it, you establish a groundedness that will be of great value.

I invoke the healing power and self-love of Witness consciousness. I feel its presence as I surrender the outcome of my experience to the Higher Self. I allow the Higher Self to work in my behalf. Transformation occurs that I could not anticipate, and I am taken to a higher plane of existence. I have transcended. I have grown.

9

Transformation

Transformation is the fourth step in Integrative Processing. In order to reach this step, you must have passed through the previous steps: You have become aware of your feelings regarding any event or condition and have taken responsibility for them; you have ceased self-rejection concerning the feelings; you have entered direct experience of the feelings.

Transformation involves the spiritual component of our individuality, or what is called the *transpersonal* in contemporary psychology. Don't be misled into thinking that the transpersonal is something outside yourself. Transpersonal, to me, only means that part of myself that is beyond my ordinary awareness. The Higher Self is the transpersonal. When we are not in direct contact with the Higher Self, we project and experience it as a power outside of ourselves. There is nothing wrong with this; it corresponds to a stage of evolutionary growth. However, an important part of self-realization is the awareness that the power is within. It is this inner power of the Higher Self that guides transformation.

There is a difference between change and transformation. Change implies a willful, intentional move. The intellect decides something needs to be different, and action is deliberately taken. At times change is necessary. Yet there are times when the aggressiveness of deliberate change will not, and cannot, be effective. The intellect eventually realizes that to find fulfillment, experience must become new, and the unknown must be entered. Willful determination fails, because the intellect can only chart a course toward the known.

Transformation becomes the recourse. Transformation implies the natural outgrowing of one set of circumstances into another, guided by the Higher Self. There is no forcing to be something that appears to be more attractive or more valuable. Surrender to the present unfailingly brings about transformation into the future. Growth takes place without effort; the Heart opens without knowledge; transformation comes without asking.

ACTIVATE THE WITNESS

Witnessing is the traditional term used to describe the detached attitude that coincides with the shift of consciousness from the Lower to the Higher Self. It may be facilitated by activating the Third Eye chakra, which we shall discuss in Chapter 11. Witnessing means just what it implies. We cultivate an impassive stance toward whatever is happening. We become the observer, watching without choice or comment as the flow passes before us. Witnessing applies to inner feelings as well as to external events, implying a sense of "being with" painful feelings instead of being the feelings.

The Witness exists
only in the moment

Self-rejecting activity of the mind, which usually takes the form of *thoughts*, must stop before the Witness can come into existence. Some teachers have said that thoughts should be witnessed, but what they actually mean, in my opinion, is that *feelings* should be witnessed. I have always found that thought inhibits the Witness state. As you shift into the Witness, you maximize the transformative potential of direct experience. You come further into *the moment,* the home of the Witness, and into the inherent feeling nature of the body.

Shifting to the Witness is an ability that will grow with practice. At first you may not be sure if what you are sensing is really Witness consciousness. Your initial sensations probably will be subtle, but you should allow whatever sensations you have to build. People experience witnessing differently. Soon you will develop a well-defined sense and an appreciation for it – it is almost a physical sensation.

Distinguish between the
Lower and Higher Selves

The Lower Self is the one we are familiar with, the one we have been talking about, the personal ego. Within it are the contents of our mind, body, and feelings. This self can be approached through psychology and growth techniques. The Higher Self is something else – it is what we discover as we go within. It is our true identity, of which we lose sight in our identification with the Lower Self. For practical purposes, we may assume that the Higher Self is the same as the Witness.

As we learn to shift our sense of "I" from the Lower to the Higher Self, we are increasingly liberated from material bondage. When in the Witness, we are no longer ruled by addiction or driven by dualistic preferences. We understand that pleasure and pain sit side by side. There is no getting one without the other. We accept both. The Lower Self still may operate in the world of duality, gaining and losing, but the Witness is content simply to observe it all.

There is a remote possibility of confusing the Witness with the clinical, dysfunctional condition known as *disassociation*. Disassociation refers to chronic lack of contact between the conscious ego and the feeling self, the result of continuous self-rejection. The person also may feel as if outside the body, disconnected from it, and in another world; blocking of feelings is complete; intense anxiety is often present. Witnessing does not imply absence of feeling. In witnessing, the Lower Self, where feeling occurs, is fully available to Higher Self consciousness, and the sense of detachment is not experienced as cause for anxiety.

The nature of the Witness is euphoric

The Witness has no requirement for anything to be any particular way; just *to be* is enough. When we live in this euphoric, peaceful center of consciousness, we feel transcendental love. Our well-being overflows, and those who are close to us can't help sharing that feeling. There is no effort involved in trying to love or in deciding to do so. We are truly detached from the self-centered preoccupation of the Lower Self. Activation of the Witness is a primary goal of esoteric teachings.

Understanding the Witness concept is of immense importance. Great psychologists like Jung and Perls have said that to become whole, we must suffer. They are talking about what we have been talking about – the need to integrate the suppressed, painful part of ourselves. The concept of the Witness, however, brings everything to a new plane. We understand that, yes, we must experience our suppressed pain, but on the level of the Lower Self. When the Witness is activated, we enter the Higher Self, and we view our pain with detachment, love, and even euphoria.

There is no magic involved in simply suffering. Suffering has transformational value when it is embraced, not rejected and resuppressed; when it is viewed from the Witness; when it is experienced with love.

*Are you accepting
with love?*

One of the tests of processing is to note whether you are accepting with love. No matter what conditions you are facing, you can activate the higher centers, the Heart and the Witness, and enter the experience from the vantage point of higher consciousness. If you are not accepting with love, you have not yet reached your full potential and effectiveness. I am not referring to the love of the Lower Self, which is attached and dualistic, but the love of the Higher Self, which is unattached and choiceless. You can feel love even when you are integrating a painful event. This may seem impossible, because we normally feel one emotion at a time. How can one feel love and pain together?

The love that comes from the Higher Self is not an emotion. It is a state of being that is open to the cosmic, ever-changing Now. The euphoric nature of the Witness is the true experience of love. It is based on the principle of acceptance, not choice. It is not dependent on any object, it just *is*. As you activate the Witness center, you awaken the healing power of love, coming from within. You then can direct it to any inner or outer condition. Don't deny the negativity that you are facing, feel it, but also feel the love and peacefulness from the Higher Self, melting the pain of the Lower Self. Love will provide the transformation.

ALLOW PSYCHIC ENERGIES TO BALANCE

Direct experience of negative energies in the Witness state creates optimal conditions for clearing and healing. This happens automatically under the direction of the unconscious intelligence of the Higher Self. It doesn't require any more thought than we give to our bodies' physical systems, such as circulation or digestion. Indeed, the stopping of thought is what makes integration possible. We stop thought when we drop self-rejection and enter the Witness. Until then thought inhibits the natural healing cycle.

The key healing attitude of the
Witness is nonidentification

Breaking identification with the Lower Self, and the desires of the Lower Self is the purpose of spiritual practice. Note that we do not try to destroy or change the Lower Self. We only shift our sense of identification, which is effected through Witness consciousness. This may appear to be in contradiction to what we discussed earlier – the need to own our experience. Yet there is no contradiction, because these functions take place on different levels of our being.

Whatever is manifesting, whether an emotion, desire, addiction, or physical symptom, it is part of our Lower Self. This self must definitely take responsibility for what it feels and puts out into the universe. But the Lower Self is not really us. We mistakenly identify with attributes of the Lower Self. Our true identity is in the Higher Self, the part that witnesses. If we cultivate the sense of nonidentification with the negative side of the Lower Self, we allow the sense of the Higher Self to grow. As we drop identification with the negative condition, we still allow it to exist in our consciousness. We experience the condition, with love. We feel as if we are "being with" the condition, in the moment, instead of being the condition.

There is an element of time involved in integration, even though in the Witness the sense of time is different. Integration does not usually come immediately. If you realize that you are working on material that has possibly been suppressed for lifetimes, you will have more patience with the time factor. Our Karma will come to us in pieces. Incidents will happen, emotions and moods will occur that are all caused by the unconscious energy we hold. Each occurrence is the opportunity either to integrate or to resuppress negative energy. Each time we successfully integrate the appearance of a negative pattern, we carve a little more off our subconscious load, but there will be many incidents before the whole load is dissolved. Certain periods of our lives may be spent in meeting one particular suppressed aspect of ourselves.

However, each time an incident is successfully integrated, you will feel the results. Your boundaries will have expanded. You will gain more freedom. You will not be as compulsive. You will not be moved as easily to react to or be motivated by negative patterns. Addictions will start to come under control. Issues that before were difficult to bear will not be as much of a problem. You are now not projecting as much into events as they occur; you have begun to release negativities. You perceive that life is going better or that others are not causing you as much trouble. But it is you who have changed.

As you continue to integrate events – primarily through processing the feelings associated with them – you will gain a clearer view of the objective nature of interaction. You will see the other's side much more easily. You will see the positive side of an occurrence that before you had been loading with negativity. Situations will be *reframed* spontaneously. Reframing is a technique that means finding the proper context for any event, so that it is perceived positively rather than negatively. When reframing happens automatically, it is a sign that integration has occurred, but you should be careful about deliberate reframing, which can easily serve as another way of suppressing feelings. Don't ever talk yourself out of your feelings.

OPEN YOURSELF TO TRANSFORMATION

When you allow energies to balance themselves, you invite the transformational power of the Higher Self to work in your behalf. This power cannot be commanded, controlled, or anticipated. It is the "grace" that comes when you do not ask – when your mind is calm and in the state of acceptance. The Higher Self will enter and will direct the outcome of both your feelings and the circumstances to which you are surrendering. This happens automatically, when you accept your experience as it is. In doing its work, the Higher Self operates on the inner psychic planes, in turn affecting the material plane. Transformation is effected in ways that appear miraculous and magical. The shaping of events is guided in practical and creative ways that cannot be foreseen.

We connect to each other
on the psychic levels

Because of the psychic connection between people, you don't have to confront someone directly when you are processing in order to clear feelings concerning them. Understanding this is an important part of taking back your power: You don't need any kind of consent, apology, confession, forgiveness, or approval from anyone. You also don't need to hurt anyone in retaliation.

But the main reason why I usually recommend not to confront others in the attempt to clear feelings is that usually, when we confront, we are into blame. When you blamefully confront another, no matter how tactfully, the results will always be unsatisfactory. Instead, clear yourself first, before talking to the other person. When you integrate emotions that concern another person, changes in the relationship will occur spontaneously. The other person will be affected and will change their behavior, possibly without even knowing why, and the need for talk will change dramatically.

When you stop blaming, you no longer put out the negative psychic energy that others unconsciously feel. You no longer buy into their game. You also no longer buy into your own projections. In no longer fighting the other, you absorb their energy as you receive it. You don't send it back mixed with your own hostility, which just fuels the other's aggression. You don't allow the other to take advantage of you, but neither do you return negativity with more negativity. The negative energy that you must absorb from the other corresponds to your Karmic debt to yourself – it is part of your projection. Don't be resentful about having to absorb it. Don't become angry about the anger. When the debt is paid, the other person's negativity that you perceive as being directed toward you will disappear.

You must maintain a choiceless
position about outcomes

One of the requirements for transformation is that you must have no personal agenda about the outcome. When you have desires, expectations, concepts, self-image, or self-interest to maintain, you inhibit the working of the balancing forces. It has been my experience, however, that the outcome is always satisfactory in ways I could not anticipate. I go beyond the duality in question, integrating the "negative" and no longer clinging to the "positive." A particular boundary is pushed back.

When you approach a problematic situation with a particular solution in mind, you don't allow the opportunity for real growth to occur. Your solution is based on what you already know and is likely to be merely the pleasant dualistic complement to what you would like to avoid. To go beyond, you must go to a place that is unknown. When you drop all concepts of what the outcome should be, you allow the higher intelligence to bring about the appropriate transformation. You make room for the new to happen, and real growth occurs.

Many believe that a religious power comes into play. This is a personal matter, but my feeling is that we are just accessing another part of ourselves – a new ability. This does not necessarily mean that a power outside of ourselves is now working for us; perhaps an expanded concept of who we really are would be more appropriate. Regardless of how you view it, contemporary psychology is coming more and more to the conviction that the transpersonal element is essential in healing.

TRUST

As we begin to function in the consciousness of the Higher Self, we realize that trust, or faith, is one of the more important attitudes that we can hold. When we trust, doubt is absent. Doubt is the negative orientation of the mind that makes inner work difficult. When we doubt, we are restricted, as in any other self-rejection. Doubt has an effect on our psychic energy and encloses us, instead of opening us to the Higher Self as trust does.

If you are to trust, what exactly are you to trust in? In many ways, it makes no difference what you trust in as long as the object of your trust is basically a positive force. When you trust in something beyond your conscious self, you open to receiving intelligent guidance and energy from a source that the conscious ego cannot provide.

If you are of a religious nature, you may choose to trust in God. If you find the right guru, you may feel trust in that relationship, eventually extending the trust to the inner guru. If the concept of the Higher Self appeals to you, you may trust in this guiding and intelligent force, or in the concept of grace. You may trust in the intelligent and supportive Universe. If none of these is appropriate for you, you can trust in the scientific principles of processing and psychology in general.

If you feel you need some*thing* to trust in, whatever you choose as the object of your trust will only be your projection. This is not necessarily detrimental, though, and can correspond to a significant and fruitful stage of growth. Trust in anything you like, as long as you trust. If you are going to create the object of your trust, however, it is better to create an abstract entity rather than project your trust onto another human, unless that person is very qualified to receive it.

Personally, having experienced that the principles we have been discussing work, I feel comfortable trusting in them. I feel that everything I perceive on the Earth plane is happening in order to cleanse my subconscious and that I cooperate by just surrendering to *what is.*

I also have a sense that the Universe is large, intelligent, and will help me if I let it. I am acquainted with the inner planes of existence, and just the knowledge that they exist is enough to invoke my trust in life. I trust that the Earth, in its natural state, is a nurturing and loving energy with which I can commune.

I trust that the evolution of the individual is leading to the awakening of higher capacities for love and creativity. Because I have experienced this, I want to keep going, even though I have no clear conception of where it leads.

I trust there is an infinite power beyond my conscious self, which will work in my favor if I let it. I choose to think of that power as part of myself, with which I have not yet come into full contact – the Higher Self.

I trust, finally, in myself; in my capacity to survive and be happy, not because of what I have or what is happening, but because *I am*.

UNDERSTAND PSYCHIC CLEANSING

We must realize that we are engaged in psychic cleansing. Even though it may not be apparent, being in a physical body presents that opportunity. When we don't yield to unpleasant feelings or resist them, but instead integrate them, we allow cleansing to take place.

In cleansing, psychic toxins are released into consciousness, becoming temporarily intensified

If you are cleansing addictive compulsions, you will feel the compulsiveness even more as it is cleansed. When you cleanse anger, you will feel more angry. When you cleanse dependency, you will feel more helpless and alone than ever. Experiencing such feelings more strongly is a sign that cleansing is proceeding, especially when the feelings occur in conjunction with a conscious program for emotional or physical healing. This period ends sooner or later, depending on how much suppressed energy is in the subconscious. You must be gentle and protective with yourself now, because you have become fragile in contrast to your former self, which may have been aggressive and hard. This is one reason why people enter the monastic life.

You enter a period of psychic fasting. By eliminating all the usual escapes from your pain, you bring the pain to the surface. You have to experience the psychic toxins as they are released in order to get rid of them. If you have ever tried physical fasting, you know that there can be a period of discomfort as all the physical toxins are dumped into the bloodstream. Nevertheless, the result is beneficial, and you feel better and healed after the fast. Psychic fasting is similar. Be patient and tender with yourself.

Emotional and physical
releasing take place together

Because of the body/mind connection, releases in the physical body may correspond to the releases in the psychic body. Physical symptoms of various types may appear. The interaction between the physical and psychic levels should not be described as one causing the other; they appear simultaneously. The acceptance of symptoms is the basis for holistic medicine. The body is allowed to manifest the cleansing symptoms, balancing itself as it does. Although the physical symptoms are accepted, there may be adjustments to be made on the physical level, such as changes in diet, supplements, environment, exercise, and so on. Usually the discovery of a chronic physical condition and its treatment on the physical level will coincide with the releasing of a psychic Karmic burden.

The releasing of suppressed material can precipitate catharsis, the emotional purging of unconscious pain and blocking. Catharsis is often accompanied by weeping. If weeping ever occurs in yourself or someone you are with, you should never attempt to inhibit it. Simply support and comfort yourself or the person, by holding them or just by being with them. Gently encourage them to stay with or even go further into the pain. Don't encourage them to avoid it, as we are inclined to do. Eventually the crisis will pass, and a thorough cleansing will have taken place.

In working on yourself, as you uncover painful emotion, include and experience it without avoidance. The attitude of including is exactly what makes deep cleansing possible. The energy in the chakras balances in a self-regulating manner, resulting in catharsis, but you cannot precipitate cleansing deliberately. Cleansing occurs spontaneously when you do not seek to avoid, but when you meet the negative.

RECOGNIZE THE HINDRANCES

Buddhist texts refer to the "Five Hindrances." As you begin working on yourself, you start to bump up against old boundaries. This may be experienced quite literally. As your auric field feels the effect of the additional prana taken in with visualizations, breath and bodywork, and inner concentration, the aura tries to expand but meets the resistance of old, self-destructive patterns of the energy body that are being disturbed. These patterns, being energy formations, have a pseudointelligence of their own, and they sense the threat to their existence. You may even think of the patterns as representing subpersonalities, if it helps you to visualize their place in your being. The subpersonalities act up because you have not accepted them.

The resistance of the patterns takes the form of the Five Hindrances and possibly others that you may add to the list. The point is that you will meet resistance as you begin inner work. It can be handled by processing, as can any negativity. There is no way past the Hindrances except to just keep going and to blast through – with gentle acceptance, of course. Resistance is lessened when you seek to integrate, not eliminate, the patterns. The Five Hindrances:

1. I WANT. Desires of any chakra can be stimulated, including present addictions.

2. I HATE. Resentment may increase, perhaps irrationally.

3. TORPOR. An energy condition of sudden sleepiness, which may come up in breathwork or meditation.

4. RESTLESSNESS. General anxiety may increase.

5. DOUBT. Doubt concerning the method, the teacher, the therapist, the progress.

As you might gather, the occurrence of even just one of these hindrances would discourage the average person. Probably many people starting on the inner path never get far because of the hindrances. Buddhists made the Hindrances a formal part of their tradition thousands of years ago, because they realized the difficulties of inner work. Make good use of their forewarning.

TAKE PART IN GROUP WORK

Working by yourself can be effective self-therapy, but you add a new dimension to your practice by participating in group sessions. A strong energy builds in the group format, which you can take in and use. This is especially true if the group takes place in a healing environment, such as a place dedicated to inner or spiritual work, an ashram, or a natural, peaceful location.

On the other hand, you must be careful not to become dependent on the group and neglect developing your own practice; group energies can definitely be addictive. You must ultimately face yourself alone, and the group cannot be there to provide continual support.

However, if you are working by yourself, a group can provide the additional push you might need to bring an issue to completion. The ideal format would be a strong foundation of regular individual work supplemented with weekly, monthly, or even less frequent group sessions. Group work may consist of bodywork, guided visualizations, encounter work, accelerated breathwork, dreamwork, or emotional processing.

part

3

Loving Yourself

I recognize that love from within is the only true source of love. I nurture myself to allow the love within to grow. I no longer enter relationships to find love but to express the love I feel within. The ability to love myself has grown because of my emotional self-acceptance. By experiencing and not avoiding my painful feelings, I have implemented real growth and transformation.

10

Love from Within

UNCONDITIONAL HAPPINESS

We are all engaged in the pursuit of happiness. From the most basic drives of survival, to the most refined tastes for art, intellectuality, and love, we seek that which fulfills us. We naturally seem to seek this outside of ourselves. Perhaps our early conditioning as dependent children receiving love and nourishment from outside led to the view that happiness is external, that it must be pursued and attained. Perhaps this tendency is another of "Nature's Traps," keeping us in the world until we become wise enough to know better.

Seeking fulfillment outside of ourselves is the materialist attitude about happiness. Whether the concern is survival, power, sensation, nurturing, significance, love, or creative needs, happiness becomes conditional upon achieving, attaining, or possessing something outside of ourselves. Even creative needs depend on successful execution and recognition before fulfillment can be attained.

Successful satisfaction of needs becomes a condition for happiness. We defend our ownership of the means to satisfy needs, whether a career, person, place to live, or self-image. We become dependent on these possessions, fearing their loss. We become anxious and resentful about our dependence, often unconsciously. We learn to hate the possessions that are supposed to bring us happiness, feeling that they actually own and control us, instead of the other way around.

Of course, legitimate needs must be met, but I am talking about something else. We have built a need system that is addictive, neurotic, and artificial. Our needs have gone beyond simple and basic human requirements, but we still look to the satisfaction of these exaggerated needs for happiness. They become the *source* of happiness.

It is unfortunate that much New Age emphasis is on learning how to more effectively get what we think we need to be happy; in other words, how to better satisfy addictions. What we need is to learn how to get rid of the addictions. The purpose of spiritual life in general is to get us to the point where we no longer assume that anything from the outside will be a source of happiness. Of course, we will still have activities, relationships, and possessions, but instead of regarding them as sources, we regard them as *expressions* of happiness. To the extent that we can do this, we are freed from dependency, poverty consciousness, and dualistic experience.

When we know that nothing from the outside can significantly and permanently help us find happiness, we are freed from the sense of lack. When we do not lack anything, we feel complete as we are and have entered *abundance consciousness*. This condition has no dependence whatsoever on our possessions; it is a state of mind. Abundance consciousness serves to attract fortunate circumstances, exactly because we do not feel that anything is lacking. We acquire material resources and harmonious relationships but are not dependent on them and do not fear their loss.

Being human, we cannot expect to live up to the ideal of abundance consciousness immediately and should not condemn ourselves when we don't. The pain that comes as a result of dependency must be accepted and experienced in order to grow beyond dependency – it is the only way.

If happiness is not to be found outside ourselves, where or how is it achieved? Sometimes we are told to seek happiness within. Often not much more is said, and the meaning may not be entirely clear. The phrase "seek happiness within" is actually misleading and is a trap many fall into when they begin thinking about spirituality. They turn away from worldly pursuits out of eventual disillusionment and try to find happiness from another source, which is now supposed to be "within." Do you see the error? The approach is exactly the same as before, but now it is thought that happiness will be found in a nonmaterial source, such as the self-projected concept of God or guru. We continue to be aggressive, demanding, concerned with our own needs, and compulsive about "happiness."

There is no source of happiness. The very concept of conditional happiness is false and misleading. We still cling to the dualistic concept of happiness/unhappiness, grasping for one, rejecting the other. If you can perceive this truth, you will realize that all efforts directed toward attaining happiness are misdirected. It is possible only to create a new "source," within or without, a new invention of the subconscious from which you expect happiness. In so doing, you fall into the dependent, dualistic pattern all over again, projecting both happiness and unhappiness.

If all efforts to "find happiness" are in vain, what are we to do? When you truly understand the futility of effort, you will simply stop trying compulsively to pursue happiness, whether in career, relationship, possession, or spirituality. Stopping effort is the first step toward liberation. Release from anxiety will follow, as will the pressure to be or do anything in an addicted manner.

However, most of us are so conditioned to be achievement

oriented that stopping effort is usually impossible. Remember, I am not saying that it is necessary to be inactive. Rather, I'm referring to the motive implicit in activity. We are *searching* for happiness instead of expressing happiness through the activity or relationship. We are victims of the core misbelief "I am not enough." You must realize that you are enough, just as you are. You don't need anything to be happy, you just need *to be*.

If you stop searching, at first you may be left with the terrible emptiness that is no longer masked by the false hope that searching brings. This emptiness must be worked with like other perceived negativities. Indeed, it is a main issue we all must face. Real work on yourself begins when you start to integrate and stop being motivated by whatever form the emptiness takes, whether it is a longing for security, sex, power, or relationship. I promise you, eventually you will become clear and experience a freedom and exhilaration that you didn't think could exist.

I realize that all this may sound like something that could never be attained, and perhaps you are asking yourself if it is necessary to go to such extremes. After all, most of us want to live a basic, simple life. Why be concerned with such abstractions? This simplistic view of happiness overlooks our basic situation. We don't understand the dualistic nature of existence, and we continue to reject much of life, including ourselves. Our subconscious will not let us alone because of the suppressed energies we carry, causing us to act self-destructively. Happiness remains elusive.

Psychotherapy has been the means by which many have found the healing and growth that results from accepting ourselves as we are. Still, at times psychotherapy can fall short of achieving maximum benefit. Often its intention is to get the client functioning, which may come down to getting them interested in pursuing goals, which perpetuates the myth that happiness will be found in the future from sources outside oneself. The real issue – the ultimately self-deceptive kind of life we lead – is not addressed.

However, this is changing. The advent of transpersonal psychology, which recognizes the spiritual component to the psyche, includes concepts similar to those we have been discussing. The intent is no longer to patch up but to understand why problems perpetuate, helping the client bring spiritual concepts into real life.

Issues of dependency in relationships, for example, are now being discussed widely. Codependency groups meet, just as Alcoholics Anonymous groups do, and people come to realize that the problem is their dependency, not the other person. Dependency is basically the impulse to search for happiness outside yourself. I would suggest that you become a true warrior and attack the central problem ruthlessly: Give up your dependent attempts to find happiness through security, sensation, power, and relationship. Until you do, you will continue to encounter misery through the very door that you hope happiness would enter.

If we are to no longer search for happiness, what do we do with ourselves? This is the point where self-work actually begins. We feel. We simply feel all that comes our way. When we are not feeling something, we exist without sensation in the Now, the eternal moment. We will still be subject to some dualism because that is the nature of the world, but we do not cling to one side and reject the other. Dualities are experienced as integrated complements instead of warring opposites. If the unpleasant comes up, it is accepted, not rejected. We understand that experiences are largely projected, and we own them, blaming no one. We have no preference about which side of the dualism we are now in because we know that both are inevitable. We trust in the flow, allowing negative experiences to be absorbed and dissolved without resistance, becoming positive experiences, and vice versa.

We activate a higher intelligence within, which guides the transformation of energies. We are emotionally unaddicted to outcomes because we no longer depend on them as a source of happiness. As we integrate dualistic experience, we discover a euphoric transcendental state beyond conditional happiness/unhappiness, which is not far away or inaccessible but easily within our grasp. This state of unconditional happiness is called love.

DEPENDENT LOVE

Although our search for fulfillment can take many forms, it could be said that what we really seek is love. This is especially true in relationships, of course, as well as in other forms of searching, as when we pursue security, power, sensation, or recognition. Love, coming from a higher center, will satisfy the emotional aspect of lower needs, but we must be aware of the different types of love. Just as there is a difference between the Lower and Higher Selves, there is a difference between dependent love and self-love.

Dependent love comes from the unintegrated Heart center. It is the complement to emptiness, isolation, and loneliness. We seek to escape from this pain by uniting with another person. At first, it is possible to experience ecstasy from union with another, especially if it is sexual. However, various problems are created when we are motivated by the unintegrated Heart, problems that are likely to undermine the relationship if they are not recognized.

The first problem is that dependent love is highly conditional. The partner is chosen carefully to begin with, and once a relationship is established, we become upset if they do not meet our expectations. Our expectations are really our addictions, which we rationalize as "needs." A relationship based on mutual satisfaction of needs is a business partnership – we give in order to get. It is difficult to cultivate a loving attitude when you are concerned primarily with the satisfaction of your own needs.

Addictive needs vary somewhat between the sexes. Traditionally men place sex high on the list and women are concerned with material security, although in this age of blurring sexual identity, both sexes may exhibit either tendency. Focusing on sex, hoping to find escape there, sets up a pattern of compulsive sexual searching. Since it is only the newness of a relationship that serves to hide the inner emptiness, the sexual attraction soon fades. The person continues to search for the elusive satisfying partner, not understanding why lasting fulfillment is never possible. The same scenario exists with regard to security, as well as any other compulsive need that we strive to satisfy through the relationship.

The difference in addictive needs does much to account for the endless battle that seems to exist between the sexes. Then come the unconscious needs that impel us to relationship, when we seek in the other whatever we block within ourselves. You might say that mutual satisfaction of needs will always be a part of relationships. My opinion, however, is that the more expectations, needs, and demands you have, the more your relationships will suffer and be a source of pain instead of love.

When you look to another to satisfy your needs, there will be times when they fail, both intentionally and unintentionally. If you are conditioned to feel satisfaction when your needs are met by your partner, you also will feel dissatisfaction when they are not. Unless you can release the dissatisfaction – by processing, for example – you can quickly become resentful, and the dualistic love/hate syndrome begins.

Another problem is that the emptiness of the unintegrated Heart is not eliminated, only suppressed, when we are motivated by dependent love. We essentially buy into and give permission for the emptiness to continue, becoming locked into a cycle of dependency/emptiness, never seeing that the existence of one depends on the other. The excitement of the relationship covers the emptiness for a while, but the emptiness continues to build in the subconscious. We need more and more of the energy of the relationship to suppress the escalating emptiness, becoming compulsive about particular aspects of it that are important to us individually. Eventually the relationship reaches the point of exhaustion, and the emptiness breaks through into awareness because there is no more energy to suppress it. We become disillusioned, thinking that the partner is the cause.

Because we depend on the other to avoid our inner emptiness, we fear losing the person. The fear results in anxiety and possessiveness. We cling to and try to control the other out of fear of loss or even of their temporary absence. We become resentful that we are dependent and can't help but to project the resentment onto the partner. Fear itself may also be projected onto the partner, so that we consciously or unconsciously fear them and become anxious and afraid in their presence. Fear becomes a major part of the negative side of the relationship; the fear of losing the person is in direct proportion to our "love." Much of the fear is suppressed, but eventually it becomes a significant source of additional resentment, often unconscious, completing the love/hate syndrome.

Resentment from all these sources becomes the motivation behind the fighting that is always present in dependent relationships.

Negative tension builds up, and the partners try to clear it through fighting. They fight, each blames the other, thinking everything would be all right if the other would behave properly. Because they blame, tension does not dissolve but is suppressed. Fighting continues, getting worse as previously suppressed tension again tries to clear along with new tensions that have accumulated. Eventually the level of suppressed resentment is such that there is no alternative except for the relationship to collapse.

Dependent love is difficult to get past if one is not aware of what it is and how it is perpetuated. Even in nonromantic relationships, when we think we are acting out of brotherly love or even being spiritual, often a good deal of dependency is present in our motivation.

I have not been describing dependent relationships primarily in order to encourage you to avoid them. If, in fact, you are able to modify your concept of relationship and exercise more discretion about how you get involved, you will be ahead of the game. However, for most of us, avoiding dependent relationships will be difficult, if not impossible. We are simply not strong enough yet; we are inherently addictive. We must not condemn ourselves in this realization; it is simply where we are on the evolutionary path. The important thing to understand is that if we handle our dependency properly, it can help us enormously in our growth. We can *use* dependency as an instrument for spiritual evolution instead of being abused by it. To do this, we must approach dependency with an enlightened sense of acceptance.

We accept dependency, whether it has to do with love or any other center of consciousness. We try to do as best as we can, but then we must accept that we are compulsive, attached, and dependent. What we do *not* accept is our reactiveness to the dependency. When our partner is not behaving as we would like and we feel pain due to the absence or threat to these behaviors on which we are dependent, we do not act out the pain and become confrontational, demanding, blaming, abusive, or vindictive. We process the pain. *This is the fastest way to growth in relationship and overcoming of dependency.*

For example, suppose you are hopelessly attracted to someone
who is unavailable. You may recognize that you are dependent

and attached, but that in itself does nothing to change the dependency. You may have been exposed to spiritual teachings that tell you that the source of all pain is attachment, and so you try your best to not be attached, to give the other person their freedom, and so on. But the attachment remains. It jumps out when your guard is down, and you act inappropriately.

Do not beat yourself up because you are dependent. Accept yourself; accept the dependency, but don't act on it. Maintain nonreactiveness to it and process the pain that results from the dependency. Don't think the other is causing your pain – take responsibility for it. Realize that your addictions are causing the pain, whether it comes up in the form of sexual frustration, financial insecurity, anger, inconvenience, abandonment, or whatever. *Process* the painful feeling instead of reacting. In so doing, you accept and honor the other as the teacher whom you have unconsciously chosen to bring up your dependency and the suppressed pain that is behind it for clearing.

We know that love is the answer to our problems. We all want it and try to maintain it, but we never can completely, in spite of our best intentions. Many spiritual spokespeople simply keep urging us to be more loving, as if this could be done intentionally. We try, only to fail, and feel guilty and inadequate. We develop a negative attitude toward loving, thinking that it is not possible. We have to understand that we are not going about loving correctly.

The mind can never generate love. No matter how hard you try to talk yourself into feeling love, you will never succeed; you are setting yourself up for continual failure. Your "love" will be a creation of the mind and will have no basis in your being. You will construct a fantasy world, possibly based on "spiritual" ideals, and you will suppress and remain cut off from your real feelings. These feelings will continually try to clear through projection, and you will end up behaving hypocritically.

You can become freed from the cycle of dependent love by processing the isolation and loneliness that is felt in the Heart center. By ceasing to be motivated by pain, eventually you will gain balance. Instead of fearing isolation and being driven by it into relationships that are often destructive, you integrate the pain of isolation, allowing it to dissipate. Isolation will transform into self-reliance, self-contentment, self-individualization, and self-love. The pain is only the birth pain of the Higher Self.

LOVING YOURSELF

When the expressions "loving yourself" or "self-love" are first heard, there may be confusion about what is meant. This is because we think in terms of the love we are familiar with, dependent love. If we try to love ourselves, we may take an approach similar to that used in dependent love, using ourselves as the object of our love. We may try to escape into ourselves, as we escaped into others. We may become self-absorbed and self-indulgent, putting our own needs first. The motive is still to escape. We reject unhappiness and, in so doing, reject ourselves.

Self-love has nothing to do with using yourself as the object of your love. Self-love means that your love *comes from within,* is generated from within, not from "loving" any object because it may please you tremendously, whether that object is someone else or yourself. Self-love is a condition of awareness, a way of perceiving, an attitude, which results in an integrated perception of the world.

The art of loving yourself begins with self-acceptance. They are essentially the same. You begin loving yourself when you stop rejecting yourself. When you practice self-acceptance, you will experience real changes in consciousness. You no longer try to juggle people or possessions in the external world in order to find fulfillment. You find fulfillment from within, simply by integrating the opposites of experience.

Do not underestimate the importance of self-acceptance. It can end the emotional pain that you feel or lead to the spiritual experience you want. Starting with the mundane, you will reach the highest of inner realization. In welcoming all your feelings, you become whole; life becomes holistic. You experience oneness. You no longer compulsively search for oneness in the external world, whether with another person or with an achievement. You accept and love yourself.

Relationships with others change dramatically when you

access the self-love within. Not until then will you experience any-thing approaching real love with another person. Even if you are with a person who is genuinely trying to love you, you will reject that love if you are not in touch with the love within. The other's love will not get through. Love must come from inside. The love that you perceive coming from another is just the reflection of your own inner love.

Love becomes primarily a relationship with yourself. It means being able to live with – and possibly even by – yourself. It means finding fulfillment within, not from any source or person outside. Turning inward whenever there is pain has always been the message of the masters; processing is a specific method through which this may be done.

Concepts that you have about love are likely to be erroneous. You should drop all concepts and wait until the capacity builds within you. Trying to force your feelings to match false concepts creates anxiety. Love may not be what you think it is.

What is love? Love is the experience of the Higher Self. Love is the euphoric nature of the Witness, simply watching all that happens. Love is of the body, the feeling nature, not the mind. Love is the unconditional acceptance and experience of all feelings. Love of another becomes the unconditional acceptance of your perception of the other. Love of another means making the other truly nondefensive because you accept them as they are, just as you accept yourself as you are. You have no selfish motivation or hidden agenda they are required to meet. You are protecting nothing, because you welcome both the positive and the nega-tive. In an environment of total acceptance, love will enter your consciousness.

You perceive yourself and the other as you are. You no longer expect anything or make comparisons because you are not evalu-ating through the mind – you perceive the other directly. You sense that you are the other, that we are all one. This knowledge is in-herently emotional. You want to exchange energies because it is the joy of life. You want to care for the other because by doing so you care for and nurture your own growth. You give because you increase yourself. You have gone beyond a limited sense of personal ego.

A key concept to self-love is whether you are living in the moment. When you are in direct experience, in the Witness state, you are in the moment. You are no longer doing with a sense of looking for future satisfaction. Satisfaction comes from being with *what is*. Of course there will always be external purpose to activity, but in the Witness, your primary pleasure comes from the activity itself, not from the eventual result. You choose activities that have the potential to be enjoyable now as well as in future outcomes.

Nevertheless, you do not confine your experience to pleasurable events. If experience swings to the other pole, and you meet unpleasant or challenging situations, you get equal satisfaction by taking responsibility and integrating them, keeping in mind your toleration point. Acceptance of negativities becomes a source of fulfillment.

You find happiness by simply being with whatever is manifesting in your consciousness right now. Fulfillment is found in the moment; you are not as concerned if the results of your work do not turn out as expected. You still may make choices about what you desire and what you are going to work toward – we cannot live our lives otherwise. However, through self-acceptance, you are no longer compulsive about the results of work. You are no longer attached to any one outcome; you can accept other outcomes.

I am not so much referring to material outcomes as I am to feelings about the outcome. If you are disappointed or frustrated, you integrate these feelings. You maintain the Witness to your feelings, allowing them to be what they are, without extending any negativity into the world. Inner equanimity becomes the basis for self-love. You are not concerned about whether you have found the proper object to love. Your fulfillment overflows, and anyone near will feel the influence.

THE HIGHER SELF AS TEACHER

In Chapter 1 we saw how a teacher might help us learn to love ourselves. Any enlightened person, whether guru, therapist, parent, friend, spouse, lover, even child, can perform the role of teacher. In light of what we have since discussed, let's expand our understanding of that relationship.

In learning self-love, we ultimately awaken the teacher within. The teacher within corresponds to the Higher Self and the Witness. We access intuitive knowledge and find acceptance and love inside; but because we are not yet in contact with the inner teacher, we enter a relationship with an external teacher to stimulate those inner qualities into awakening. We experience those qualities with the external teacher that will later come from within.

When a relationship is formed with the external teacher, it is felt emotionally. A connection is made, and it may be hard to describe why or how this happens. Perhaps it might just be assumed that at various points of our lives, we might enter into such a relationship or even serve as a teacher for another. When the link is formed, the healing relationship begins. All varieties of emotions are experienced with the teacher. At first there is a strong positive attraction, corresponding to the "honeymoon" stage, but soon negative emotions begin coming up as well. If there is love, there will be fear and resentment; our love for the teacher is dependent love, even though we may not like to think so.

The teacher appears responsible for causing our feelings, positive as well as negative. What we do, however, is to project feelings onto the teacher. The teacher functions as an especially clear mirror, reflecting the contents of the subconscious. This happens exactly because the teacher has no expectations of us. *If we maintain awareness of ourselves* as we function in the relationship, we can see ourselves clearly.

The unconditional acceptance of the teacher is what causes the mirroring. The teacher accepts all feelings directed toward him or her, love as well as fear and anger. Usually when we love others, they respond with conditional love. When we resent others, they return our resentment; they do not accept it. In neither case do we receive unconditional acceptance. The teacher accepts our resentment as well as our love. Acceptance is the key to the healing relationship. Acceptance makes us conscious that we are projecting. We become aware of how we actually create our experience. At the same time, we become aware of the real love being extended to us through unconditional acceptance. We feel, possibly for the first time, unconditional love. We learn that acceptance *is* love.

The teacher becomes a surrogate for working out unfinished emotional issues. We bring all our patterns into the relationship. We project attitudes concerning authority, security, approval, love, and so on. We work out our Karma in a therapeutic relationship with this one person. The relationship with the teacher becomes intense, but the teacher's stance continues to be nonreactive, not buying into anything we do, not reacting to our love or our fear, simply accepting. Of course, the teacher will appear to react to our love, but the love we offer is not of the level as the love we receive from the teacher. We think we offer love, but we offer a mix of our positive and negative Karma.

Acceptance has a deep correspondence on the energy level, which is why it is effective as therapy. The teacher knows how to accept all that is directed toward him or her, which can amount to substantial energies. The method of acceptance is no different from what we have been discussing. The teacher only has an expanded capacity for accepting energies. Once we have had the experience of unconditional acceptance from the teacher, we may develop the capacity to give the experience to ourselves. The teacher serves as the model for how we can relate to ourselves. Our Higher Self, the Witness, becomes the teacher within.

This kind of relationship is the foundation for psychotherapy, where the projecting of the client onto the therapist is called "transference." Freud is credited with this discovery. His, and Jung's, opinion was that an important aspect of therapy did not take place until transference began. Until then there was no real interaction between therapist and client. The analytic schools would analyze the transference, to make the client aware of the patterns, but the humanistic therapist simply accepts. Acceptance is the more powerful form of therapy because of its subtle effects on the energy level, where blocking occurs.

I do not believe it is essential to have a relationship with an external teacher to awaken the Higher Self, although undoubtedly it can be helpful. You must decide for yourself. In modern short-term therapy, where the emphasis is on results, such a relationship is not common anyway. I have done most of my inner work by myself. Twice I have been privileged to enter a relationship with a teacher. The approach that I have described in this book has formed the foundation for my work, with the external teacher appearing at certain points in my life. Perhaps this approach also would work for you.

LOVE THROUGH THE BODY

Awakening the feeling capacity is primary in developing self-love. The feeling center has become underused, and we substitute thoughts for feelings. We linger in the mind when we should be with our feelings.

One of the best ways to develop the feeling capacity is through work with the body, including breath, bodywork, and meditating on the chakras. You can begin self-love by accepting and experiencing body sensations that come up during these sessions. You start to get in touch with yourself. You develop the capacity for sensitivity by being sensitive to your body. The feeling nature grows so that you sense your body as yourself, but also as a friend. This is a friend who has always been with you and has always worked to help and sustain you. The relationship with yourself can be thought of as starting with your relationship with your body. Of course, you have other dimensions besides the material, but the material reflects and represents the other aspects, which may be approached through the body. I have found working with the body to be a most fulfilling path to the Higher Self.

When you nurture the body, do not become self-indulgent. You are not trying to find pleasure through the body but are providing the body with optimum conditions to establish a fundamental condition of well-being. The sense of physical well-being can build to become a basis for emotional health, since body and feelings are so closely connected.

Begin with the basics concerning what the body needs: proper nutrition, exercise, safe and clean environment, and the attitude of self-love – the acceptance of all aspects of the body. When you accept physical sensations as cleansing in progress, you are loving your body. When you accept and experience feelings *about* your body, whether positive or negative, you begin cleansing those feelings that affect you subconsciously.

You should not try to love your body as an object. That would be an extension of the idea of dependent love. Accept and experience whatever feelings exist without trying to control or change them; you will be led to the transcendence of dualistic feelings and the beginning of self-love. As you enter your body more fully, you will become aware of a new sense of emotional being, a new connectedness with life. You become one with your body and simultaneously one with your experience. Emotional growth coincides with your connection to your body.

part

Working on Yourself

4

I devote a regular period each day to practice. I understand that bodywork, meditation, and breathwork are instrumental in bringing about self-integration. I joyously look forward to my practice as a time of relaxation and recharging. I feel my powers growing as I consciously use these special techniques.

11

Practice

In this chapter we discuss specific techniques that can be of immense help in our work. In all of the traditional approaches to enlightenment, the emphasis has always been on practice. Practice is a regular routine of specific exercises through which the capacity for integration and growth is activated. Practice balances the energy system and unblocks the chakras. The effects are felt on all levels, including physical and psychological. Stress is relieved. Sensitivity increases. The psychic capabilities awaken and come into play. Feelings and emotions are integrated. Addictions are outgrown.

Practice is the means to clear the subconscious. Negative emotions will enter awareness when released from the body during practice. You can expect that the tendency to project will continue, or even temporarily increase, as buried feelings are loosened. Practice must be approached with the understanding that integration of suppressed material will be required as it is released. However, practice will be instrumental in helping to integrate the material.

If you are serious about working on yourself, you should consider getting into the habit of devoting time, on a daily basis, to practice. Regular practice will develop your capabilities more quickly than just an intellectual acquaintance with self-work. Practice becomes a scientific way of activating, cleansing, integrating. Practice is also helpful because you learn the principles of working on yourself in a controlled environment. You will then be able to more easily apply them during the activity of everyday life.

A practice routine need not infringe greatly on your schedule. What's important is to do it every day. Short sessions performed daily will do more than longer sessions done irregularly. As you start to enjoy practice, you will increase your session time automatically. You will look forward to it as a period of relaxation and recharging.

The program that I present in this chapter can be used indefinitely. As you become more proficient in practice, you may want to add additional elements, but you also may find that this is not necessary. You'll find that you'll go deeper and deeper with the same basic tools. Because of the depth of this system, it may appear complex, but do not be intimidated. You do not need to understand or apply everything at once. Take whatever elements appeal to you and start working with them. When you are ready to learn more, it will be there, waiting for you. Set aside a regular time, no matter how brief it may be, for your practice. Practice has four parts: Bodywork, Activating healing energy, Breathwork, and Meditative processing.

BODYWORK

Physical activity in a healing regime is of two basic types, both of which are important. The first type is exercise. Any kind of exercise is good: manual labor, aerobics, dance-kinetics, sports, jogging, and so on. Exercising only a few times a week will keep you in shape and serve as the basis for a healthy body and vibrant energy system. A stagnant energy system leads to stagnant feelings, encouraging depression and compulsiveness.

The second type is *bodywork*. Bodywork should not be confused with exercise. They serve different purposes. Exercise vitalizes the body, while bodywork is of a psychophysical nature, affecting chakras and consciousness. Many types of bodywork are available, but I feel that yoga postures (asanas) are among the best. I would encourage you to become familiar with the principles of yoga if you are not already. Include a short session at the beginning of your practice. The stretching and loosening of the body is very relaxing, opening the feeling centers, making it easier to enter the meditative states that are desirable for inner work.

If you need technical information on yoga postures, books and classes are available almost everywhere. However, the particular benefits you experience with yoga depend entirely on how it is approached. There are several ways to approach yoga, only one of which is useful for consciousness development and psychophysical bodywork. If you have tried yoga and did not feel it was working for you, the fault may lie in your approach. In making these recommendations, I am drawing on my exposure to a variety of yoga schools, my personal practice, and my past experience as a yoga teacher.

In recent years, there seems to have developed – as a sign of the times – an emphasis on "power" yoga, in which the physical side of yoga is emphasized. Postures are performed more energetically than intended in classical yoga. The object is to get a good workout, to build endurance, to firm and contour the body to achieve esthetic and health-oriented goals. While it will accomplish these goals, yoga used only for this purpose with no consideration of its higher capabilities for consciousness development is a tragic misuse. We denigrate yoga in the service of the ego. We are driven by our compulsiveness. We reinforce our endless seeking, striving, grasping.

Yoga for consciousness work should be meditative in nature, with minimal exertion. The postures should be performed passively. You should think of them as "poses of relaxation" – not as a discipline or task in which you must excel or from which you will benefit. The sense of seeking, striving, trying to achieve anything through the practice is counterproductive and should be put aside. The purpose is to provide a vehicle to bring us into greater contact with our feeling selves, through the body. Yoga should relax us, not challenge us. We should come more and more into the moment, through the body, not remain fixed in the mind, driving the body to perform and accomplish.

Meditative yoga maintains an effortless inner attitude

Do not think of yoga postures as exercise but as meditation. Enter with a meditative attitude; drop all intention and effort. Relax all parts of the body except those that are tensed in holding the pose. Maintain a sense that the body is assuming the pose by itself, not being directed by the mind. Let the wisdom of the body take over and direct the body to what it needs. Let the body find its own point of comfort. Do not push with the mind. Simply watch and witness. Observe and feel what is happening in the body as you go through the sequence of poses, without trying to interfere or change anything. Do not feel that you have to do any posture perfectly or that you are competing with yourself or anyone else. Do not judge yourself either good or bad. Keep relaxing more and more deeply into the posture. The object of your meditative focus is to go deeper and deeper into feelings in the body that come up, both physical and emotional, as you stretch muscles and loosen chakras.

Witness physical sensations, choicelessly accepting. You should gently push the body to the point where you are experiencing a comfortable amount of strain; this can be enjoyable and relaxing. You are training yourself to be self-accepting, getting into the body's feeling centers and out of mental self-rejection. Other feelings that come up will be emotional. You may experience a variety of negative emotions, along with their associated thoughts. You should welcome these feelings, because they are cleansing. Be with the feelings in the Witness, neither reacting to nor rejecting them. In this way you access deep, hidden levels of body-held suppressed negativity and open the door to transcendental experiences of higher consciousness, approached through the body.

Hold the pose

Learn to hold poses for a significant length of time. Most people do not hold poses long enough. Of course, be careful not to cause physical injury, but stay in the pose until you feel a physical or emotional shift. You will go through stages of release. You will think you are stretched out and relaxed, and suddenly you will notice muscle tension that you have been holding in some part of the body to which you have not been paying attention. Then you can consciously relax that part of the body and stretch out further. Keep scanning the body as you hold a pose, looking for areas that are tight.

Usually, holding for one to five minutes will be enough. However, if you really want to work on a certain part of your body where you think you are holding suppressed energy or on a particular blocked chakra, you could hold for fifteen minutes or longer. Try to maintain the effortless attitude, even though certain muscles probably will be under stress. Witness this. Before beginning an extended holding, always make sure the body is warmed up by performing basic warm-ups or other postures, and always be careful. You probably shouldn't do extended holding until you are somewhat advanced in yoga. Don't strain the body to the point of injury, but also be aware that the body usually can endure more than you think. You have to use your inner sense to find the right balance. The stress that is put on the body during holding is needed to cause the release.

Extended holding can precipitate a crisis. The body may begin trembling and shaking, and your emotions may become intensified as deep cleansing in the chakras takes place. Hold the pose for as long as you think reasonable, but after you release the pose, continue opening to the feelings until they dissolve. I have seen healings occur, in both myself and clients, as a result of extended holding.

Maintain the breath

It is important always to keep the breath flowing smoothly when doing yoga. Keep breathing as you hold the pose; do not hold the breath. As you breathe, focus your awareness on the areas that are being stretched out and strained. Breathe into the area. Expand and contract the body in those areas, if possible, as you breathe into them. Doing so will focus healing energy, which will facilitate the release of body-held negativity. Use a gentle Integrating breath, which we will discuss shortly.

Work on specific chakras

Certain poses will work on certain chakras, releasing suppressed material in those centers. This key function of yoga is usually not appreciated. In addition to a balanced series of postures, then, you may want to emphasize poses that are appropriate for you. If you feel that you have a good deal of a certain type of suppressed negativity, work on the corresponding chakra. If you feel sad or hurt, work on opening the heart; if you feel invalidated, emphasize the solar plexus, and so on. Hold the pose, and keep breathing into the chakra. Here are some basic yoga postures that work on the chakras:

	CHAKRA	POSTURE
1.	Survival	Forward Bend
2.	Power	Spinal Twist
3.	Sensation	Bridge
4.	Nurturing	Peacock
5.	Significance	Cobra
6.	Heart	Bow
7.	Expression	Plow
	Upper chakras	Shoulderstand, Headstand

ACTIVATING HEALING ENERGY

Activating healing energy includes invoking the Witness and entering the alpha level of consciousness. These are essential skills in processing that you should apply before and during all processing sessions, whenever needed.

Two kinds of healing energy

There are two kinds of healing energy: positive (yang) and negative (yin). Both kinds are considered basically positive healing forces. As you become familiar with them, you will automatically draw whichever is needed for any particular healing; there is no need for conscious choice.

The alpha state

As you activate healing energy, you enter the alpha state. Alpha refers to the rate of electrical vibrations of the brain. The normal waking rate, the beta state, is from 13 to 30 cycles per second. In alpha, brainwaves slow down to between 8 to 12 cycles per second. You can even go deeper, as you acquire expertise in meditation, entering the theta state of 4 to 7 cycles per second. Much research has been done on the benefits of the alpha state. Healing occurs naturally and the conscious mind is relaxed. The body is relaxed and feels different. Meditation begins: The Higher Self and the Witness begin to function. The psychic abilities are awakened. Sensitivity to the energy flow (as perceived through the feelings) increases. Visualizations and affirmations are more effective. Clearing begins, almost spontaneously. Integration is facilitated.

Although the alpha state may be induced satisfactorily by meditative skills, an interesting and helpful aid in learning how to achieve this state is through the use of *entrainment* technology. Entrainment means applying an outside influence on the brain to bring the vibrations to the desired level. Entrainment may be effected through several avenues, but I prefer using sound, having found it easy and effective. The sound vibration is coordinated with the target brainwave frequency. When consciously used along with the proper exercises, alpha can be achieved effortlessly.

Entrainment aids usually come in the form of sound wave tapes and CDs or "mind machines." In both cases, earphones are worn for best results. I would recommend that the material does not contain any spoken or musical information in addition to the entraining frequencies. Spoken accompaniment that is often included in these tapes is intended to reprogram the subconscious, of which I am not in favor. Our goal is to access the deeper healing states and to bring about healing through self-processing, not reprogramming. But do not feel you are at a disadvantage if you do not have the assistance of entrainment technology – people have meditated successfully for centuries without it, and your eventual goal is to not be dependent on it.

Learn to visualize

To perform inner exercises effectively, you must call into play the skill of *visualization*. You visualize in order to direct energy in certain paths around the body. What you are actually directing is the pranic energy taken in with the breath. You are moving it in the energy body, but the sensation is physical. Visualizing has two components, seeing and feeling.

If you want prana to move in a certain path, you *see* it happening. This is different from imagining a picture in the mind. Instead, you use your inner sight. For example, if you want to visualize the navel center, you imagine it in your mind's eye, creating a mental picture. It is better, though, to see it as if your eyes were inside your body, at the navel. Inner seeing is developed by using the imagination.

As you are seeing inside, you may also *feel*. Sense the prana in the physical-psychic body. You might feel a current, a warmth, an expansion/contraction, a pressure, a vacuum, or other sensation. You may have your own way of feeling the energy, but you should feel something. Again, you may have to start with imagination, but after a short while, the feelings will be real.

In the end, it is your *intention* that enables you to direct prana. If you intend that the prana perform a certain function, it will, sensing the intention. You do not have to doubt whether you are visualizing well enough. Doubt will impede the effectiveness.

Activate healing energy

The following exercise constitutes a powerful shamanic induction for activating healing energy and the alpha state that I have found to be quite useful for inner work. There are four steps; they are all important for the success of meditative processing. I will first describe the purpose of each step and then lead you through the exercise.

1. Breath Relaxation

Consciously using the breath is the first powerful step for activating alpha. Simply breathing quietly and regularly will begin the shift into the alpha state and deep relaxation.

In all the exercises that follow, you will be using the Cleansing breath, which we will discuss shortly. However, do not be preoccupied with doing the breath "properly." Your aim is to just let the breath relax you into alpha. To do this you must start with being as relaxed as possible and not concerned with performance. However, if you were to single out any one part of the Cleansing breath to emphasize now, it would be the *connected* breath.

2. Aura Strengthening

In this step, you draw on and increase your supply of the masculine, yang healing energy of the universe. You use this energy to strengthen your aura.

If your aura is weak, you are low in vitality. *A strong aura is needed as you practice; it will repel outside negativity so that you process only your own energies, not those of some other psychic origin.* When you perform this exercise, you strengthen the aura and minimize the influence of outside negativity. You awaken your capacity for *self-protection.*

Everyone, especially sensitive people, absorbs negativity from our surroundings. It is unavoidable and should not be a cause for alarm. In the end, the negativity to which we are susceptible generally corresponds to the negativity we have suppressed. For this

223

reason, it is correct to accept the outside negativity and allow it to trigger our subconscious and to process the resultant experience. In practice, do not become overly concerned with where your negativity is coming from – doing so will only distract you from the work. Protect yourself by strengthening your aura with reasonable, not compulsive, use of this exercise and then trust in your guidance, surrender to your experience, and process.

This exercise is important if you have boundary issues, meaning you find it hard to maintain or even be aware of your personal boundaries: Others encroach on you or you encroach on others. Boundary issues occur because of our inclination for dependent relationships. We use the energy of others not only in romantic relationships, but in all types. On the psychic level, we form tangible ties to others. This exercise breaks those ties and trains you to access energy directly from the proper inner source instead of other people.

This exercise may activate issues with the archetypal male/father and survival issues. The feelings that come up during it reflect your relationship to the inner male and, consequently, relationships with men. By processing these feelings as they are, you strengthen the inner male and counter the weakness to find male energy outside yourself.

3. Grounding

In grounding, you establish a link with the earth that absorbs negative energies as you release them. *Doing so is essential to discharge both casual negative energies that you may have absorbed and suppressed negativity that releases from the subconscious.* If a path is not provided for negative energies when they are released, they will linger in your psychic atmosphere. When you establish the path, they will follow it and become neutralized. Note that the path itself does not act to release negativity, except perhaps for superficial negativity that does not correspond to our Karma; processing releases the negativity.

Grounding also draws in the powerful, archetypal feminine, yin healing earth energy. Both sexes need a balance of both the yin energy of the earth and the yang energy of the sun. By consciously drawing in more of your opposite-sex energy from the universe – which is the same as getting it from inner sources – you can reduce the compulsive need to get it indirectly from the other sex.

As we access the archetypal feminine, we awaken our capacity for *self-nurturing*. This is extremely important, not only for our personal development in general but especially now, when we are more sensitive because we are intentionally dropping self-rejection and all the addictive means that we may have used to keep ourselves going.

The feelings that come up during this exercise reflect your relationship to the inner female and, consequently, women in general and the mother. By processing these feelings as they are, resolution will occur.

4. Entering the Witness

If you are sensitive or if you have been practicing, the first three steps will have brought you at least partially into alpha. This last step will bring you all the way.

Witnessing is vital in processing. *Witnessing provides the power and perspective to confront the strong negative energies that are surfacing.* The Witness is the key inner orientation for processing feelings. It gives you the ability to detach from negativity and not be overcome by it.

As you practice, you will gain an appreciation of what the Witness feels like. It is a sense of being detached from whatever is going on around you or inside you but also sensing your connection to it on a deeper level. Your sense of physical perspective may change. You feel the healing power and joy of self-love. When you have become familiar with the sensation of being in the Witness, you will know when you have to reactivate it in order to maintain the sense of *disidentification* that is so important when working with lower chakra feelings. After you become proficient, you will be able to activate the Witness in seconds or less. Just remembering to do it will be enough. Witness consciousness can be entered during activity as well as meditation; maintaining the Witness during activity will become second nature.

EXERCISE

As you work with these steps, you will intuitively feel which of them may be more important for you. You may emphasize that particular step, taking more time with it, but be careful to perform all the steps. A suitable amount of time for the whole exercise is eight minutes, but you may adjust this as best suits you, taking less time or extending and really getting into the exercise.

The exercise is a powerful stimulus for bringing up feelings that are held in the subconscious, especially the invoking of the archetype male and female. If strong feelings come up for you during the exercise or if you experience *blocking,* recognize what is happening. Contain the feelings or the blocking for further processing immediately after you complete the entire exercise.

I usually recommend using the sitting position for the Cleansing breath in this exercise, but you also may perform it lying down, if that appeals to you. I would suggest that you do not always lie down; use the sitting position at least occasionally so that you can get an idea of the subtle difference in the energy flow between the two positions.

1. BREATH RELAXATION

Feel the connection to your body. Allow yourself to come into *the moment,* through sensing your connection to the body. *Drop all sense of striving.* Drop all intention to achieve anything, even in these exercises. Come more and more into the moment, the place where healing occurs and where the Witness resides.

Begin a gentle *connected* breath, with a 1:1 ratio. Breathe easily and smoothly. Watch the breath as it goes in and out. Feel it in the body. Again drop all sense of striving, of needing to make anything happen. Allow everything to be as it is. Gently keep breathing, with the conscious connection of inhale and exhale. Allow the breath to take you to deep alpha levels of relaxation and quiet in the body.

(2 minutes)

2. AURA
STRENGTHENING

Continue the connected breath but do not pay attention to it. Let it find its own level.

Visualize your aura around you. See a sphere perhaps six feet in diameter with colorful, charged electrical particles inside.

As you inhale, visualize a beam of luminescent, silver-white light shining down from the sun, entering the top of your head, and going down to your solar plexus, where it forms an energy ball about one foot in diameter. See the light as dazzling, powerful, dominating, burning away negativity it encounters.

As you exhale, visualize the energy ball at your solar plexus expanding outward to fill the entire space inside your aura. Visualize the particles extending to the edge of your aura, where they form a shell. Visualize (*see and feel*) the shell as strong and impenetrable. Visualize vibrations outside the shell being deflected as they try to pass through.

Feel deeply the archetypal, yang, masculine qualities of the light, and your relation to them: strength, protection, dominance, willfulness, competence.

(2 minutes)

AURA STRENGTHENING

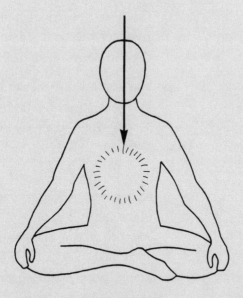

Inhale – Bring in Yang Healing Energy from above

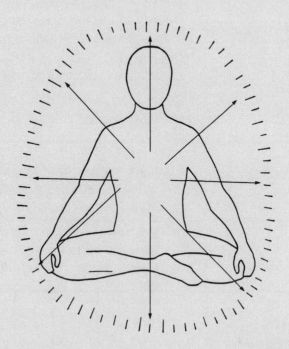

Exhale – Visualize Energy strengthening the aura

3. GROUNDING

Continue the connected breath. Remember to both see and feel as you visualize.

Visualize a link from the center of the earth to your first chakra, the Survival center, located at the base of the spine.

As you inhale, visualize blue-green earth energy coming from the center of the earth along the link, touching your first chakra, and filling up your entire body. Visualize the energy as vibrant, warm, nurturing, loving.

As you exhale, visualize the blue-green color absorbing negativity, turning to a reddish-black color, and being pulled by the earth through the first chakra, back to the center of the earth, where it is neutralized. See it being neutralized and dissolving into the earth.

Invoke the presence of the archetypal, yin, feminine by simply inviting her. Allow the qualities of the feminine to come forward, and *feel them deeply:* softness, caring, receptivity, compassion, nurturing, sensuality, unconditional love.

(2 minutes)

GROUNDING

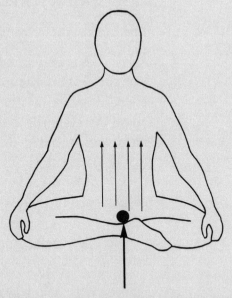

Inhale – Draw up Yin Healing Energy from the Earth

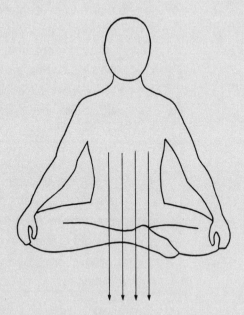

Exhale – Discharge Negativity into the Earth

4. ENTERING
THE WITNESS

Continue the same breath.

Keeping your eyes closed, look up with the physical eyes to the Third Eye point. This point is between and above the eyebrows, on the forehead. You should strain the eyes slightly, looking up as far as possible. Look into the blackness with the physical eyes. Keep straining as long as comfortable – it is the straining that activates the psychophysiological response.

Visualize both yang energy coming from above and yin energy coming from below, meeting at the Third Eye as you inhale. As you exhale, you can visualize the energies spinning clockwise or just being still in the Third Eye, whichever feels best. You may want to use only one of these energies, depending on which you need most.

Invite the Witness to come forward. *Feel* the qualities of the Witness: detachment from the Lower Self body, thoughts, and feelings; disidentification; choicelessness; unconditional happiness.

(2 minutes)

ENTERING THE WITNESS

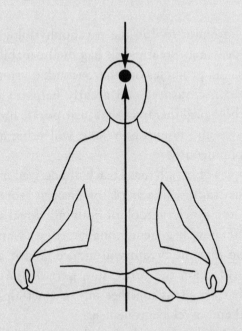

Inhale – Bring up both Yin and Yang Energy

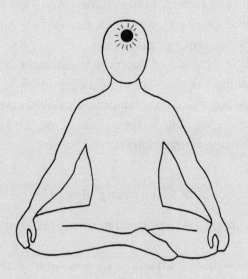

Exhale – Hold Energy at Third Eye

BREATHWORK

Breathwork is a major tool in the psychophysiological aspect of Integrative Processing. Breathwork has dual capabilities. First, it calms, relaxes, and promotes healing. Second, it brings suppressed material into consciousness and greatly helps to integrate the material. Psychological therapies that incorporate breathwork can be nonaggressive and noninvasive, and will bring about healing gently and spontaneously.

The principles of breath that I teach are derived from my exposure to various traditional schools of Eastern esoteric science. I see the breath as a powerful tool for both individual and therapist/client work. When we begin emotional work, we want to be in the deep relaxation that the breath will induce. When working with clients, I always begin the processing part of the session with breathwork that brings us together into a quiet alpha state, and into emotional and psychic attunement.

We have spoken of prana, the invisible energy that is contained in the air. In breathwork, it is prana with which we are working. As the breath is drawn in, prana is also drawn in. Visualizations are used to send the energy to various parts of the physical/energy body to perform cleansing and healing.

Maintain an attitude of acceptance throughout breathwork. Accept all feelings. You will become aware of physical and emotional feelings, but make no attempt to change them; instead, surrender to them. Enter the Witness, and allow the Higher Self to direct the balancing of the energies.

The Cleansing Breath

The Cleansing breath is performed in sitting meditation, as part of regular practice.

Do not perform any breathing exercise immediately after eating; wait an hour or two, until digestion is complete.

Make sure that clothing is not tight and constrictive on the body. Even the subtle pressure of the elastic around the waist from undergarments can contribute significantly to the sense of being split from lower body chakras. I recommend wearing only loose clothing for breathwork, such as a robe, with no undergarments, or even no clothes when possible.

During deep and regenerative breathing you may feel the need to yawn. Yawning is a physiological response to the prana that is taken in. Do not be confused by this impulse, but rather regard it as a sign that recharging is taking place. Allow yourself to yawn, but try to maintain the flow of the breath as you do. Usually it is easier to yawn near the end of the exhale. During the yawn, you probably will need to open the mouth and exhale partially through the mouth.

There are several elements to the Cleansing breath. Your aim is to eventually incorporate all these elements simultaneously.

Nose Breathing

Breathe only through the nose. As the air flows through the nasal passages, it is filtered and warmed; these are essential steps for optimal absorption of the breath by the body.

Posture

The most critical aspect of posture concerns the spine. The spine must be held in an upright, relaxed position. It should not be forced absolutely straight but kept in alignment with its natural curvature, so that a sense of delicate balance is achieved. You may have to shift vertebrae, moving some forward or back. The head is loosely held upright. The shoulders as well as all the muscles are consciously relaxed.

Correct alignment is important because the chakras connect to each other through the nerves that run through the spine. Small changes in the alignment of the spine therefore will affect the electrical exchange between chakras, influencing the energy flow and the feelings.

The best position to achieve alignment is sitting with no back support, not leaning against anything, including a wall or back-rest. It is hard for many of us to do this is because sitting with an unsupported back immediately begins releasing negativity held in the chakras. If you accept the pains and strains that come up, you cleanse the blocks in the chakras. Sitting in this manner for breath-work and meditation is the main practice of the Buddhist Vipas-sana tradition.

Over the years, my capacity for sitting has increased, and I feel there has been a correlation between this and my inner cleansing. A practical approach for you if you are a beginner might be to start sitting unsupported for as long as you can. When you feel you have reached your toleration point, lean back against a support to continue. You will gradually build your capacity.

I have become used to sitting in the traditional cross-legged position. I find it induces more of a grounded feeling than sitting in a chair. The overall energy pattern of the body is optimally config-ured, with no leakage out of arms or legs. Prana that runs down the limbs is returned to the body. Circulation in the legs is reduced, and more blood goes into the brain.

Cross-legged sitting is easiest in the so-called easy pose, where the legs do not actually cross. There is no need to strain to get into the half or full lotus position. Sitting on the edge of a firm cushion with your pelvis tilted forward slightly will make it even more comfortable.

If your legs are too stiff for cross-legged sitting, you can use the kneeling pose, sitting on your legs and ankles, perhaps with a pil-low or bench between your butt and your ankles. This pose is per-fectly fine, although it is not considered quite as energy retentive as the easy pose and is harder to maintain for long periods. If neither of these suits you, you can use a chair. Just make sure you sit on the edge of the chair, and do not lean back. In all of the poses, your hands should be either on your knees (palms down) or clasped in your lap.

Progressive Filling

When taking a breath, fill the lower part of the torso first, progres-sively working upward until the very uppermost lungs are filled. You should fill in stages, with each stage corresponding to one of the first seven chakras:

Easy Pose

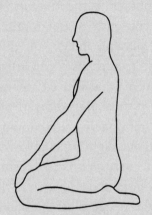

Kneeling Pose

Sitting Pose

CHAKRA	BODY LOCATION
1. Survival	Base of Spine
2. Power	Perineum
3. Sensation	Lower Abdomen
4. Nurturing	Navel
5. Significance	Solar Plexus
6. Heart	Chest
7. Expression	Throat

Of course, air is not actually sent into the lower areas, but you can expand them during the inhale because of the action of the diaphragm. The diaphragm is the muscular horizontal membrane under the lungs. As you push air down into the lower lungs, they in turn act on the diaphragm and expand the abdominal and perineum areas outward. You feel as if you are sending air into those areas, but a large part of what you are feeling is the prana.

When filling, you must not allow the abdomen to become bloated. Keep some tension in the abdominal muscles, allowing the abdomen to push out slightly as the lower lungs are filled.

The upper chest corresponds to sections of the lungs that extend upward toward the shoulders, areas that we normally don't fill. You should fill the upper chest consciously, relating it to the Throat center.

After the lungs have been progressively filled, you exhale in opposite order, emptying the upper lungs first and then the lower areas.

You can get a sense of how to begin progressive filling by first exhaling. Empty the upper chest, midchest, solar plexus, navel area, and lower abdomen, contracting each area as you exhale. Then you must bring into play another diaphragm of the body, the *perineum*. This is not usually taught to beginners, but I think that knowing about it is to your advantage.

The perineum is on the bottom side of the abdomen, running between the genital and anal areas, right in the crotch. If you experiment, you will find that you can contract this diaphragm independently of other areas of the body. The sensation is that of lifting and tightening the muscles of the crotch.

Besides contracting the perineum, you also can contract the anal area, called the "root lock." You tighten and lift the area, separately from the perineum. Control of these areas is part of advanced yoga and is instrumental in activating and clearing the lower chakras. The anal contraction corresponds to the first chakra, the Survival center. The perineum contraction corresponds to the second chakra, the Power center.

To complete the exhale, contract the perineum and then the anal area, pushing out the last air from the lungs. You should have a tight, solid feeling in the lower body.

As you inhale, release the lower contractions, expanding the body and allowing air to rush in. After filling the anal and perineum areas, the lower abdomen fills, followed by the navel, solar plexus, midchest, and upper chest.

If this is too involved for you, you can skip over contracting the lower areas individually and just contract the lower abdomen as a whole. This is how the breath is usually taught to beginners.

Blocks in the breath reflect blocks in the chakras

The progressive fill is an important tool for locating your blocks. Observe yourself carefully as you breathe. Watch the body. Sit quietly. Witness. Try to breathe in a smooth, continuous fashion, but you probably will find that this is not possible. Your body will jerk, and your breath will be uneven. As you fill your lungs from bottom to top, you may feel slight pain, discomfort, or tightness in certain parts of the body. These sensations correspond to blocks in the chakras.

The blocks are worked by accepting and experiencing them. Continue the breath, making sure to breathe into all parts of the torso, especially into areas that may be difficult to breathe into or into areas where you may never breathe. Watch without comment or choice as the breath encounters the blocks. Accept the sensations. Allow yourself to just *be with* them.

Allow your breath to come to its own equilibrium as you continue to practice, and for smoothness to gradually develop as you integrate feelings that arise as cleansing proceeds during breathwork. In time, the unevenness and discomfort will diminish, corresponding to the diminishing of the blocks in chakras.

Tongue Position

The tongue acts like a switch in the energy circuit of the body. When the tongue is pressed against the roof of the mouth, as far to the rear as comfortable, the switch is closed and energy will circulate. Maintain this position at all times while doing the Cleansing breath.

This position of the tongue stimulates the flow of saliva, which is regarded as beneficial and a help to circulating energies. Try to develop the ability to swallow whenever necessary without disrupting the flow of the breath. It may be easiest to do this toward the end of the exhale but before the turning point to the inhale is reached.

Throttling

After the tongue is in place, you may further adjust the throat muscles, resulting in a partial constriction of the air passage. If you experiment with the muscles of the throat, around the vocal cords, eventually you will find the proper position. You will know you are constricting the throat correctly when you are able to accomplish two functions: throttling and inner sound.

As air is both inhaled and exhaled, the constriction of the air passage serves as a throttle to control the rate of flow into the lungs. The feeling is a steady flow into and out of the lungs, with the constricted throat muscles doing the throttling.

Inner Sound

At the same time, the constriction of the throat causes the air to make a sound as it passes through. The sounds originate from the central throat region, not in the mouth or nasal cavities. On the inhale, adjust the muscles of the throat to make a deep "aah" sound. On the exhale, make a hissing "ee" sound. If you can make these sounds, you are constricting the air passage correctly. The sounds have a vibratory influence on the energy system, raising and purifying the vibrations. In modern times, this principle has been rediscovered and called "toning." As you add the toning element to the breath, you add a new dimension to the effectiveness of your practice.

The sound should not be too loud but should not be faint either. It may vary in your breathwork, depending on whether you are emphasizing it. Sometimes you may wish to focus entirely on the sound, increasing the benefits of the vibration. Try to physically sense the high-frequency vibration as it travels through the energy body. Send the vibration to chakras on which you are working by visualizing it happening. The inhale sound encourages the inflow of prana to that area, and the exhale sound is the outflow of stagnant energy from the area.

You may use the inner sound as the focus of meditation, feeling the vibrations as they resonate through the body. At the same time, be conscious of the throttling effect produced by the constriction of the throat.

Connected Breathing

In connected breathing, inhale and exhale are joined so that there is absolutely no pause between them. The inhale transitions smoothly and effortlessly into the exhale and the exhale into the inhale. There is no resting of the lungs between expansion and contraction. This does not imply rushing or hurrying between inhale and exhale. On the contrary, the breath is taken slowly and steadily, but without any sense of pause.

Why connected breathing has the effect that it does is something of a mystery from the physiological standpoint, but linking inhale and exhale will take you into deeper mystical experiences with the breath. The physical breath, with its in-and-out movement, represents the yin/yang, dualistic nature of the universe. Connecting inhale and exhale serves to integrate our experience of duality, connect the left and right brains, and make our experience whole.

There is also something about linking inhale and exhale that augments cleansing effectiveness. It allows prana to build up instead of escape during a pause. Linking inhale and exhale is one of the most important parts of the breath cycle. It is an area where your expertise and realization will continue to grow. Linking inhale and exhale will take on new meaning and experience throughout your practice.

The connected aspect of the breath can be an effective focus point for meditation that will take you to deeper states.

Ratio

Ratio of breath refers to the ratio of the time for inhale and exhale. In a ratio equation, the inhale is always first and the exhale is second. In the Cleansing breath, the ratio is 1:2, which means the exhale is twice as long as the inhale. You may inhale to the count of eight, for example, and exhale to the count of sixteen. In a breath with a ratio of 1:1, inhale and exhale are of equal lengths, regardless of the time.

Rate

When you are counting, the length of each count should be about one second, although you don't have to time your breath with a watch. Start with whatever lengths of cycle are comfortable, but keep the 1:2 ratio. You may start with 4:8, inhaling for four seconds, exhaling for eight. You may then go to 5:10, for example. Gradually build up to 8:16 as the final ratio.

During the exhale, suppressed energies are released from the chakras. Be patient during the long exhale, and watch as feelings may jump into consciousness to be integrated; do not resist them. I find that I sometimes get a better sense of being in the moment with the exhale if I imagine that I am actually holding the breath instead of exhaling, although, of course, I continue to exhale. The exhale is so slow that it just feels like holding.

Depth

Depth of breath is controlled by the volume of air that is taken in. Depth will vary from a very full breath to a very shallow breath, depending on where you are in your breathwork.

At the start of a breathwork session, you probably will want to use a deep inhale, which expands all the areas of the torso. Filling to maximum capacity brings in maximum prana, but be careful not to strain too much. A comfortable sense of fill will do.

As meditation continues, your requirements for breath will change, and you will learn to adjust automatically. Your breathing may become very shallow as you go deeper into a breathwork meditation. This can be an exquisite and delicate feeling, when you are sensing energy movements in the chakras with almost no physical breath.

Additional Breathwork Techniques

These are additional breath techniques that you will employ to focus and move energy in the body. Allow your body to tell you when you need to use them.

Third Eye

Stay focused on the Third Eye point for the entire breathwork meditation, as when you entered Alpha.

Orbiting

Orbiting is an exercise that serves to move energy around the body when the energy is stuck, and to vitalize and balance all the chakras together, influencing the feelings. This is one of the best for steady, quiet, meditative breathwork. If you are using this technique, you will not be using the progressive fill.

Assume there is a path from the base of the spine up to the top of the head, in the back of the body. Assume there is another path in the front of the body, from the top of the head down to the base of the spine. These two paths together constitute the orbit. Visualize energy traveling up the path at the back, along the spine, as you inhale, and down the path at the front of the body as you exhale. Both see and feel. Imagine a bright, luminescent, blue ball of energy.

Chakra Breathing

Chakra breathing is one of the most important techniques we use. This technique is effective with either the Cleansing breath, when you are in quiet meditation and wish to heal a certain chakra, or with the Integrating breath, when strong feelings are surfacing.

In chakra breathing, you breathe directly into any chakra, directing prana to it. With any chakra located in the torso, expand and contract the area of the body that corresponds to the chakra. There may still be some sense of progressive filling. Visualize healing energy going into the chakra as you breathe. Don't reject any feelings that come up. If you want to work with all the chakras, start with the first, the Survival center, and work up to the Crown chakra at the top of the head, with a full inhale and exhale for each center.

For example, try breathing into your solar plexus. As you breathe, carefully sense the motion that takes place. Feel the body gently expanding in this particular area on the inhale, and contracting on the exhale. Use a 1:1 ratio of breath. When you have sensed the expansion and contraction clearly, you are breathing into the center.

After breathing in this manner for a while, reduce the volume of air, still sensing the movement in the body. Keep reducing the volume of breath to only the slightest possible amount, and then to the point where there is no air actually entering or leaving the lungs, but only the suggestion of breath. You still may be able to sense a expansion/contraction in the area of the solar plexus, even though there is no comparable motion in the physical body. What you are sensing is the motion of the chakra – or, rather, the motion of the energy body, since the chakra is composed of energy. You have reduced the volume of air to zero only for the purposes of this exercise; when you normally breathe into a chakra, there should be some amount of air entering and leaving. Resume normal inhale and exhale and end the exercise.

You may now sense the Third Eye and Crown chakras in the same manner. Of course, you can't expand the body at these centers, but you can still feel the motion of the chakra itself.

Sensing chakras requires sensitivity. If you succeed, you can assume that you already have a fair amount of psychic skill. If you can't sense the chakras, don't worry. The ability will come with practice.

When you are meditating, you may choose which breath and ratio you need. If strong emotions are coming up, go to the Integrating breath, breathing into the appropriate chakra. You may increase your breathing rate slightly. Change positions, if necessary. Continue until the feeling has shifted and the intensity has lessened.

You also may connect any chakra to the universal energy source above, and the grounding earth below as you breathe into it, which we will discuss shortly. Visualize strong white light coming from above, entering the chakra as you inhale, displacing negativity to the ground as you exhale.

The Integrating Breath

The Integrating breath is a variation of the basic Cleansing breath. We use it in two ways: first, whenever suppressed feelings or emotions are coming up strongly and there is a need for larger amounts of prana to help integrate them. This can happen either in practice or during stressful events.

Second, if we push this breath more strenuously, we can use it for "accelerated" breath sessions, when we wish to go especially deep into emotional clearing. The oxygen and prana build in the body, dramatically bringing suppressed emotions into awareness and at the same time implementing integration. Sessions can reach the point of radically altering consciousness, shifting through levels of inner awareness rapidly. Emotional issues integrate, self-love is intensified, and body/mind healing is augmented. Catharsis can be achieved almost at will.

The Integrating breath, when used in this manner, offers an alternative to the more gentle healing of the Cleansing breath. You may choose either breath to be the focus of your breathwork, depending on your preference. The gentleness of the Cleansing breath will, over time, give you a completely adequate approach to inner integration. The Integrating breath is a more active approach, tending to precipitate a healing crisis. There is no danger in using the Integrating breath, but it does call for more of the warrior spirit. Here are the important points:

- Try to breathe mainly through the nose, but you may also breathe through the mouth if you need a large volume of air. Do not alternate between nose and mouth during the same breath cycle; for example, if you inhale through the mouth, exhale through the mouth.

- Posture is not important. The Integrating breath is usually performed lying on the back, but any position may be used. You may want to change positions during the session, even going into yoga poses, which are particularly helpful now to work with the breath in freeing up blocked energy.

- Do not observe the progressive fill. Instead, breathe directly into the chakra(s) involved, expanding and contracting primarily that part of the body, when possible. For example, you may breathe into the abdominal area, Solar Plexus, upper chest, or all of these. Experiment in different areas to see what effect the breath has on the emotions that surface.

- The same tongue position as the Cleansing breath is helpful but not mandatory.

- Do not close the throat or use throttling or inner sound. Instead, there is a sense of "letting go" on the exhale. The body completely relaxes on the exhale, and the breath is allowed to find its own way out. Relaxing on the exhale is a critical part of this breath. Do not try to control the exhale in any way. Just relax all the muscles of the chest, and let gravity push the air out.

- Connected breathing is the most critical aspect of this breath, and you must be very careful to observe it. The purpose of connected breathing here is to build the level of oxygen and prana. If you pause between inhale and exhale, the oxygen and prana are allowed to dissipate, and no energy collects to enable the breath to perform its function.

- Do not observe any set ratio. As the exhale is released, let it find its own rate; this may either be faster or slower than the inhale.

- The rate of breath applies only to the inhale, because you are letting the exhale find its own rate. You may use any inhale rate, ranging from slow (6 to 8 seconds) to fast (½ second). Experiment to see what effect the different inhale rates have on you; it varies with individuals. Do not try to control the exhale rate; let it happen by itself.

- Vary the depth from shallow to full.

A typical accelerated breathwork session with the Integrating breath will last about one hour. When you begin the session, you want to use a full and fast breath to bring in as much oxygen and prana as possible. As you proceed, you will intuitively change the rate and depth to control your experience.

Breathing in this manner gets the energy moving in your body. You will feel various physiological sensations as well as emotions. The first sensation is usually that it becomes difficult to keep up the fast breathing rate required for the breath to have any effect. You will feel that you have to push very hard; be careful not to slow down your rate to the point where the breath is ineffective. You might become sleepy and drift off, forgetting to breathe for a short period. This is not dangerous – you will always wake up when you need more air.

Other sensations may be tingling in hands and body, a sense of the energy rushing about the body, pressures or pains in parts of the body, or similar occurrences. These are all energy sensations and mean that you are proceeding correctly. Negative emotions will start to come up intensely and should be processed. You should be ready for feelings that you may never have confronted before. For all these reasons, you should be somewhat experienced in inner work before launching off into a heavy session with this breath, and you may want to have a friend, therapist, or other breathwork professional with you to watch and guide you.

After clearing negative emotions, more blissful states of consciousness will come about. Feelings of universal love, oceanic oneness, heightened and expanded consciousness are all possible. This breath can lead to truly altered states of consciousness. The accelerated form of the Integrating breath is too intense to be used on a regular basis, even though the benefits are great. Using it in a more gentle way, not pushing as much, will be easier to manage and also will be beneficial, along with the Cleansing breath. You should incorporate both of these breaths into your practice; each serves to activate you in a different way.

Hyperventilation

In using the Integrating breath, the only possible physiological difficulty you might encounter is hyperventilation. In hyperventilation, the oxygen/carbon dioxide ratio in the body becomes unbalanced, and you get too much oxygen in the blood. The symptoms include involuntary tightening of the muscles, dizziness, lightheadedness, rapid or forced breathing, and in rare instances eventually passing out, in which case you will always come back to consciousness.

Hyperventilation occurs because the exhale is tensed and controlled instead of being relaxed and uncontrolled. If you feel like you are hyperventilating, keep breathing but slow down your breathing to a normal rate, and be very careful to relax your body completely on the exhale. Relax all muscles, and just let gravity take out the air.

Breathwork Meditation

As you incorporate breathwork into a regular practice, it becomes a kind of meditation in itself. Our intention here is to be *nondirective* – to bring ourselves into a place where spontaneous releasing of the subconscious will occur without any specific seeking out. Release will happen in most types of meditation unless you are engaging in "suppressive meditation," but using the breath will be even more effective.

You should keep in mind the basic principles of acceptance as you sit to breathe. Although the breath is performed to achieve a certain result, you should not become compulsively goal-oriented. It is best not to look forward to results, not to live in the future, not to get nervous about performing correctly. Maintain your sense of being in the moment, and your sense of the body.

As you proceed with the breath, cleansing may begin. Physical, emotional, intuitive, and psychic feelings may surface. They will usually be of a disturbing nature; that is why they were suppressed originally. Do not resuppress by rejecting, resisting, or trying to control the feelings, but process them – accept and experience them – as we have discussed. You may want to occasionally reactivate the Witness. Eventually you will find you can be doing any meditation and also be resting in the Third Eye.

Try to incorporate all the various parts of the breath, possibly emphasizing what it feels like you need at that time. It is also good, as you develop your practice, to take one aspect and concentrate on it on a regular day. Establish a weekly routine, using that aspect on a consistent day of the week. The seventh day can be used to combine all of them, or even to take a break from practice. Each aspect activates cleansing differently, also adding variety to practice. As you continue to practice, the different aspects become part of the unconscious mind and they will all automatically occur at once, whenever you sit to breathe.

Day/Breath

1. Progressive Fill

2. Chakra Breathing

3. Inner Sound/Throttling

4. Connected Breath/Ratio

5. Orbiting

6. Third Eye

It is usually best to maintain the upright sitting position for breathwork, but if you feel so inclined, you may experiment with other positions, such as lying down or a yoga posture. The important point, except if you are using a yoga pose, is that the spine be kept straight. Sitting and leaning back is not good because the spine is curved and the front of the body compressed, making it difficult to sense the body and open the chakras.

MEDITATIVE PROCESSING

For meditative processing, you are going to meditate as we discussed in Chapter 8. Use a focus point if you prefer, or use the breath as the focus point. It is usually best to be sitting or lying on your back, with the spine straight, unless your body is indicating that it needs another position, such as the fetal position or a movement. I have found that both sitting and lying are good, and I use both equally. If I have a specific, urgent feeling that I am working with, I usually sit. If I want to nondirectively enter deep alpha or theta and experiment with altered states, I usually lie down. Allow yourself to be spontaneous.

This final phase of practice naturally results from the preceding two steps. You will drift into a deeper, relaxed state, no longer concentrating specifically on the breath. Your focus will be either directive or nondirective, depending on whether emotionally charged material is surfacing.

The Body

Whether meditation is directive or nondirective, it is important to remember to stay in contact with the body. Always watch the body. Be sensitive to feelings that are coming up in the body. If any sensation has arisen, take it as an energetic clearing in progress, and witness it. Allow it to lead to other feelings, both physical or emotional. Breathe into it. Give priority to body-based feelings, both physical and emotional.

Nondirective Meditation

The essence of meditation is to bring the activity of the mind to a halt. Thoughts block the meditative experience. In our work, we distinguish between thoughts and feelings. We allow thoughts to cease, so we can more deeply sense feelings. When the energy of the feelings has dissipated, meditation can go into other areas of inner experience.

If no strong feelings are coming up for you, allow yourself to simply be in the alpha state. Enjoy its peacefulness. Keep reactivating healing energy and the Witness. Keep returning to your focus point if you are using one. You may even use the body itself as a focus point, simply staying in the moment without seeking or striving.

Directive Processing

If strong feelings spontaneously come up as a result of your meditation, you will shift to processing them. If feelings do not spontaneously come up, you may deliberately choose to work on any specific emotional issue that may be occupying you, at the time. You might devote a period of a few weeks to working on recurring fear, resentment, or loneliness. If you need a stimulus to bring up the feeling, visualize in your meditation the incident or occurrence that is associated with the feeling. Process the feeling by owning, accepting, being with, and witnessing. Breathe into the corresponding chakra, enhancing the clearing and integrating effect. Use bodywork whenever appropriate. Bring in healing energy and self-love by entering the Witness before, during, and after each session. You may relive past unfinished situations or just work with whatever is happening currently in your life.

CLOSE PRACTICE

It is important to make a formal ending to the practice session. This trains the mind to close "the door to the subconscious" until the next session. The subconscious will learn that since it is being given a voice into consciousness during practice, it need no any longer resort to projection in order to be heard.

Closing

Ground down to the earth one final time, to disperse all negativity. See the negativity being absorbed and neutralized by the earth.

Bring in more white light from above. Feel it as joyous and powerful, filling any dark places that have resulted from negativity releasing.

Close the door to the subconscious by willing that it be so. Deliberately bring yourself back to normal consciousness.

Emotional Clearing Practice Summary

Emotional clearing practice has four main parts:

BODYWORK. When possible, use a brief yoga or other bodywork session at the start of practice to relax you and to open the chakras. (5 to 15 minutes)

ACTIVATING HEALING ENERGY. Perform this each time you sit for practice and during the session to reactivate the Witness. (5 to 10 minutes)

BREATHWORK MEDITATION. Use a different breathwork aspect for each day of the week, on a regular basis. (5 to 10 minutes)

MEDITATIVE PROCESSING. Use directive or nondirective meditation, depending on what is coming up. (10 to 30 minutes)

I have indicated approximate times above, but as you become comfortable with your routine, feel free to adjust times as you need. It would be optimal to practice twice a day, from twenty minutes to one hour each time, possibly with one short session and one longer session. If you can't find time for two sessions, do one session per day. Don't think you have to learn the practice routine all at once. Feel free to go step by step. The above exercises are a synthesis derived from traditional Yogic, Buddhist, and other esoteric disciplines. Stay with it, and you will definitely get positive results.

I understand that the conflict I undergo is the result of being attached to one side of any dualistic experience while trying to avoid the other side. I understand that no amount of the "positive" will ever be fulfilling and that to heal myself, I must integrate the "negative" directly, through accepting and experiencing it. In so doing, I transcend the emotional roller coaster I have been riding. I find true fulfillment. I have grown.

12

Integrating

In working on ourselves, we integrate both sides of any dualistic experience. Our problem is that we reject one side and cling dependently to the other side, creating pain. We develop compulsive needs. We allow ourselves to be driven.

To integrate a dualistic pattern means to stop chasing after the positive in an effort to avoid the negative; to accept and experience the negative, on a feeling level. As we allow ourselves to simply feel what we previously were resisting, we start to come into balance. The pain of the negative is released instead of suppressed, and we no longer perceive it as an urgent need that we are driven compulsively to satisfy.

What must be understood is that no matter what extremes we take to satisfy compulsive needs, we will never get enough, because of the dualistic nature of existence. When we achieve more of the positive, it only brings with it more of the negative. Compulsive seeking can be felt in any center of consciousness. This chapter covers integration of some of the more basic areas, but let's start with the general condition of depression.

INTEGRATING DEPRESSION

There is no question in my mind that the buildup of suppressed feelings results in the chronic depressed and manic-depressive conditions. Depression is not a disease or illness that we catch, even in its most severe forms. It is not genetically acquired, even though persons who are susceptible to it may tend to be attracted to one another and may even incarnate in family groups, as will occur with other characteristics as well. Depression is the result of ignorance and mismanagement of experience. We fall into a pattern of suppressing feelings instead of allowing them to release, which results in addictive tendencies, depletion of energy, and the condition we call depression.

If you are experiencing significant depression, you need to enter on a dedicated program, either by yourself or with help, of releasing these suppressed feelings. Many feelings – basic feelings such as anxiety, anger, loneliness, jealousy, sexual compulsiveness – are likely to be already conscious, waiting to be engaged properly so they can be cleared. If you work with them, you will be led to deeper core feelings and patterns that will ultimately result in complete healing and balance.

If you are conscious only of the depression and not of any negative feelings in particular, then you are in a *repressed* condition – without awareness – and working to uncover and release the feelings is even more urgent. The repressed feelings attract adversity, failure, accident, and ultimately result in break-down of the physical body.

Don't react to depression by trying to escape or compensate through other activities. Don't blame circumstances, events, or other people for your depression. It is possible to lose perspective and project depression onto unrelated areas of life, thinking that you are depressed because of this or that condition without under-standing the real cause. Instead, process the depression.

Processing the experience of depression, even though it is the result of suppression and not a real feeling in itself, may proceed exactly as with any feeling. Recognize that depression is an ener-getic condition. Feel it, witness it, as an energetic experience. Detach and break your identification with it. Use the powerful tools of breathwork and bodywork. Activate healing energy, enter alpha, and especially breathe into the feelings of depression. Allow the healing energies of the universe to come in as you accept and watch. As you engage the feeling of depression, surrender entirely to the sensation. Allow the depression *to be*. Doing only this can bring tremendous relief, because you are no longer trying to avoid.

Ceasing resistance to the depression will change your entire energy flow. As you sit with depression, the feelings that are behind it eventually will come into awareness to be processed. These can be any feelings; no one particular type of feeling is behind depression. Do not think you are getting worse when this happens. Recognize that the subconscious is being revealed to be healed. Trust that you are being guided and protected.

Depression is the condition of energy depletion

Suppressing feelings requires large amounts of psychic energy. The resulting energetic depletion is the condition we call depres-sion. When you work with feelings of depression, you will sense a recharging taking place. The Higher Self will draw energy to you automatically to replenish your exhausted reserves. When the experience of depression itself is integrated, it becomes the natural complement to expenditure of psychic energies. Depression becomes the time to recharge, to heal. It can be joyous and restful, once surrendered to. Physical imbalances that may correspond to the energy depletion also will come into alignment.

Mild depression will arise from normal cycles of living. Since we are active beings, a certain amount of depression is inevitable; it is the complement to activity. If you can accept and open to depression, you will recharge your energy reserves instead of suppressing the depression with rejecting attitudes, such as becoming depressed about the depression.

Depression can be suppressed and stored in the energy body; the depletion becomes larger and is unable to recharge. If you have a pattern of avoiding depression, you probably have a good deal of suppressed depression. You will have to work with it in a reasonable manner, not exceeding your toleration point. Do not react to your depression; do not become motivated by it. Eventually acceptance will bring you to the point where you experience depression as the natural recharging of energies.

Chemical substances
act as suppressants

All chemical substances used to modify feelings, including depression, do not serve actually to resolve the feelings but only to *suppress* the feelings from conscious awareness. This includes natural substances such as St. John's wort as well as prescription drugs. Unfortunately, that it may be of "natural" origin does not change the way any mood-altering substance works: by suppressing feelings. If we regularly turn to substances as the means to control feelings, we are only digging ourselves deeper into the dark hole of suppression.

I view the medical establishment's reliance on pharmacology as the primary strategy for handling mood disorder as materialistic ignorance of the highest degree. Brain chemistry is the *result* of feelings, not the other way around, and trying to change brain chemistry to change feelings is simply absurd. Whether it's lithium, Prozac, illegal drugs, alcohol, caffeine, nicotine, St. John's wort, or any of the newest, latest designer drugs, all chemically induced mood changes take us *out of* our feelings. Integration becomes impossible. We enter a no-man's land of self-rejection, cut off from our soul and the eventuality of real healing. The popularity of mood-altering substance use today is a compelling comment on both the poverty of the world's emotional state and the utter lack of comprehension about how to handle it.

However, in spite of my condemnation of substance usage, at times it may be called for. If conditions are so severe that it is impossible to function, perhaps extremely judicious use of substances is justified when coupled with other forms of psychological work – meditation, breathwork, bodywork, processing, therapy, or support groups. But you should recognize that progress with inner work is not really possible when substances are used; feelings are not available for processing. They are kept suppressed by the substance. You are merely treading water and will eventually experience a backlash from the suppression that the substance causes. If you are using any form of substance, your priority should be getting off it so that work may proceed.

Release yourself from the illness and "syndrome" trap

The medical establishment is fond of labeling depression an illness. I wish to make clear that, in my opinion, implying that depression is an illness is a disservice to the person as well as an impediment to resolution. Illness is usually interpreted to mean something has been "caught"; it is beyond the individual's control, and the "cure" must be effected by outside intervention. Even though the motive behind the labeling of the patient's condition as illness may be benevolent – trying to assuage feelings a patient may have of being "bad" – the subtle shift of responsibility away from self and into a blaming or victim mode (it's the illness, not me) undermines the most basic healing orientation, that of taking full responsibility for oneself and one's condition.

The medical establishment currently is encouraging this distortion of responsibility by identifying and blaming a multitude of other "syndromes" for behavior or experience. I understand the need for a label to identify types of behavior, but what is implied is, again, that an illness is present. Instead, we need to understand that behavioral acting out is a form of *defense* from underlying feelings, especially in the case of obsessive-compulsive syndrome and other similar ones, and that painful inner experience such as depression and even disease is the result of unconscious mismanagement of personal psychic energies.

INTEGRATING FEAR

Fear is of the Survival center. Fear comes into awareness as anxiety, insecurity, apprehensiveness, nervousness, or paranoia. We become fixated on issues of work, money, health, physical protection, and life itself. A certain amount of fear is necessary to survive in the world. Fear protects us. When fear is integrated, cautiousness and groundedness result, balanced with the instinct to provide for basic survival needs. Our impulses are tempered; we are sensible.

Unintegrated, we fear fear itself. We don't allow for fear as part of our groundedness; we reject and resist fear. We perceive fear as undesirable, something that should be eliminated instead of occupying a balanced place in our lives. In being motivated to eliminate fear, we suppress it. Fear builds in the subconscious until we become obsessed. We start projecting onto inappropriate situations. Fear builds to the point where we actually attract situations to us that correspond to the fear.

Fear cannot be defeated
by manipulating reality

It may take many years to learn that no matter what we do externally to fight fear, it will never be enough. Fear will always remain, because it is within. Some people never learn this. They spend their entire lives being motivated by fear, never eliminating it. Fear does not go away just because we make changes. It's true that we may find apparent temporary relief in a certain area, but the fear will emerge in another area. We just change the object onto which it is projected.

For example, you may have financial needs, but you project onto the situation and feel stress out of proportion. You become further confused and anxious when you find that it is not possible to satisfy your "needs," no matter how much money you acquire.

Your income may increase, but on the psychic level, your suppressed fears keep bringing you more expenses. You never get ahead. It is not the situation that is causing the stress but the suppressed feelings. Moreover, when we allow ourselves to be motivated by fear, we become dependent on whatever means we use to combat the fear, which leads to more insecurity and unrest.

Using other people as a means to eliminate fear results in unhealthy dependent relationships. We become resentful of our dependence, and it becomes impossible to maintain love. Unfortunately, fear is one of the main reasons for relationships today. We turn to relationships to try to eliminate fears regarding security, finances, loneliness, self-esteem, or sexual lack. We must learn that we can never escape from fear by means of buffers. Our fears are compulsive and must be integrated, not fought.

Are you being motivated by fear or love?

We need to be aware – it is all too easy to be unconsciously motivated by fear. To check your motivation, simply ask yourself whether you are being motivated by fear or by love. These are the two major types of motivation. When fear is the motivation, our interest is in the results of the activity; we don't really enjoy the activity itself. When love is the motivation, we do whatever we do because of the joy in the doing. We express our love in the doing. Any kind of reward is secondary.

It is possible to live a life based on the motivation of love, but not many of us achieve this. We are almost entirely motivated by fear. Fear on the Survival level usually comes into consciousness as anxiety about money and security, leading to greed and selfishness. Of course, we need money to survive, but if we were motivated by love, the money would follow. You may want to look closely at whether fear or love is ruling you. If you can add just a little each day to being motivated by love, your life can transform. Note that this doesn't mean being motivated by the fear of not having or losing a "loving" relationship.

The problem is that we can't be motivated by love when we hold suppressed fear. To be motivated by love, you must first clear the fear; otherwise, fear always will creep into your motivation. Facing and integrating the fear will result in its eventual balance.

Accept and experience your fear

Fear is integrated like any other emotion. When you feel anxious or insecure, or are about to make a decision or be motivated in order to eliminate fear, stop and process first. Accept the fear, enter the Witness and the direct experience of the fear. Do not be afraid of the fear. Feel the fear, without resistance. Open to it, in a controlled way, until you sense a change in the energy. If you have a chronic fear problem, you will have to do this over a period of time. Work with all emotions related to the Survival center, such as anxiety about loss of property or possessions, the compulsive desire for protection, insecurity in general, and the ultimate fear of death. Do not blame anyone, including yourself, for your situation.

Always remember to breathe into the emotion. Breathe directly into the Survival center. Use bodywork to free up the energy congestion in the root chakra. Bring light into the area, and clear negativity by grounding. Emphasize working in the Survival center in your practice if fear is a particular problem for you. You will bring about the condition of being motivated by love.

INTEGRATING SEX

When we have suppressed and blocked the Sensation center, we feel compulsive, distorted cravings for sex, sensuality, or other physical sensations. I have found that cravings can be handled effectively by working with them on the energy level, accepting and experiencing the craving without acting on it. Processing techniques will give you the power to do this. Do not condemn, try to fight, eliminate, or avoid cravings. They are very strong, and you will only fall into additional suppression.

Free up the energy in the chakras

In working on yourself, the goal is to free up blocked energy in the second and third chakras. Start with basic, semiregular physical exercise. Follow with a regular practice of bodywork, emphasizing these centers. Use contractions of the perineum and lower abdomen to stimulate release; these areas can be especially helpful. Use meditation and breathwork to bring in light and prana, and grounding to remove negativity. The lower chakras can be difficult to work with, so entrenched is our sexual repression, which I feel is the main reason for problems in this area.

As you work with the center, desires will be stimulated, and all kinds of feelings will surface. None of the desires or feelings should be condemned; that is what caused them to be suppressed in the first place. They must be accepted and inwardly experienced but not acted on, because at this stage, they are still compulsive.

Accept but don't act on compulsive sexual impulses

We have become conditioned to think that sexual impulses must be satisfied immediately. The reality, however, is that life, even under the best of conditions, does not allow for immediate expression of sexual impulses. Then we feel cheated. We feel as if we are missing out on our normal right. We develop a judgmental attitude about sexual impulses, unconsciously condemning them because they seem to bring more frustration than joy. We start suppressing sexual impulses as they come up, adding to the sense of sexual frustration. Suppression builds, and we become blocked and compulsive.

Suppression of sexual impulses may originate in other ways, relating to our personal history. What is important is not why we suppress but the recognition that this is what we do. Intellectually understanding the cause of the suppression will do little to change the pattern of suppression. The pattern has become established on an unconscious level and is maintained by the suppressed energy. It has reached the point of repression, where we suppress unknowingly. Working with the feelings of frustration that are conscious will bring eventual integration.

What needs to be acknowledged is the reality that sexual fulfillment is created and balanced by sexual tension. We reject and suppress the tension, creating the blocking. Part of our rejection is due to the intense nature of the sexual impulse, especially in men.

As we reject sexual tension, we try to escape from it. We pursue sex for its own sake instead of as the means to share and bond energies with a loved one.

If you begin accepting and experiencing sexual tension without acting on it, you can make major changes in your energy and growth patterns. This may sound like much to ask for, and it is. Only seekers who are committed to their growth and practice would want to extend such an approach to its logical conclusion, which would involve periods of sexual abstinence.

The esoteric physiology of celibacy is well understood by the masters of the East. They teach that as the sexual impulse is accepted but not acted on, the energy builds to the point where it rises to the other chakras and serves to stimulate them into awakening. The sexual center becomes integrated and serves as the main energy source for personal transformation. Transmutation of sexual energy is the basis of all advanced spiritual practice but should not be attempted until one is ready, when the paths in the body are opened so the energy actually can rise instead of building in the lower chakras.

In practical terms, accepting but not acting on means allowing the sexual impulse to exist, even possibly taking part in lovemaking, but without orgasm. Relinquishing orgasm is not the problem that it may first appear to be, because the buildup of sexual force is released upward, into the other chakras, instead of outward as in conventional orgasm. In the esoteric practice of *Tantra*, the focus is on controlling and transmuting the sexual force, relating it to the Kundalini energy. Transmutation is facilitated by the right kind of practice, involving yoga postures, breathing, and locks. Contraction of the perineum is the main lock used to diffuse and disperse sexual energy out of the lower centers and into the higher centers.

The important factor is to accept before not acting on. I feel many spiritual seekers make the mistake of suppressing their sexual impulses in the name of celibacy, even though they may not think they are doing so. The impulses must be consciously and deliberately accepted, even celebrated, but not acted on. Compulsive sexual impulses dissolve, like any other integrated feeling. After a while, the energy is likely to rise up higher into the body, without having to be forced. If the impulses are not accepted, the energy does not rise up to the other chakras. It becomes suppressed and held in the lower chakras.

Transmuting sexual energy may not be something you are ready for yet, but knowing about it may help influence your attitude about needing immediate release from sexual impulses. I might add that once sex is integrated and celibacy established, sexual frustration evaporates. There is no sense of continuing frustration or even the need for ordinary sexual release. Instead, there is a joyful sense of liberation from being a slave to sexual tension. On the other hand, sexual activity without conventional orgasm can still be entered into, without compulsiveness. It is like having the best of both worlds.

In my own experiments, I found that it took a few months to get past the initial frustration of not having the energy exit through the usual path when it built up. The energy instead rose to the top of my head, where I could feel the pressure building, and released back down into my body. After a few more months, I felt a tremendous release of sexual tension in the lower abdomen, the area of the third chakra.

This release occurred only after I had reached the point of fully accepting the sexual impulses I was feeling. Before that I thought I had accepted but had not; I was unconsciously resisting. The release happened one day when I was holding the cobra pose and witnessing the sexual impulse at the same time. I fell into the complete acceptance and experience of my sexual impulse and almost simultaneously felt a release of suppressed sexual tension. Included was suppressed tension of which I had not even been aware. The relaxation in the chakra was tremendous.

In this one experience, I cleared a good amount of the suppressed material that I had been carrying in the Sensation chakra. A major healing was beginning for me, as the sexual energy activated centers above it. I went into a period of cleansing the Solar Plexus and started to go through the suppressed negativity of that center as it came up.

Most of us are suppressed in the sexual centers. Therefore, it is difficult to go without normal sexual release. The very suppression blocks the energy from rising up and out of the lower into higher chakras, and release through orgasm is the sole alternative. If you begin working on this center, your experience of sex will gradually transform. Your capacity for noncompulsive enjoyment of sex, as well as the related areas of food, alcohol, or drugs, will increase. If you are dealing with one of these other substances, you can treat it exactly like sex.

INTEGRATING ANGER

Anger is the manifestation of the unintegrated Significance center. We experience it when our importance, worth, or intrinsic value as a human being is unvalidated. Anger is probably the single most projected emotion. We constantly avoid responsibility for anger, thinking that others are the cause of it. We constantly blame, rejecting ourselves.

*Do not try to think
away your anger*

There is no rational basis for anger. It cannot be controlled by intellectually identifying whatever is making you angry and trying to change your reaction through reprogramming yourself or others. Types of therapy in which you try to reprogram your thoughts to alter your feelings can be dangerous. If you use such an approach and appear to be successful, you have merely resuppressed your anger – or any other feeling – and it will come forth another time. Unusually strong negative feelings always represent suppressed energy. They must be released on the energy level through conscious processing. Reprogramming is not the answer. Reprogramming starts with the assumption that feelings must be avoided; this is doomed from the start. All feelings must be accepted in order to be cleared.

You also may experience what could be called "ordinary" amounts of anger, anger that does not involve suppressed energy and is not as strong as suppressed anger. Processing is the best approach I know for handling either ordinary or suppressed anger. We have already discussed the ineffectiveness and self-destructiveness of venting anger on those who appear to have hurt us. Processing, breath, and bodywork will release anger effectively without alienating others. Let's summarize the steps of integration with regard to anger. These same steps can be applied to any feeling, including depression.

1. AWARENESS. Own your anger. Understand that whatever is "making" you angry is just bringing up your own suppressed anger. There is no rational reason why you should choose to be angry. Your subconscious is just taking the opportunity to project and clear itself.

2. ACCEPTANCE. End inner resistance to your anger. Do not think you have to avoid it. Accept it but do not act on it or blamefully extend it into the universe. If you blame or attack others who appear to make you angry, you reject yourself and resuppress the anger.

3. DIRECT EXPERIENCE. Surrender to the experience of the anger. Feel it in the body, as the energy moves. If possible, use bodywork that acts on the Solar Plexus. Feel the anger, in the moment, with no thought of changing it. KEEP BREATHING.

4. TRANSFORMATION. Activate the Witness through concentration on the Third Eye. Allow the energy of the anger *to be* and to find its own equilibrium. Allow the outcome to be directed by the Higher Self. Allow change to happen on the inner psychic planes without your conscious knowledge or intention. The anger will be dissolved, not suppressed, and creative change will occur spontaneously.

If anger is a problem for you, you have to accept that it will take time to bring yourself into balance. Learn to work with anger during meditation; you will gain the ability to do so in confrontation. At one period of my life, I felt tremendous waves of anger when I sat to meditate. Things would happen that would disturb my meditation, and I would become angry. I decided that my subconscious was cleansing and that once I sat down, I would not get up to change anything in my environment until my meditation was over. I would sit. The phone would ring and the answering machine would not be on. Neighbors would start to play music and my windows were open. My cat was locked out and would start scratching on the door. Carpenters next door started hammering. And this was when I had moved to the seashore to find quiet from the city!

I would release large amounts of anger during these meditations. Many times my body started trembling and shaking, but I would not break from the experience of the anger. The crisis would last up to ten minutes at a time, over a period of several months. I realized that I was drawing these events to me and reacting to them in order to cleanse. I didn't need the stress of the city to provoke me; I provided my own provocation. Anger was cleansing because I wasn't in a stressful environment but in a *healing* environment. Gradually my meditation started to calm down. You also may go through a similar period, when anger or another emotion may start to cleanse. If you work with whatever is cleansing, you can make a lasting change.

Anger relates to the Power center. We feel angry because we have not integrated the complementary sides of the Power duality: our capacity to control versus our helplessness. We reject helplessness and feel anger when our power, really our infantile desire for omnipotence, is threatened or blocked. We must accept that we have this desire for omnipotence and that we are also helpless and powerless much of the time; helplessness is actually the basis for our sense of power. This unintegrated dualistic conflict causes anger; we cannot avoid it at our present stage of growth.

When the Power center is integrated, you still will have flashes of anger as you exercise your will. The anger will dissolve and pass away quickly if it is not resisted but accepted. When integration in this center matures, you will experience personal power balanced with surrender to the Higher Self, because when the conscious ego is not capable of acting, it means the Higher Self is taking control. Recognizing this, you integrate the expression of personal and higher will. But do not try to reach this realization intellectually. Process your anger, and you will become clear.

Anger also can relate to the Significance center and issues of thwarted or invalidated self-image, self-esteem, recognition, and worth. If you feel pressures in these areas, pressures that are most likely to occur in the workplace, do not be compulsively motivated by the feelings. Don't be motivated by the anger into making demands or into confrontations with others. Process the anger and allow it to link to the core feelings hidden behind. Recognize that the events are only triggering the lack of worth you are holding within. Clear yourself, and you will find that the conditions you encounter will magically transform.

INTEGRATING THE HEART

Feelings of the Heart stem from our need for relationship. We have a genuine need for relationships of all types: to be part of a community, to work with others; to be a parent as well as having been a child; to be intimate as well as a need to be alone. Relationships are also important because others serve as mirrors, reflecting our suppressed qualities and stimulating growth. In our society, we have developed a special compulsiveness about one specific kind of relationship: romantic love. We search for a partner; we hunger for intimate relationship, but satisfaction often remains elusive. Can this need ever be realistically fulfilled?

This is not an easy question to answer. When we are compulsive in relationships, we prevent a relationship with integrity from developing. We become dependent on the relationship, even when it is not living up to what we expected from it, and the dependency results in stress and the likelihood of the relationship failing. Because we are not fully enlightened yet, it is probably safe to assume that most of our relationships will be of a dependent nature, in spite of our best intentions. However, there is no problem in this, if only we can accept the pain that dependency brings.

Pain is felt whenever what you are addicted to in the relationship is threatened or absent; this pain is the simplest method of identifying addictions. You may respond to the pain by arguing that your needs are legitimate or that your partner is being unfair. You may rationalize your needs endlessly, but in the end, it comes down to being addicted and dependent. Moreover, you attract the kind of person who acts exactly to trigger your insecurities. Such is the precision of Karma. You will be with someone who will make you conscious of your addictions; that is why you chose them.

Whenever you feel pain in any type of relationship, whether insecurity, sexual frustration, rejection, anger, hurt, invalidation, or loneliness, you must remember that *you* are responsible for the pain because it is caused by your suppressed energies that are surfacing. These energies surface when you are denied those qualities or behavior in your partner to which you are addicted and which enable you to continue to suppress your pain. If you can remember this and not blame the other, you make it possible to maintain the relationship. The relationship can be used to help identify what you are addicted to, and it becomes a powerful vehicle for growth. However, if you blame the other, growth does not occur, and the relationship collapses.

Use your relationship as a vehicle for growth

I have noticed that usually most of the time spent in relationship is harmonious, except for a small percentage, varying from 10 to 30 percent, let's say. If your relationship fits this description, you may assume that you have a perfect relationship. You will be happy most of the time, and when those times of complete alienation come up, you can dig in and make leaps in your self-work. The relationship becomes win-win.

This is how to make a relationship work. There is no "perfect" relationship, because *we* are not perfect. The relationship serves as a mirror for our imperfections. When disharmony surfaces, you must process. Become aware of and take responsibility for your negative reaction – remember, it is your addictions that are being threatened. You must accept your pain without resistance or *blame*. You must experience the pain, understanding that it is suppressed material that you are clearing. The transformation will come. Your partner will sense, without fail, that you have changed and will change in return. There is no need to fight, discuss, explain, argue, or persuade. These are all self-defeating because even if you win, you lose: Your addiction continues.

However, it is hard to maintain perfect acceptance in the face of continual relationship stress. Even when we take responsibility and are processing, there comes a point when we are forced to say "Enough." You must strike a reasonable balance between processing and confronting. Do not use processing as an excuse for tolerating a bad situation or as justification for unassertiveness. If processing has not brought a transformation and your toleration is reached, you may have to discuss your feelings in a nonblaming way if you haven't already, saying something like "When you do such and such, it brings up my feelings of _____. Could you please do something different?" If your partner cannot respond and if your toleration is truly reached, or if your partner keeps blaming you when you have taken responsibility, the relationship may have to be abandoned.

Relationship addiction can tie into any level of being, such as Security, where we depend on the other for material support; Sexual, where we are compulsive and using; Power, where we control the other because we gain energy from them; or Heart, where we seek to escape from loneliness. Of all of these, the escape from loneliness may appear to be the most justified. It may be hard to understand why wanting a relationship to ease loneliness would be called an addiction, because isn't this what relationships are for?

Integrate loneliness

The question of loneliness is one that we all must confront. We must understand that because we are compulsive, no amount of being with others, even a special loved one, will eliminate loneliness. What happens is that the newness and excitement of a relationship, especially if it is sexual, will cover loneliness temporarily. After a while, it no longer has the same effect, and loneliness returns. We may then look for another relationship, but we continue to suppress our loneliness, becoming superficial and using others. Eventually our Karma will create a situation designed to teach us once and for all that we cannot escape from loneliness.

If you have not developed your capacity for loving yourself, you will be lonely regardless of whom you are with. You will not be able to accept love from others, even if they are genuinely loving. You may have experienced this in reverse – possibly you have been with someone who could not accept your love because they could not touch the love within themselves.

Integrating loneliness is the only way I know to work with it. Integrating the pain, the isolation, the separateness that you feel will result in its eventual transformation. Even though it sometimes seems as if it may never be possible to eliminate the experience of loneliness completely, there is no question that it is much more painful when we have developed the habit of suppressing it. When loneliness is integrated, you will gain a sense of personal empowerment. You will feel more complete unto yourself and will choose to be with others to share yourself and your joy, not in the hope of finding happiness because you are with them. Relying on myself is a lesson that I have to relearn from time to time. Whenever I feel sad and turn to a friend for support or to find happiness, it rarely works. I am reminded that I must go within and welcome whatever feelings are there.

Surrender to sadness

There is much suppressed sadness in the Heart center. You must take time to go into sadness, experiencing it without avoidance. Sadness can become the focus of the Witness. You can experience an emotional peak in its transformation; you enter the paradoxical ecstasy of emotional pain. Sadness can be approached much like depression, as an opportunity for healing and bringing in energy. As you surrender to sadness, you invoke the ecstasy.

I am conscious that I am engaged in the work of healing. I maintain a positive attitude as I welcome and experience all parts of life, not only the pleasant. I use affirmations not to avoid my experience but to enhance it and to help me with my self-acceptance. I am conscious of my environment and how it may influence me. I no longer buy into situations. I use my dreams as another approach to working on myself.

13

Practical Inner Work

In this chapter we explore additional topics that will expand your understanding of and the scope of application for Integrative Processing. I include some practical tips on how to make the most out of your efforts at inner work.

HEALING

Integration is concerned with healing. There may be emotional stress in your life that must be brought under control; blocks, addictions, and negative patterns may be keeping you in pain, and this pain must be healed; physical symptoms may be present that have resulted from inner imbalances; or you may just feel the need for an approach to activate growth and sensitivity to yourself. What you are concerned with is nothing less than *healing*.

Several elements are central to healing: concern, understanding, patience, nurturing, and courage. You may have an item of your own to add.

Concern means caring enough about yourself to be interested in taking the time to explore, with an open mind, what might be done to implement healing.

Understanding is certainly required, but we have seen there is appropriate as well as inappropriate understanding. You must know the limits of understanding.

Patience is required for the necessary cleansing and rebalancing of the energy system. We have been abusing and suppressing ourselves a long time. Realistically, we cannot expect overnight change.

Nurturing is an attitude applied toward yourself and may be thought of as the first step in loving yourself. You nurture yourself by activating your Nurturing center and contacting the archetypal feminine of the earth.

Courage is required to face negativities instead of rejecting them. The warrior spirit will build as you experience the first results of working on yourself successfully. Contact with the archetypal masculine of the sun will bring courage.

*Illness is the body's attempt
to cleanse negativity*

Healing in regard to physical health is an area that we have only touched on so far. The same principles that are used in integrating feelings or events can be used here.

Awareness is the first step. So much negativity has been

suppressed that it manifests in the physical body as illness. You should own your illness instead of blaming external factors, such as accident or virus. Such conditions are attracted and succumbed to because of the suppressed negative energies within. While illness may be perceived to be synonymous with decay or breakdown, on another level illness also represents the body's attempt to *cleanse itself* of the negativity. As you process the illness, you cooperate with this purpose, and you allow the negativity to be released.

If you accept and witness illness, it heals. If you resist illness, you resist healing. Acceptance of physical symptoms does not mean that you are agreeing to continue having the unhealthy conditions in your body. It just means that you cease resisting the energy imbalance that is present now. As long as you resist the imbalance, healing cannot occur. The healing power of the Higher Self cannot enter.

Direct experience of the energy imbalance and the physical symptoms from the vantage point of the Witness allows the healing power to start working. Enter alpha and bring in both yang universal energy from above and yin earth energy from below. Experience the feelings of the imbalance; do not deny them. Feel the healing power of the Higher Self as it enters the body and begins its work. The pain that accompanies healing represents the cleansing of negativities into consciousness. To whatever extent you are able to open to the pain by witnessing it, you work with the healing force.

The healing transformation will come after you maintain direct experience for the necessary amount of time. It is essential that you *trust* in the process of the Higher Self, which may bring forth possibly even more suppressed negativity and physical symptoms as healing continues, in order to cleanse. Eventually a healing crisis may be entered, and complete cleansing will take place.

EMOTIONALITY

People who may be described as "overly emotional" are not necessarily more in touch with their feelings than those who may be thought of as having subdued emotions. Both conditions are poles of the dualistic condition of *emotionality*. As we touched on in discussing the second reaction and the self-rejecting behavior of dramatizing, emotionality means reacting emotionally and superficially to feelings instead of feeling the feelings. An overly emotional person may therefore be as much out of touch with core feelings as a person with subdued feelings.

If you are overly emotional, you should emphasize two aspects of your practice: Witnessing and grounding. The overly emotional person is usually closely identified with feelings, both core feelings and the emotional reaction. Breaking the identification is essential. Understand that you are not your feelings. Learn to watch them with an impassive, detached viewpoint. Practice witnessing when stressful situations come up. Ground down to the earth using the grounding exercise regularly. See yourself standing on the earth, strong and steady, not being blown by the winds of feeling.

If you are a person with subdued emotions, it does not necessarily mean that you are out of touch with feelings, but it does probably mean that you are too much in the head and not enough in the feeling center of the body. Do not fall into the trap of going to the other dualistic pole, thinking you must cultivate emotionality and be more emotionally outgoing and "expressive." Instead, what you must do is come more into touch with your inner feelings. As you do this, your outward expressiveness will naturally develop to the point where you will be comfortable with yourself and not intimidated by the emotionality of others. You will find your inner strength. Emphasize working with the body, opening to feeling through opening to the body, sensing the energy currents in the body. Emphasize breathwork, which will help to increase your sensitivity. Allow yourself to come into a balanced experience of left/right brain.

POSITIVE ATTITUDE

Positive attitude is often spoken of as a requirement for healing. I agree, but I also feel that this subject is sometimes misunderstood. Many people think that having a positive attitude means never admitting that they have any problems, either psychological or physical. They think that a positive attitude means denying negative conditions and that if they hold an image of complete positivity in their minds, the image will materialize.

The problem with this approach is that it leads to suppression of negative conditions, instead of integration and release. If you are constantly telling yourself how excellent you are, there is no room left for the perception of the negative side of life, which certainly will not go away just because you are trying to deny it. Your idea of the positive is just a concept and is not related to the natural balancing of energies in the feeling body. Indeed, insistence on seeing only the perceived positive will reinforce the existence of the negative, since one depends on the other. In our work, we have learned that we must acknowledge the negative. Yet maintaining the right kind of "positive attitude" can be of benefit.

For me, positive attitude results from the proper understanding of all we have been discussing. When we know that we are clearing long-held negativities; when we feel ourselves growing, positive attitude comes naturally. We become positive about accepting and experiencing the negative. We become positive about all of life, not just about whatever is immediately pleasing. The finite mind surrenders to whatever the Higher Self brings forth, and we become the Witness. Such a positive attitude can supply the energy and enthusiasm to enable us to confront our Karma successfully.

Affirmations

Affirmations are a type of positive attitude. They can be of benefit when used correctly but can be detrimental when used incorrectly. Affirmations are used correctly when the intention is to recondition the unconscious mind to be accepting. As with positive attitude, they are used incorrectly when the intention is to avoid whatever is perceived as an unpleasant experience or feeling. My opinion is that the current New Age/personal achievement fields overemphasize affirming, visualizing, and "manifesting," and the need for real work on ourselves has become obscured. Affirmations have appeal because of the sensationalistic promise of getting whatever you think you need by merely calling for it. Even if affirmations were to work as easily as some would have us believe, there are limitations to their use.

The mind tends to
maintain self-rejection

When we try to bring something into our lives, we usually start with a concept of what we think we need – a concept of the mind. The mind, however, is the source of our self-rejection. Consequently, the mind cannot be relied on to provide solutions. What the mind generally comes up with are better ways to avoid experience, continue self-rejection, and maintain addictions. Any solution of the mind will be dualistic. Even if the solution is achieved, it will not provide the happiness that is expected. There may be apparent relief at first, but the new condition will change into or be accompanied by its complement. For example, if you try to affirm prosperity, you also will maintain your sense of survival anxiety. Prosperity that comes to you will be balanced by your increasing insecurity. The two are dualistically dependent and cannot exist without each other.

What about using affirmations to attempt to satisfy what we think are genuine needs and not addictions? Unfortunately, it is difficult to maintain objectivity about this. We think we are satisfying real needs but, in reality, we are driven by compulsiveness. The use of affirmations to attempt to satisfy compulsive ego needs is what might be called "low-level" New Age activity. It is a mild form of magic, leading to a deepening of the isolation of the individual ego. In contrast, when a situation is processed, the intelligence of the Higher Self works for us, providing a solution that the mind could never imagine. The solution will be genuinely creative and lead to circumstances that result in the dropping of addictions.

Affirmations cannot change beliefs
or clear suppressed feelings

When we use an affirmation to try to change our circumstances, we generally try to recondition a belief, since we know that beliefs are responsible for drawing events to us. Unfortunately, beliefs cannot be changed that easily. Beliefs are supported and maintained by suppressed feelings. Feelings, in turn, are created by beliefs. A mutually dependent cycle exists.

For example, you may experience fear when a certain belief about security is threatened, even though the belief is irrational. If the fear is then suppressed, it maintains the belief. The fear is then projected, drawing threatening events to you and confirming the belief. Beliefs cannot be abandoned, changed, or transformed until the underlying suppressed feelings have been cleared. Belief systems should not be attacked directly, but you should work on yourself with whatever belief system you have, outgrowing it through integrating the related feelings.

Suppressed feelings are the source of power that attracts negative events into our lives. Feelings are where the power is, not beliefs. A belief, in itself, has relatively little power. It is unrealistic, therefore, to assume that substantial change can be made by trying to recondition a belief when the subconscious energy of the corresponding feeling remains to both support the belief and continue to attract events.

Nevertheless, affirmations can be helpful to recondition certain negative *mind-sets* to be accepting. Let's explore how to use them productively. The use of affirmations falls into three classes: accepting feelings, accepting conditions, and changing conditions.

Accepting Feelings

The mind, our thinking center, is a different part of ourselves from the feeling center. Although there can be a correspondence between them, they are often in conflict. You may be feeling tired and in need of rest, but the ambitious mind pushes the body into unreasonable activity to accomplish a goal of the mind. Such self-rejection is typical of the mind.

The mind can be reconditioned to be accepting with affirmations. In contrast, feelings cannot be influenced with affirmations, except to suppress the feelings. Feelings will not evaporate simply because you try to affirm them away. Suppressed feelings are composed of energy, while affirmations are of the mind. They are different levels of being. Feelings must be cleared and experienced in order to clear. You should observe this distinction when formulating affirmations.

What happens in practice is that trying to use an affirmation to change a feeling serves to bring the undesired feeling more into consciousness. If you are unaware, you will then try to resuppress the feeling, through one of the forms of self-rejection. If you are aware, however, you could use the opportunity to integrate the feeling. For example, if you are angry, but try to reject your anger and yourself by affirming "I am in a pleasant and joyous mood," your anger will become worse. If it seems to go away, which is unlikely, it has only been suppressed. The same will happen with any other negative feeling you try to eliminate through affirmation, such as fear, anxiety, sexual or food hunger, resentment, or loneliness.

Affirmations should be used to help you accept feelings, not avoid them. If you wanted to use an affirmation to help you get past your self-rejection about anger, you might affirm, "It is OK to accept and experience my anger." You would avoid becoming angry about the anger as well as possibly fearful and depressed.

You must be careful about how you apply affirmations. You need to distinguish clearly between thoughts and feelings, accepting feelings, and using affirmations to change your mind-set regarding the acceptance. The mind is the source of the *opinion* about the feeling. The opinion is what should be changed.

Accepting Conditions

When you recondition your mind-set to accept conditions, you are not resigning yourself to endure circumstances that may need to be changed; acceptance means only that you have stopped resisting what your experience is *now*. In accepting present conditions, you allow growth to occur. When you resist, you perpetuate the very conditions you fight.

Suppose you believe that you are poor. This in itself is subjective, and certain people may consider themselves poor with a million dollars in the bank. You cannot recondition the belief about being poor directly because of the suppressed emotional energies – such as insecurity, fear, or anxiety – that maintain it. If you affirm "I am wealthy," you bring up the suppressed anxiety about being poor. Accepting and experiencing the anxiety would be beneficial, but usually it is resuppressed. The affirmation may even work against you, bringing about undesirable conditions because of the suppressed negativity that is stirred up.

However, it is possible to recondition your opinion about being poor. You can accept your poverty along with the suppressed emotions concerning it, whether the belief of poverty is justified or not. Your opinion that it is bad to be poor is a mindset. When you accept being poor, you can begin integrating emotions about being poor that have been suppressed and continue to bring about the condition of subjective poverty. You take the first step toward creatively dealing with the situation. You will be more relaxed about it. You still might prefer having more money, and that is fine, but you will have dropped the compulsive aspect of suppressed emotions.

Remember that you are affirming in the present. "It is OK to be poor" does not have a future reference; you are not conditioning yourself to be poor in the future. It simply means that it's all right, it's not a disaster, it's not so bad to be poor *now*. The intention is to become at ease with the present condition, not to reject it and therefore yourself.

You can try affirming conditions right now. Take any "negative" condition you have been fighting. Affirm "It is OK for me to be/have/feel _____." Say this mentally to yourself ten times. Do you feel the immediate relief from giving yourself permission to be/have/feel what you previously condemned? Do you feel the release in the body, in the feeling centers as suppressed emotions clear?

Suppose you have an addiction. Affirming that it is OK to have the addiction does not mean giving yourself permission to continue *to act on* the addiction. You are just affirming the present: that it's OK, it's not a disaster, you are not worthless, you are not guilty because you have an addiction now. This has no bearing on the future. The future will be that you do not act on addictive impulses but release the tension through processing techniques; you observe nonreactiveness. You accept but do not react to or extend negativity into the universe.

What if you are sick or in real physical or emotional pain?

You have to trust that these extreme conditions result from the buildup of suppressed energies and that the principles of acceptance and invoking the Higher Self will see you through. When you fight a condition, you impede the flow of energies as they try to balance themselves. Affirming the experience will help you accept it.

Changing Conditions

If you have reached the point of accepting and integrating current feelings and conditions, you may use affirmations to help shape future conditions. Suppose you are still poor, according to your belief system, but have integrated the poverty. You have become at ease with "poverty," thinking it not so bad after all. You may have used an affirmation to help change your mind-set. Or you may still be insecure about poverty, but you have accepted the insecurity. You are not fearful about insecurity; you remain in the Witness with it. You do not self-reject.

Affirmations will work effectively now to change conditions because, in having integrated, you have released the subconscious feeling energies that create your poverty. Energy is no longer present to oppose the affirmation, as before. In other words, we can change things only after we have accepted the present; when we are not motivated to seek change by the desire to escape. The present consists of the conditions and feelings we experience and the beliefs that create them.

When affirmations are used for change, you make the assumption that the conditions you desire already exist, such as "I am wealthy" or "I am becoming wealthier every day." The affirmation is repeated mentally or written.

Use affirmations to enhance your experience, not to escape from it

If you have accepted and are integrating conditions and feelings, would you need affirmations at all to bring about change? It is likely that you wouldn't. As you surrender to *what is* and invite the participation of the Higher Self, situations will change spontaneously, in a positive way that you could not foresee. Still, some fine-tuning may be called for. Affirmations and visualizations can be helpful at this stage. They are not to be used out of desperation and lack, trying to counter suppressed energies, but simply to exercise discretion about how things are shaping. Is it possible to make lasting and substantial changes by affirming? I would have to answer both yes and no.

No, because all the great religious philosophies I have studied, whether Buddhism, Hinduism, Taoism, even Christianity, have basically taught acceptance of the negative. Psychologists have supported this viewpoint. In working on ourselves, the focus is on release of suppressed energies through acceptance. If affirmations could change these energies and the events they bring, I'm sure the use of them would not have been overlooked.

Moreover, although I have been active in spiritual, psychological, and New Age circles for years, I cannot say that I have ever met anyone who actually has had success with affirmations in bringing lasting material or psychological change into their lives. However, I have met people who have used affirmations to further suppress their unwanted qualities, and this has been plain in that their suppressed negativities would jump out whenever possible. These people also have a sense of self-imposed concepts, rigidity, and hypocrisy about them. The real changes that I have seen have come through the more traditional approaches of acceptance, meditation, therapy, and spiritual practice.

On the other hand, affirmations have a definite place if used correctly. People who misuse them are not aware of the basic principles we have just covered. Affirmations can be instrumental in bringing about self-acceptance, which is the beginning of self-love, as well as material change when used at the right time. I would encourage you to include reasonable and intelligent use of them in your practice. Here are typical affirmations, in the three modes of (1) accepting feelings, (2) accepting conditions, and (3) changing conditions:

Survival

1. It's OK to be insecure.
2. It's OK to be poor.
3. I am getting wealthier every day.

Sensation

1. It's OK to have sexual impulses.
2. I am comfortable with unsatisfied sexual desires.
3. My opportunities for sexual fulfillment are bountiful.

Significance

1. It's OK to feel angry.
2. It's OK to be inadequate.
3. I am comfortable in limiting situations.

Heart

1. It's OK to be lonely.
2. I accept my alienation.
3. I love myself for accepting my _____. (perceived weakness)
4. I form loving relationships easily.

I would like to make a point concerning processing in general that is related to our discussion of affirmations. Since in using an affirmation we hold a thought in mind with the expectation of attracting a corresponding condition, perhaps you are wondering if holding negative feelings in awareness during processing might serve to further attract negative conditions. The answer is no.

The principle of affirmation is usually interpreted as meaning that thoughts held in the mind attract similar conditions. However, it is not primarily thoughts but *feelings* that draw conditions to us. Feelings are where the power is. Subconscious negative feelings are already actively working to draw conditions to us, even though we are not conscious of them. Simply bringing these feelings into consciousness during processing does not increase their tendency to do so. On the contrary, when we start to work with feelings, their attractive pull is lessened, for several reasons.

First, bringing feelings into consciousness makes us aware of the contents of the subconscious. Awareness itself lessens the unconscious attractive power. Next, when we enter the direct experience of the Witness, we have stopped identifying with feelings.

Disidentification breaks the power of the negative feelings to attract events. It is when we identify with negative feelings that they have the power to attract events, and we can identify with feelings whether we are conscious or unconscious of them. As integration proceeds, the negative energy becomes released, and the attractive power of the subconscious is completely dissolved.

ENVIRONMENT

The question of environment is a difficult one. There is no doubt that we are influenced by our environment. We are routinely exposed to a vast variety of negative stimuli, including noise and air pollution, crowding, work stress as well as genuinely dangerous conditions and people. In urban areas, these factors are intensified. We absorb the negativity, and it affects us. When processing, we question if we are working with our own energies or ones we have picked up from the outside.

An additional factor about large cities is the lack of prana; cities are prana deficient. Living in a large city results in a condition of chronic prana deficiency. Most people are not aware of how significant this can be. Lack of adequate prana means lack of ample psychic energy. Basic addictive tendencies are developed to get the energy merely to function. We become dependent on stimulants, ranging from coffee and sugar to T.V., drugs, and sex.

When I am in the city, I immediately feel more stressed, and my lower centers start showing their negative sides. I become anxious, worrying about survival issues (money). I feel overwhelmed and powerless. I am sexually stimulated and at the same time frustrated. I am easily angered. These emotions are precipitated by the combination of the basic negative factors mentioned above with the lack of fresh prana. Without prana, the chakras are literally starving.

In negative environments, it becomes easy to reach the point of *overload*. We are confronted with too much negativity and we go beyond our toleration point. We shut down. We start suppressing all the negativity around us and end by also suppressing ourselves. However, the issue is not that simple.

To use an analogy, if you are caught out in the rain and are cold, wet, and miserable, you could process the situation as a response to your condition. You could own, accept, experience, and transform being miserable out in the rain, possibly catching pneumonia as your toleration point is exceeded. Or you could walk to the nearest shelter and get out of the rain. I would recommend walking to the shelter and also would recommend this kind of solution to any problem whenever possible. Use processing when it is not possible to walk out of the rain.

We are all caught out in the rain in one way or another and have the option of walking to the shelter, *but we don't*. The reality is that we choose to stay out in the rain. This is because the negativity outside of us coincides with the negativity inside; we are attracted to it unconsciously. We are drawn into the turmoil, it reflects us, we identify with it, and it becomes our own. In the end, we probably have created it. The enlightened person simply steps out of the rain. The unenlightened person stays in the rain, fighting it, perpetuating the conditions. The question of environment then takes on a different cast. Because our environment reflects ourselves, this may be why it is so hard to walk away.

We attract and absorb energies
that are already within us

Because we absorb only those energies that correspond to those that we are already holding in the subconscious, it is correct to accept negativity that appears to be coming from the outside, even in highly negative environments. Our reaction to an external condition corresponds to our Karma – it is part of the projection mechanism. If our environment makes us depressed or angry, it is only stirring up those feelings in the subconscious. The negativity should be accepted.

The problem with negative environments then becomes one of overload. Even though feelings that come up should be integrated, we become overwhelmed by the amount of negativity, we begin suppressing, and growth becomes stagnated. Therefore, we must control our environment to the extent that we do not exceed our toleration point and reach overload. At the same time, it must be understood that if we shield ourselves from each and every piece of perceived negativity outside of us, we cut ourselves off from our projected subconscious.

Also remember that it is important to open yourself to positive influences and energies, to receive the blessing that such sources can provide. You must, therefore, find the right balance in confronting life so that you are nurturing yourself as well as meeting your projections but are not being overwhelmed by the negativity of the world. If you find that you cannot shield yourself from a particular negative person or circumstance, you can be sure that you are being presented with a Karmic lesson that must be integrated.

BUYING INTO

We "buy into" something when we identify with it or when we choose not to walk out of the rain. We take situations seriously, not suspecting that we are largely the creator, through our projections. When you're "buying into" something, you might try the following to help get a perspective on what's happening.

Imagine that the other people who seem to be causing the problem for you are actually *cardboard cutouts*. See them as flat, one-dimensional, painted, and pasted cartoon figures. Look behind them, and see the wooden sticks that hold up the figures. When you visualize a figure, see it doing whatever it is that sets you off. See it in a fixed pose that does not change. Understand that you have created the figure to test yourself. This need take no more than an instant of time; you don't want to hold the image so long that you drop out of the interaction. Visualizing this may even help you come up with a smile in the middle of a confrontation.

It might appear as if you are depersonalizing other people when you see them as cartoon figures, but this is not so. You are only dramatizing and deflating your tendency to buy into your projections. In fact, you depersonalize others when you buy into situations; then you really do see them as cutouts. You assign your projected roles to them. You do not see them as they are.

PROBLEM SOLVING

Processing techniques can be used for problem solving in general as well as for handling feelings and situations. The problem can be a practical matter, a question about a person or relationship, or whatever.

Hold the problem situation in mind, with no thought for the solution. Turn the problem over to the Higher Self intelligence. A solution will be presented to you that will be unique and creative. All creative people use a similar approach, even if they are not aware of it. The steps are:

1. AWARENESS: Clearly formulate the problem, but not the solution, in your mind. You might even write it out.

2. ACCEPTANCE: Accept that you don't know the solution. Enter the "don't know" state of Zen.

3. DIRECT EXPERIENCE: Keep the problem in your consciousness by witnessing. Internally, assign the problem to your Higher Self, then forget about it. The first three steps might take minutes, or less.

4. TRANSFORMATION: Wait for the solution to appear, by directly coming into your mind or by appearing in dream form or in other symbolic representation. This might happen immediately or after a period of time.

DREAMWORK

Dreams are an important means for the subconscious to communicate its contents to the conscious mind. As you begin working on yourself, your dreamlife is likely to become more vivid and significant. Spontaneous clearing will begin during dreams.

The usual psychological, analytical approach to dreams is to try to understand what they represent – to "interpret" them. Although analysis may be appropriate at times, in our work, we approach dreams as we would any other event. The dream is seen to be the dramatic metaphor that triggers the accompanying feelings. Bringing feelings into consciousness is considered to be the purpose of the dream; intellectual content is considered secondary and possibly misleading.

For example, you may dream of a particularly nasty interaction with your spouse, and that they hate you. If you take this at face value, you may think that your subconscious is trying to warn you about something concerning your spouse. You may become paranoid. You may get lost in analysis, ignoring the feeling. If you take a processing approach, you would consider that the dream is surfacing suppressed, complementary feelings about the relationship or even about yourself that you are projecting onto the spouse. You do not allow the dream to undermine the relationship. You accept and experience the feelings, clearing them.

Dreams become significant when the feelings that accompany them are strong. Feelings are the essential part of the dream, which may be overlooked in the search for "meaning." If you don't realize that feelings are being cleared, you resist and resuppress. Note, however, that just having had the feelings in the dream is not enough to clear them. You must intentionally include the dream feelings in your conscious processing practice and work with them in order to make use of the revelation that occurred in the dream. If you don't do this, the purpose of the dream is thwarted and the feelings resuppressed.

Do not reject yourself by rejecting your dream feelings; do not look for intellectual meaning that is probably not there. Integrate the feelings either upon awakening or during your regular meditation. Working with dream feelings can become another powerful approach to working on yourself.

As I open to myself, I look deeper than I ever have before. I take responsibility for and accept feelings that I have always rejected because they were too painful. In going so deeply within, I surrender to the Higher Self, and I begin deep and lasting transformation.

14

Opening to Yourself

I would like to relate some examples of my work with clients to give you further insight into how I approach the counseling relationship and a deeper view of Integrative Processing in action. I think this will be helpful as you begin to work on yourself.

In learning any skill, there are times when a personal teacher may be advantageous. Although I have tried to present the fundamentals of Integrative Processing as a self-therapy, it is also a powerful therapeutic modality when used within the therapist-client relationship. It could prove useful if you found a counselor who was sympathetic with these principles to help you get started, or if you feel stuck, or if you simply want the advantage of a therapist's ability and support. Working with a counselor might be especially helpful if you have no previous exposure to inner work. If you have previous experience, then perhaps no assistance is required. If you are inclined to seek help, I would recommend working, if at all possible, with a Certified Integrative Processing Therapist (CIPT), all of whom I have personally trained.

The central focus in Integrative Processing Therapy is the deeply relaxed state in which the unconscious is accessed and healing spontaneously occurs. It is the meditative state, where the therapist acts as facilitator, helping the client to enter alpha, enabling them to go deeper than they can on their own. This is effected primarily by the therapist entering alpha and energetically influencing the client through a psychic vibrational resonance that the therapist has been trained to induce. Entrainment technology also may be judiciously used, along with breathwork. The therapist also consciously channels healing energy to the client. The client is supported by the energy of the therapist, feels safe, and is guided through the process.

Developing the special sensitivity for guiding a client through deep alpha-state process is a major part of the training for certification that I perform with therapists. The training is based on the new paradigm of psychological healing that is the foundation of processing: *inner experience of feelings* as the key to integration. The therapist is trained to bring the client *into* their experience. The therapy session becomes an experience in itself, where the subconscious is accessed and experienced as the means to clear, and not just a dialogue between therapist and client.

In the alpha state, there is no attempt to recondition the unconscious to achieve behavioral goals. Alpha state is used only for healing of feelings, through communion with deep levels of the subconscious soul, not reconditioning, which I consider intrusive and undesirable. Negative behavior, including addictions, usually derives from self-rejecting attempts to avoid feelings and will change spontaneously and dramatically after feelings are released; the attempt to change behavior without first clearing underlying feelings is futile.

In the following stories, I have briefly summarized astrological factors that helped me identify each client's patterns for readers who are interested and have some knowledge of astrology. If you are not one of these, you may safely skip over this material.

SANDY

Sandy is a thirty-two-year-old, attractive woman with a charming personality and a gift for making friends easily. She has been unable to settle into any specific career since college and has supported herself by doing temporary office work. She was prompted to seek counseling by a series of crises in her romantic relationships. I met with her once a week for three months and then once a month for eight months, and still see her occasionally. I also met once with Richard, the man with whom she was involved in her longest relationship, which covered a six-year period.

Sandy was emotionally suppressed and addictive. She consumed large quantities of alcohol and drugs, and had a tendency for sexual straying. She had no concept that this behavior constituted self-rejection and that she indulged in it to shield herself from painful feelings. A large part of our time was spent in overcoming her resistance to the idea that there was something wrong with this behavior. She viewed it as recreation.

Sandy's astrological chart showed the following stressful elements: Saturn closely conjunct Moon in the twelfth house. This represents a depressive and emotionally blocked nature, resulting in a fear of intimacy. Saturn, the planet of fear and limitation, is blocking the planet of feelings, the Moon. Being in the twelfth house further exaggerates the unconscious nature of her feelings, implying a highly repressed condition. Fear of feelings as well as the feelings themselves, such as depression, need to be integrated. Next, Venus square Mars adds to her sexual magnetism but also represents a lack of integration between her loving and sexual sides. Then South Node in the fifth house suggests that whenever she fell back into self-defeating behavior and avoidance of feelings, she would seek escape in love affairs, entertainment, or acting like a child.

In her relationship with Richard, she unconsciously chose a man who was not emotionally expressive, so that she would not feel threatened. Intimate relationship with an emotionally expressive person would have been stressful for her, pointing out her own lack of emotional contact with herself.

At one point in her relationship, she experienced the sudden need to escape, and did so by flinging herself into a weeklong sexual affair with someone she had just met. She soon rejected this person, who had become attached to her, causing him to feel pain and disappointment. As we examined this incident and I met with Richard, the details that triggered her behavior came to light.

It seems she had always wanted a commitment in her relationship with Richard. For six years this had been an issue, which included the discussion of children. Richard was unable to commit and remained emotionally distant. She did not realize that she was dependent on the aloofness. When Richard, who had been working on himself, finally began to open emotionally to Sandy, telling her that he really deeply cared for her, she panicked. She could not handle the expression of real emotion because of her inner blocking and fear of intimacy, and she escaped into the weeklong fling, not the first of her affairs outside the relationship. After learning about the affair, Richard decided to call it quits for good, greatly hurt that Sandy had reacted to his finally opening to her in what he felt was an enormous step for him by throwing herself into the arms of a stranger. At this point, Sandy and I began meeting.

Although not actively working on herself, Sandy was familiar with meditation and seemed motivated to make changes in her life. She seemed to have finally realized that her life was misdirected and that something important was missing. We spent time discussing the concepts of emotional self-acceptance and how critical it was for her to accept and experience her feelings instead of trying to escape from them through alcohol, drugs, or wild sex. Once she understood and agreed with this concept, we were able to start work. The focus of our work together consisted of entering alpha and bringing up her feelings in a controlled way so she could integrate them. Her primary problem was an irrational fear of feeling itself. We had to go into this basic fear and then the actual feelings she was blocking.

I would lead her into awareness of fear in general. She became able to feel the fear that had been unconscious. I kept pointing out the fear, making sure she felt it was safe to feel it, telling her that it would not hurt her and that she should not fear the fear but just be with it. I had her enter her body and continuously breathe into the root chakra with the Integrating breath, sometimes breathing gently and quietly, sometimes more forcefully, bringing up the fear. Occasionally I had her hold yoga poses: Forward Bend, Hero, Bridge, Hip Rotation. Together we activated the Witness and brought in healing energy to the fear.

As she witnessed, I had her access the feelings of self-love that resulted from her facing the fear. I would assist her by resonating with her as I brought up my own feelings of self-acceptance and self-love. After about four sessions, Sandy reported that she thought she was "beginning to get it."

Then, gradually, as the fear emerged, so did one of the primary feelings she was suppressing: her resentment and anger toward Richard for his lack of commitment and support. I reasoned with her that she attracted this kind of partner and was heavily projecting her own inability to commit onto him. Gradually I was able to start getting her past the blame that was keeping her in self-rejection and making release of the anger impossible. She was able to understand that she was reacting to her own fear of intimacy, not to her partner.

I had her feel the anger, instructing her to keep shifting from the blame to the experience of the anger. I told her to use her thoughts of Richard as a stimulus for the anger but to understand intellectually that the blame was a mistake and to set it aside. During our second month, she reached the point of being able to access her fear and anger in a nonblaming way, and began to cleanse significantly.

The next major emotion to emerge as cleansing continued was depression, which was a large part of her motivation for escapist activities. Depression became the focus of our work for the third month; she had a large amount of suppressed depression. I emphasized accepting and experiencing it in a controlled and reasonable manner. She started attending yoga classes and became involved with a women's group, shifting from her usual habits of diversion by means of substances. At the same time, we worked more with this chakra, breathing into it and bringing in healing energy. She learned to sit with and witness her depression instead of reacting to it. During this period, Sandy became dependent on our meetings. I did not discourage this but kept redirecting her focus inwardly.

As we further examined her relationship with Richard, another aspect emerged. When I met with Richard, he mentioned that he felt Sandy wanted to be too dependent on him in terms of material support, almost as if she wanted him to be her father. This was reinforced by a gap in their ages. (He was older and more financially established.) Richard said he was not comfortable with this role, feeling he was being used. As I discussed this with Sandy, she started to see the possibility of her projecting a fathering role onto Richard, although at first she was annoyed and rejected the idea, which was also how she reacted whenever Richard tried to discuss it with her.

Her own father was an alcoholic and was functionally and emotionally absent. Sandy had been attracted to an emotionally distant man as her biological father and now had repeated the choice in selecting Richard as a partner, in an unconscious attempt to bring up those feelings for clearing that the relationship triggered.

We examined those feelings. She wanted to be supported and protected in her relationship but felt as if she had to acquiesce when Richard pointed out that he felt her demands were unreasonable or were just not what he wanted in a relationship; nevertheless, she remained resentful. She created the structure to support her resentment: Her partner would not support her. Traditional psychology might say she transferred her resentment about her father not supporting her to her partner, but a more basic cause lies in previous-life Karma.

I asked her to try to accept these feelings of resentment about not being supported by her father. I had her bring up her feelings of utter dependency as a child by regressing her to an early age after entering alpha. She relived the dependency and the experience of complete fear of being left alone, of turning to him when he was drunk and being slapped by him. Constantly, as she relived these events, I would bring her out of blame and into the experience by reminding her to drop blameful thoughts and enter the feeling; to bring her self-love and healing energy to the pain of being alone, of being hurt.

We worked on the regression for three sessions. In the third session, I had her go back to a fantasy about herself as a child, to a time not of the earth, a dreamtime. She saw herself as a very young girl in a light blue dress, in a place of blue-gray clouds. She saw herself as innocent, tender, open, and loving. I asked her to bring her father to her, so she could speak to him. What immediately appeared was an image that she could not physically identify, but she could feel as Richard, her present partner. She was struck by the realization that he had been her father in a previous life. He was unable to speak to her because he was bound by his own chains, but she could sense that he loved her and wanted to express his love even though he was unable. I told her to reach out to him.

At this point, Sandy entered what I could only describe as a major catharsis. Tears and release of emotion flooded her for at least twenty minutes. She was physically shaking and convulsing. I held her and let her go on with the release until she was finished.

The release of emotion convinced me that the fantasy was true – her partner had indeed been her father in some previous life. They had come together again in order to heal their relationship. Richard was the first to have taken those steps, but Sandy was not yet ready and reacted by trying to escape.

Sandy later told me that she discussed this session with Richard. This in itself was a giant step of growth for her, because she had never been able to talk meaningfully about her feelings before. Today she and Richard are no longer lovers but remain supportive friends for each other.

As Sandy and I ceased our work together, I had the impression that she had gone through a turning point in her life. She under-stood herself much better. She no longer reacted to her fears or her projections unconsciously and compulsively, and her use of drugs and alcohol was coming under control. She had an approach for working on herself and trust that she was going forward in her growth. She had cleared a large amount of the subconscious nega-tivity that had been driving her. We still meet whenever she needs some help in clarifying events or feelings.

JIM

Jim is forty-three years old. He has always been interested in the quest for higher consciousness and the pursuit of spiritual goals. He has had a fair amount of therapy, is conversant about the basics of psychology, and has the capacity for self-objectivity.

His current crisis takes the form of conflict within his marriage of four years. He finds himself at an irreconcilable position with his partner and is experiencing great anxiety at the possibility of losing contact with his two children from the marriage. This prospect is even more painful because this is exactly what happened with his two children from a previous marriage, when he was in his twenties.

In spite of his spiritual idealism and his desire to be a loving person, he experiences tremendous anger when dealing with his partner, feeling he is being manipulated and treated unfairly. On several occasions he went over the edge and became physically abusive. This violence further alienates his partner, who feels she must protect herself and the children from him, and he becomes further enraged at being separated from the children. This cycle has built up over the past year.

Although there is enough feeling on the surface to begin work, looking at Jim's chart provided some interesting insights. Knowing that the issue centered around children, I looked at the fifth house. The only significator here is the North Node. The North Node represents the area of life where we are to focus if we are to move ahead in our personal growth; the South Node represents going backward. Jim was correct in focusing on children as a means to his own growth, but the afflictions to the North Node indicate that he has a tremendous amount of negative Karma to contend with as he does. The Node is opposite Sun, square Moon, and square Venus, indicating basic conflict with the individuality, the emotional nature, and the love nature. Children will bring up pain in the form of conflicts that must be integrated.

Even more telling are the parallels to the Node. The Node is strongly parallel to Pluto and Mars as well as the Sun. Having Pluto, Mars, and Sun aspecting any point is a powerful and potentially violent energy, indicating difficult Karma. The patterns that need integrating: Sun parallel Pluto – manipulation, power struggles. Jim attracted an intensely manipulative person but then projects on top of that, perceiving her as heartless and controlling; Sun parallel Mars, Mars opposite Ascendant – large amounts of suppressed anger, manifesting also as conflicts with authority; Mars parallel Pluto – the potential for violence, either as victim or perpetrator.

In spite of these afflictions, Jim was highly idealistic, actively trying to be loving and spiritual, as indicated by the positive side of his chart: Sun conjunct Venus; Venus sextile Jupiter; Neptune trine Ascendant, sextile Mercury, sextile Pluto, trine Uranus. However, with South Node in the eleventh house of ideals, being idealistic represented going backward, avoidance of issues, and self-rejection.

In our first month of meeting once a week, we talked about all aspects of processing but focused mostly on awareness. I felt that Jim would not be able really to begin working with his negative energy until he had clearly recognized and then owned his feelings. But it was also important for him to look at his idealism.

Jim heavily entertained idealistic goals, thinking that things would resolve if these goals could be achieved. Living in a spiritual community was one. Entering into a helping profession was another. I tried to point out that these might be the result of an integrated personality but that they would not lead to integration, and that dwelling on them only served to suppress his real feelings. The idealism was Jim's self-rejection, taking him out of the moment and the experience of himself as he was. It took time for him to understand that he had to drop the focus on ideals as a means to accept the feelings. We came back to this issue often.

Tied to the idealism was the guilt that he felt in not being able to live up to the ideals. Jim had to see that the guilt was misplaced and was another form of self-rejection – his defense against really having to feel his feelings. We discussed this as well.

We went into the issue of anger. I pointed out to Jim that his anger was suppressed from previous times and was being brought up only by present circumstances, not being caused by them, no matter how painful the anger was. We talked about this until he grasped the idea of emotional responsibility and could intellectually own his anger.

As we explored the concept of owning the anger, Jim said that he felt he had the right to be angry with and to express his anger to his wife, that he was being honest in doing so, and he further resented that she would not "accept it." This kind of expectation for unconditional emotional acceptance from the partner seems to be typical of men in our culture. Just as Sandy was projecting her unfulfilled needs for a father on her partner in her expectation that he support her financially, and then resenting him when he refused, Jim was projecting his quest for mother fulfillment. His expectation was that his wife receive him unconditionally, at any time, on any emotional-sexual basis, and he became resentful when she wouldn't.

I explained to Jim that once he had established his own emotional self-acceptance, he would no longer be dependent on a woman's acceptance. Furthermore, Jim's sexual needs were strong and compulsive. It appeared that he was unconsciously trying to get rid of tension from the suppressed anger through sexual release, another common behavior trait, although more common in men than women. There was no way to deal with this directly, but to expect that sexual compulsion would decrease as the anger was cleansed. As I ventured these ideas, Jim perceived the truth of them with the clarity and courage that was to typify his work on himself.

We worked on clearing the anger. Our primary tool was the accelerated Integrating breath. I had Jim lie down, activate healing energy and the Witness, enter alpha, and then start to breathe full and fast. Jim's anger usually would be the first feeling to come up. I encouraged him to drop blame and shift to the energy experience. I had him report to me constantly about his feelings. By his reporting that he was experiencing the anger and not the blame, I could monitor where he was and that clearing was proceeding. We worked on accessing self-love as he was feeling the anger, all the while continuing with the breath. Jim took to this kind of breathwork easily, and altogether we did nine hour-long breathwork sessions. Jim said that he always felt better after the sessions, and he experienced dramatic catharsis in about half of them. I felt he was getting tremendous benefit in releasing feelings.

Jim reported being able to activate the Witness and feel the healing of self-love at home, in his own practice. There he worked with both the Cleansing and Integrating breaths, finding them useful at different times.

In counseling Jim about how to deal with his wife, I stressed nonreactiveness – not reacting to or expressing the anger that came up in the encounters with her, but containing the anger for later release through processing. This was difficult, and Jim was not able to succeed immediately. Only after a period of time, after we had been working together, did he begin to develop the skills of nonreactiveness.

Behind the anger were the feelings of being used, manipulated, and controlled. My impression was that Jim was correct in feeling this, that his wife really was behaving this way. But I had to point out that Jim had drawn this situation to himself in order to become conscious of the exact same energy blocked in his subconscious. He had to intellectually accept this possibility before he could work on clearing the power issue. If he fought back and got involved in a power struggle for the children, the energy would only be suppressed again because of his nonacceptance. He had to accept – emotionally – that his children were being torn from him, and he had to process the pain that he felt. I pointed out that this pain was present in him before the situation developed, that the purpose of the situation was only to bring it to the surface.

This insight proved to be a turning point. Jim had never before taken responsibility for the pain of losing his children. I further tried to point out that he was addicted to his children, that he had idealistic plans for them, that he was trying to find his own fulfillment through them, that they were to bring meaning to his life. What had happened was life's way of showing him that he was looking for fulfillment in the wrong place – outside of himself. The very expectation and heavy hope upon his children had already created the pain of loss – the two went together. He now had to face and integrate the pain of the loss to go beyond being blocked at this level.

His craving for significance that was to be fulfilled through his children was another result of his unintegrated Solar Plexus center, the home of his anger. He had to stop looking for the satisfaction of this craving through his children. The compulsive craving for significance was another feeling that he had to integrate and stop being driven by.

We worked with the concept of acceptance and surrendering the outcome of the acceptance to the Higher Self. Jim was familiar with this concept from his previous spiritual work, but he had never before brought it to such a personal level. Gradually he developed a reverent attitude toward his pain. Surrender became a working force in his life.

In his personal practice, Jim continued applying the principles of processing. His work was mainly with his rage, his helplessness and pain about losing his children, and his sense of insignificance. He learned to activate alpha and the Witness and to bring healing to these painful feelings. He would use thoughts of his wife and children to bring up the feelings and then consciously drop blame and settle into experiencing the feelings. Sometimes he would just work with the breath and be with whatever came up. He worked with simple affirmations to implement his self-acceptance: "It is OK for me to be angry; I accept the pain of losing my children." These affirmations also served to bring up painful feelings, which he then witnessed.

About two months after we first met, Jim reported that he was able to confront his wife and maintain nonreactiveness to his feelings of anger. This was both because the anger had subsided due to his regular practice and because he had developed the skill of nonreactiveness in sitting with his feelings. Nothing had really changed in the actual situation, but Jim realized that the possibility of maintaining contact with his children was real and feasible, and could not be blocked by his wife once he had released the extreme feelings that compelled him to see the situation in a distorted way and to act irresponsibly.

At this writing, about ten months have elapsed from our first meeting. Jim has been able to clear much of his suppressed feelings with success and reports that he is more stable in regard to communication with his wife. In not having fought her, he realizes that to a certain extent he has not played into her game and given her more justification for possession of the children. In being nonreactive, he has forced her to become more reasonable, both in response to the change in him and because she would be acting irrationally if she didn't. The relationship with this woman is obviously Karmic; they probably have a history that goes back into many lives.

As Jim maintains nonreactiveness to her and integrates the pain that she appears to be causing, he frees himself from the negative aspects of the bond between them. Because of Jim's courage and aptitude for intense inner work, and his comprehension of the power of acceptance, I feel he will continue to grow. His present circumstances will prove to be the springboard to a valuable life of inner transformation.

ELLEN

Ellen is thirty-eight years old. She has been operating a retail clothing store for the past two years with her partner, thirty-seven, with whom she has been romantically involved for three years. They are experiencing marginal success with the store and are thinking about whether to continue the business or to drop it as well as their relationship. The factors Ellen related that prompted her to seek counseling: continual and unresolved anxiety about financial concerns and the problems in her relationship. The fact that Ellen is conscious of her anxiety is a sign that she will be able to work productively with it. Many people remain unaware of feelings like these, but continue to be unconsciously driven by them into self-destructive attempts to compensate.

Ellen's chart showed the following relevant stressful aspects: Sun in the second house of money square Saturn. Saturn, the planet of fear and survival, is in disharmonious aspect to the Sun, which represents will and individuality. Ellen experiences great fear when she tries to satisfy material needs. Next, South Node in Taurus indicates that a primary life orientation of seeking material security signifies going backward for her in her personal growth. In order to go forward she has to focus on the North Node in

Scorpio, spiritual regeneration. If she did so, her material needs would be provided automatically.

It appeared that Ellen was being driven by irrational survival fears. Not being integrated, the fear was continuing to attract conditions of failure and insecurity. She was experiencing manifestation projection; she then reacted to the condition she had created/ attracted, experiencing even more fear, entering an expanding cycle.

As we spoke along these lines, Ellen said she had previously been a painter and felt she was expressing her spiritual self in her art, but had decided she needed more of a financial base. The opportunity for the clothing business arose only because of her relationship; she felt she would be unable to run it alone. Her partner did the business, and she did the selling. As they began to run the business, their relationship got worse. Ellen thought this was because they had more contact and were bound to experience stress.

My first step in working with Ellen was to advise her about the depth of her fear and that it was irrational; not that there was no reasonable cause for it in the past, but that she was projecting the suppressed fear onto inappropriate events in her current life. Her capacity to understand the nature of suppression, projection, and clearing would determine if she could make progress with inner work. She was able to grasp these concepts and to take responsibility for her fear.

Next was the actual acceptance of the fear. I explained that by allowing herself to be motivated by the fear into the mechanics of the business, she was rejecting herself. She was reacting blindly to the fear. She feared fear itself. She rejected herself by expecting that the future attainment of a stable business would resolve her fears – she hungered after the idea of future attainment. She was blocking her feelings of fear with the fantasy of success in the future.

We worked on acceptance and direct experience for about six sessions. As her acceptance increased, her experience of her fear increased. We worked on separating her fear from the object of her fear. Using the object (the business) to bring up the fear, I told her to drop thoughts of the business but to stay with the fear. She developed the capacity to be with only the fear, not her projections. She went deeper into the experience of pure fear. She noticed that after most of these sessions she would feel better, even though she mentioned once that she found the actual experience of processing the fear "like going to the dentist."

I responded that I admired her bravery but also noted that this was a cue that we needed to work more on self-love. We spent more time on activating the Witness together, bringing up the non-identification and healing power of the Higher Self, and especially on just cultivating an appreciation for the complete peacefulness of alpha. I would enter meditation with her, and we would build the energy together.

We developed a program for her practice at home. I taught her the breathwork meditations that I detail in Chapter 11, along with a personal prescription: Since her energy block was between her Survival (Saturn) and Solar Plexus (Sun) chakras, she was to alternate breathing into these two centers. Ellen used mainly the Cleansing breath, because she felt more comfortable with its gentleness than the intensity of the Integrating breath.

As our work continued, it emerged that as a child, Ellen had broken her coccyx – the tailbone at the base of the spine – and had had a difficult healing. The coccyx relates to the first chakra. My interpretation was that this "accident" was the result of the fear she carried in the first chakra – the energy had built to the point of releasing through injury. I urged her to go back to the incident and work with all the feelings related to it. She reported experiencing more fear, vulnerability, and helplessness, but there was no particular cause in her childhood to which she could trace the feelings, except for the injury. She worked with clearing the feelings related to this traumatic injury for about a month, going back and reexperiencing the injury, opening to all the feelings surrounding it. She always reported that she felt better after her sessions and that she was aware that suppressed feelings were, indeed, being cleared.

I felt satisfied that Ellen was progressing in her work. After about two months, however, she reported that her fear and anxiety had become worse, along with some problems in the business. She had even started smoking marijuana, something she did not do regularly. Looking at her chart again, I noticed that transiting

Saturn was conjuncting her natal Sun. This signified a period of about three weeks when her fear issues would be intensified. I told her that this was a critical time, that the worsening represented a healing crisis and the opportunity for emotional clearing, that it would be over in a few weeks, but that she could realize great benefits if she stayed with her inner work now and did not reject what was happening.

We met twice a week for three weeks. I tried to encourage her to work on her own, but she felt she needed support now. Our work was more of the same, with Ellen sitting with her anxiety, bringing in healing energy and evoking self-love, and doing breath-work. I did some energy polarity work on her, between the Root and Solar Plexus chakras. She showed admirable bravery, faith, and aptitude in opening to the shadow side of herself.

This period proved to be a turning point. After it had passed, Ellen reported feeling better than she had in the last few years and that things had cleared somewhat in the business. After a few more weeks, we decided to meet once a month. Ellen was obviously committed to her personal practice at home, and I felt she had the capacity to carry on by herself. We had been working together for about four months.

Throughout all of our sessions, Ellen never experienced any peaks of emotional catharsis, any crying or relating her fear to an incident in her childhood or past lives; nevertheless, she appeared to be undergoing genuine cleansing of suppressed and abnormal fear. In one of our next meetings, she related an incident that occurred during her practice at home.

She had been reading a book on codependency and started thinking about whether her relationship was codependent. She was sitting with her fear during her meditation, when she suddenly realized that she feared her partner. Immediately, she came into contact with her anger – her anger against her partner, on whom she depended and feared. This realization triggered a catharsis of the anger. She went into deeply emotional weeping, seeing how her unconscious resentment of her partner had been a major cause of the emotional and sexual problems they were having. She connected her present relationship to her father – how she had basically the same feelings about him. She knew enough to allow the catharsis to continue, and kept crying for about two hours.

When we first met, I had immediately spotted that Ellen's relationship was strongly codependent. I chose not to bring this up because I felt that her fear issue was primary and was enough for her to handle. I always feel that inner work should be mostly nondirective and noninvasive – that I should not merely tell the client what I observe but must lead them and allow them to discover their inner truth at their own pace. I was pleased that she had come to the dependency issue by herself.

Now, about eight months since we first met, Ellen continues to work on herself. She reports that her fear and anxiety have subsided drastically but that it is still an issue. I have told her that it may be the work of a lifetime, and she has accepted that the fear may never clear entirely. However, she is no longer motivated by it; she allows it to exist as a subpersonality. She is no longer afraid of it and takes loving care of it. These are the conditions that will allow the fear to continue to clear and normalize.

Nothing has changed much with her business, but she thinks that the situation may not be so bad; after all, she and her partner are making a living. She feels eager and ready to work on her next phase of growth – her relationship and what she brings to it. We continue to meet monthly, but she does most of her inner work on her own.

GROUP WORK

Sometimes integration can be accomplished more easily in a group than in any other format. The group becomes the source of energy that each individual can take in and use to support their work. The collective energy of the group can build to a very significant level and can be a major aid in transformation.

In the workshops I direct, I like to include some interpersonal contact work in partnering and small groups, but my primary intention is that the group energy be used to facilitate individual work. This is useful in two ways.

If a person is new to processing and inner work, the group energy provides a strong training benefit; the steps of Integrative Processing can be learned more easily by tuning into the group-mind. If the person already has an established practice, the group energy can provide a powerful stimulus to bring issues into integration that may have been resistant.

I usually begin group work with some physical loosening up and a few yoga postures. As a group, we enter alpha, activate the Witness, accessing healing energy and self-love. These steps alone are very powerful, when everyone performs the same visualizations simultaneously. When we begin deeper work, I remind people that emotions and issues that come up usually can be related to one of the lower chakras and that by breathing into that center, they can further enhance integration. Breathwork is a primary tool that we use. Breath provides a nonintellectual means to clear the subconscious emotions that form the basis of the conflict we experience. Breathwork sessions become very powerful and emotional as inner release is facilitated.

In an accelerated breath session, I ask people to lie down on the floor, and instruct them to begin the Integrating breath, starting with a full and fast pattern. They are to regulate the intensity of the physiological and emotional aspects they experience by slowing down or speeding up the rate of breath, breathing into the body or appropriate chakra, and sensing the feelings in the chakra or anywhere else in the body. As we proceed, I talk the group through the steps of processing. While we are working, we continually activate feelings of self-love and the healing power of the Higher Self to cleanse the negativity that is surfacing.

This is very intense work. Given permission to have feelings and the techniques to draw feelings out, people experience meaningful catharsis. It must be noted, therefore, that this type of work must be approached cautiously and reverently.

I hope discussing personal work has been inspiring for you. Sometimes it is difficult to see the depth to which we must open to ourselves. Perhaps this has now been somewhat clarified. Your everyday feelings, conflicts, and circumstances are the very ones with which you must work. If they are ever to be transformed, you are the only person who can make it happen.

Often we assume that there is no question that our situation is being caused by forces outside ourselves; we react blindly and with no real awareness. If this book is to have any value for you, you must realize that you are creating your experience, as it is manifesting right now. You must take responsibility and begin working on yourself.

If you do, you will no longer be dependent on whether other people change or don't change. You will feel your individuality as you never have; and with this individuality will come strength, peace, and inner communion. You will surrender your conscious will to the Higher Self; but you will be fulfilled as never before.

Do not allow this tremendous opportunity for personal growth to go unused. I wish you the best of everything.

Resources

WORKSHOPS

John runs three-day and longer workshops in *Emotional Clearing*. Participants learn how to work with feelings on the path to higher consciousness and are empowered to achieve deep emotional integration, clearing, and growth. The program includes both training in techniques that will become a permanent, life-enhancing resource and powerful experiential group work to facilitate emotional breakthroughs. The experience gained in these workshops can be vital in any healing program that recognizes the connection between physical and emotional illness. Workshops take place in New York, San Francisco, and at other places around the country according to demand.

PERSONAL THERAPY

Integrative Processing Therapy is a spiritual, feeling-oriented method of facilitating emotional release and growth within the therapist/client setting. Therapists who have been trained by John are located around the country. Names of therapists are posted on the website.

PROFESSIONAL CERTIFICATION

This powerful training has been designed for professional therapists of any discipline, but may be taken by those who wish to gain skills to help others in a semiprofessional capacity, such as teachers, medical personnel, or any type of counselor. With the emphasis on feelings as they are happening right now, this approach can provide important complementary tools for a therapist who might be primarily analytical in orientation, or who wishes to become more familiar with the application of Eastern or spiritual principles to therapy. Therapists already familiar with such principles will find a formalized system that will enable them to effectively work with clients. No prerequisite training or credentials are required.

For more information about workshops, therapists, or certification, check the *Emotional Clearing* website or call 1-800-988-6560 to leave your name and address for information to be sent to you.

RECORDINGS

Emotional Clearing Guided Meditation Cassette

John has recorded guided meditations in which he speaks and leads you step by step in clearing feelings. These meditations are the same that he uses in workshops and in private sessions. There are two meditations on this cassette-only release: 1. Grounding and Alpha Healing Induction. 2. *Emotional Clearing* Guided Meditation.

Desert Dawn

John is a dedicated musical artist. Here, his intent is to communicate directly on the right brain, emotional level, in order to complement the largely left brain, intellectual mode of writing. This album contains music that John has composed and recorded specifically to induce the deep relaxation, alpha healing state. It can be used for meditation, emotional clearing sessions, bodywork or yoga, or simply for setting a soothing and striking mood. A double album, with over two hours on two CDs or cassettes, John plays all the electronic and acoustic instruments. Samples are available on the website.

AlphaJourney CD

Being a musician and a meditator, John has a sharp interest in exploring the possibilities of triggering deep meditative, healing states with sound. Incorporating the research of others in the field with his own exploration, he has produced a CD that contains various key binaural-beat frequencies of pure sine waves that will entrain brainwaves to the alpha and theta state, where meditation and healing spontaneously occur. This is *not* an album of music, but of *tones* that entrain the brain to match a certain frequency. The recording contains no spoken guided meditations, but is intended to bring you into a deep inner place where your own process and personal imagery will unfold. Any of the various entrainment level tones can be indefinitely played by setting the CD to repeat a certain selection. Available in CD only. Complete instruction included.

To order any of the recordings, call 1-800-247-6553 for credit card sales.

WEBSITE

Visit the *Emotional Clearing* worldwide English speaking website at:

http://www.emclear.com

The website contains articles, talks, interviews, other tapes, musical and creative offerings, and other information from John that complements the book. In the interactive dialogue section, readers may post their own stories and receive as well as give support to others about their emotional journeys and their experience applying the principles of *Emotional Clearing* to their lives. John occasionally also gives feedback, but he hopes that this forum will become a widely used, self-supporting place for opening the heart through sharing, being heard, and helping each other.